1666

1666

Plague, War, and Hellfire

REBECCA RIDEAL

Thomas Dunne Books
St. Martin's Press
New York

THOMAS DUNNE BOOKS.
An imprint of St. Martin's Press.

www.thomasdunnebooks.com
www.stmartins.com

The Library of Congress Cataloging-in-Publication Data is available upon request.

ISBN 978-1-250-09706-4 (hardcover)
ISBN 978-1-250-09707-1 (e-book)

Our books may be purchased in bulk for promotional, educational, or business use. Please contact your local bookseller or the Macmillan Corporate and Premium Sales Department at 1-800-221-7945, extension 5442, or by e-mail at MacmillanSpecialMarkets@macmillan.com.

First published in Great Britain by John Murray (Publishers), an Hachette UK company

First U.S. Edition: October 2016

10 9 8 7 6 5 4 3 2 1

To my daughter, Edie

Contents

Maps

Cast of Characters

Charles II	King of England, Scotland and Ireland
James, Duke of York	Charles II's brother and heir and Lord High Admiral of the navy
Margaret Cavendish	author and scholar of natural philosophy
George Monck	Lord General and 1st Duke of Albemarle
Prince Rupert of the Rhine	Charles II's cousin and former Royalist commander
Nell Gwynn	actress within the King's Company
Isaac Newton	Cambridge scholar and mathematician
Robert Hooke	member of the Royal Society
Aphra Behn	government spy
Christopher Wren	mathematician and member of the Royal Society
Samuel Pepys	navy clerk
John Evelyn	writer, gentleman and navy commissioner
Nathaniel Hodges	London physician
Thomas Farriner	baker living on Pudding Lane
Thomas Vincent	Puritan preacher living in Hoxton
John Milton	poet, pamphleteer and republican figure
Michiel de Ruyter	head of the Dutch navy
Cornelius Tromp	Orangist Dutch naval commander
Johan de Witt	leader of the Dutch Republic

Author's Note

IN LATE-SEVENTEENTH-CENTURY ENGLAND, the new year officially began on 25 March, however 1 January was also recognised by contemporaries as the beginning of the year. To overcome this discrepancy, dates between 1 January and 24 March would often be chronicled by contemporaneous record-keepers in a 'split year' format (e.g. what we would recognise as 1 February 1666, would be recorded as '1 February 1665/6'). For clarity, this book takes 1 January as the beginning of the year. For the most part, this book uses dates according to the Julian calendar; by the seventeenth century this was ten days behind the Gregorian calendar used on the Continent. The reader should also note that, where appropriate, obscure spellings within quotations have been modernised.

I am much deceiv'd if any have so dearly purchased their Reputation . . . than [through] an expensive, though necessary, War, a consuming Pestilence, and a more consuming Fire.

John Dryden, Preface to *Annus Mirabilis:*
The Year of Wonders, 1666

'O, wonder!
How many goodly creatures are there here!
How beauteous mankind is! O brave new world,
That has such people in't!'

William Shakespeare, *The Tempest*

1666

Prologue

Moorfields: Saturday, 1 September 1666

HE WAS USUALLY dressed in white with a black mask. The opposing colours were a nod to life and death. Carrying a wooden baton, he shuffled awkwardly to and fro as an eclectic crowd of spectators eyed his every move; they had travelled from all over London just to see him. He was an uneasy mix of stupidity and cunning; his voice was shrill, his temper was short; and taut strings of silk tugged at his tiny arms and legs, manipulated by an operator hidden from view. For now, his name was Polichinello, but within a couple of decades Londoners would come to know him as 'Punch'.[1]

On this late summer afternoon, Samuel Pepys was part of the audience watching this 'puppet play' in Moorfields. It was a place of trees and open fields to the north of the city and was lined with shops, taverns and brothels, and filled with an assortment of characters – from booksellers and ballad singers to laundresses, pickpockets and gentlemen. The horrors of the previous summer – the carts, the bodies and the smell – had all but gone. They were now nine months into the year that some had warned, and many had feared, would herald the biblical End of Days. Centuries of religious conditioning had led the Christian world to see disasters and major events as signs of God's providence, and the year 1666, with its link to the biblical Number of the Beast, had been earmarked by religious factions from as early as 1597 as the beginning of the apocalypse. The king's own grandfather, James VI and

I

I had written a tract rooted in the Book of Revelation arguing that he and his contemporaries were living in 'this our last age' and, over the course of the previous two decades, religious fervour had escalated. Yet despite the prophecies and the undeniable bad fortune of the previous year, the world appeared to be intact and London at least was almost wholly returned to normal.

While the exact nature of Polichinello's performance is unknown, puppet shows thrived on satire and farce, subverting the narrative of well-known events, fables and histories. It was the third time in just over a week that Pepys had seen this particular show and he thought it to be 'The best that ever I saw.' Joined by his wife, Elizabeth, her friend Mary, and their acquaintance Sir William Penn, this cheery, albeit windy, Saturday afternoon would continue with food and wine at a nearby alehouse. It was a typical afternoon in the historic metropolis of London.

Only it wasn't typical. Within hours a fire would begin in the heart of the city. It was to be a fire that would transform the London they knew for ever.

PART I

1665

I

The *London* Burns

... for it is observed that in most Families of England, if
there be any Son or Daughter that excels the rest in Beauty
or Wit, or perhaps Courage or Industry, or any other rare
quality, London is their North-star, and they are never at rest
till they point directly thither.

Edward Chamberlayne, *The . . . present state of england*[1]

Tuesday, 7 March 1665

THE DAY STARTED like any other. A pale winter sun brought
the dawn. Casting a mottled-grey glow on glazed windows
and icy puddles, it offered light but little warmth. London was a
month into a deep frost. Across the capital, people woke to clang-
ing church bells and the hubbub of the streets: barking dogs,
clattering carts, calling pigeons and chattering early risers. Candles
and fires were lit, chamber pots were emptied, food and drink
were taken, and the people of the metropolis prepared for the
day ahead. The butchers, bakers and tallow-chandlers; the booksellers, grocers and coffee-house keepers; the apothecaries,
goldsmiths and city drapers made the short journey from their
living quarters upstairs to their shops and businesses below. The
rest of the city's inhabitants stepped into the big wide world;
their misty breath swirling and rising above the medieval streets.

On this day, if someone had viewed the capital from above,
they would have found a city that had long given up the fight to

contain itself. A vast canopy of tiled roofs, Gothic church spires, and stone chimneys emitting thick black smoke, covered a warren of passageways and streets below – some unevenly paved, others hard mud and stone. These streets, 'so narrow and incommodious' in the centre of the city, according to John Evelyn, cleaved through a discord of overhanging timber-framed buildings, replete with heavy wooden trade posts suspended overhead. To John Milton, who resided at Artillery Walk to the north-east of the city, it was a place 'Where houses [were] thick and sewers annoy[ed] the air'[2] – indeed, that air often made visitors sick, with Thomas Ellwood being forced to leave three years earlier due to 'the sulphurous air of that city'.[3] Writing some decades later, the poet John Gay asserted that mornings were the best time to travel because 'No Tides of Passengers the Street molest'.[4] Those navigating this labyrinth on foot, and there were a great many, kept close to the walls so as to avoid the waste from the 'troublesome and malicious . . . Spouts and Gutters' above and the Hackney carriages and sedan chairs in front and behind.[5] During busy periods, fighting for 'the wall' was common. In 1664, Samuel Pepys recorded how 'two men . . . justling for the wall about the New Exchange, did kill one another, each thrusting the other through'.[6] Thanks to its meandering streets, it was, as French philosopher Samuel de Sorbière declared, the type of city that required 'a Year's time to live in it before you can have a very exact Idea of the Place' and while brick buildings could be found in the wealthier areas, the medieval dominated.

Once a modest Roman settlement, the ancient city walls had surrendered to London's growing population and prosperity, allowing the capital to spill out of its old boundaries and form a metropolis of three parts. There was the mercantile heartland within the historic walled City of London, reached by the six city gates and controlled by the Lord Mayor, aldermen, and powerful livery companies. Here, many of the former 'great houses' once owned by noblemen had been turned into tenements, with the most affluent residents living in the centre.[7] Umbilically linked by the Strand to the south-west was the City of Westminster. Containing the palaces of Whitehall and Westminster, it was the formal seat of the nation's political and royal power. Finally, there was the ever-expanding cushion of suburban sprawl that buttressed the walls and tumbled into the surrounding fields and farmland: north, east, south and especially west. These expanding suburbs, alongside the grand houses lining the Thames and Westminster, offered a glimpse of London's architectural future. In Bloomsbury, the Earl of Southampton was in the process of building what Evelyn described as a 'noble square or piazza' – it was in fact the first garden square of its type in London; in Lincoln's Inn Fields, the colonial merchant and Treasurer of the Tangier Committee, Mr Thomas Povey, had an 'elegant house', containing vases imitating porphyry, stables tiled with delftware, fountains and 'pretty cellar and ranging of his wine bottles';[8] in Piccadilly work was well underway constructing grand new residences for the Earl of Clarendon, Sir John Berkeley and Sir John Denham.[9] All of which looked to the vast, silver River Thames to the south.

Today, an array of characters could be found going about their business. On the river, there were the watermen – like Mr Delkes who carried 'pins always in his mouth'[10] and occasionally pimped out his pretty daughter – bobbing in boats at the wharfs waiting to carry Londoners to and fro. There were the merchant sailors who prepared a cluster of vessels for passage across the Atlantic, transporting Quaker prisoners to work as indentured servants on 'the plantations' of the English colonies of Jamaica, Barbados or Virginia (most likely the former).[11] There were also the many fishermen, out to catch and then sell sturgeon and trout that were in the river in abundance. In the city, Mathew and Thomas Aldred, who had recently set up shop treating 'melancholique and distracted persons', could be found close to Angel Alley in Bishopsgate.[12] Near to the Rainbow Coffee-House of Fleet Street, Thomas Grey sold lozenges for coughs, colds and consumption between 'the two temple gates'.[13] Along Fleet Street, the artist Mary Beale might have been seen packing together her worldly goods ready to retreat to Hampshire after living in the capital for several years. On cold days such as this, a seventy-six-year-old gentleman named Thomas Hobbes could often be seen leaving the Duke of Devonshire's house, wearing a black velvet coat and 'bootes of Spanish leather, laced or tyed along the sides with black ribbons', to take his morning walk.[14] Those needing to leave the city might have made their way to the Red Lion tavern in Lambeth, where Thomas Fisher and Thomas Ryder ran a daily coach service to Epsom, leaving at 8 a.m. promptly. To the west of St Paul's Cathedral, a 'Choice collection of Rarities' (including Egyptian mummies, the 'Thigh-bone of a Gyant', and 'A Mermaid's Skin'), could be seen for a small price.[15] If money was short, Londoners might consider visiting 'one George Gray, Barber and Periwig-maker', where he would 'give 10 or 12s per ounce for long Flaxen hair, and for other long fair hair 6 or 3s per ounce';[16] wigs for men and women were a burgeoning trade.

There were an estimated 460,000 people living and working in London,[17] sustained by a vast network of agriculture and industry the length and breadth of the country, and beyond. Coal was shipped from the Tyne, lead from Derbyshire, tin (vital for creating pewter) from Cornwall, fruit and vegetables from the neighbouring counties of Hertfordshire and Kent, cloth arrived from Wiltshire and Sussex, clay pipes for tobacco from the Isle of Wight, and livestock for butchering from Ireland. Further afield, glassware was transported from Delft, fashionable exotic spices and silks arrived from the East Indies, and tobacco and sugar from the Americas. Ale, cider and wine were the safest drinks to consume, but water of varying quality was available. Wells were scattered around London and filthy water from the Thames could be accessed via a large water wheel at London Bridge. The cleanest drinking water available though was supplied by the New River Company outside the city. Established at the start of the century, it had constructed a forty-mile long artificial waterway, beginning at the fresh-water springs of Chadwell and Amwell in Hertfordshire, and ending in Clerkenwell, London. For a price, residents could have a lead pipe installed to feed regular fresh water into their homes.

Like every city, London consisted of both the real and tangible world of food, drink, money, streets, houses and goods, and the illusory, the imagined and the ideological. The Restoration of the monarchy in 1660, following over a decade of republican rule, gave another twist to the kaleidoscope of seventeenth-century habits, creating new patterns of daily life. Sundays remained sacrosanct, but every other day saw shops remain open until 10 p.m. Coffee houses and Royal Society meetings offered a space for a select but vocal few to discuss natural philosophy and conduct experiments, while taverns and commercial and cultural centres like St Paul's Churchyard and the Royal Exchange roared with life and frivolity. The Royal Exchange in particular was a cradle of news and gossip. Positioned between Threadneedle Street and Cornhill, 'the Exchange' as it was often called had stood for nearly a hundred years as a centre of trade. The brainchild of Sir Thomas Gresham (whose other project included the college at which the Royal Society was based), it contained a square piazza lined with several levels of shops, stalls and meeting places.

Alongside traditional festivals and fairs, Londoners enjoyed an evolving and vibrant mix of public entertainment – from the theatre, bearbaiting and gambling to new forms of music, dance and an invigorated interest in Continental fashion (buckled shoes, the precursor to the three-piece suit and, most notably, the periwig). There were new spaces to explore, such as the royal parks and shopping arcades, while for those higher up the social ladder, spectator sports such as tennis and horse racing became popular – Charles II himself was reputed to play tennis every morning, and the court trips to Newmarket to watch horse racing became increasingly popular, with two excursions each year. In short, there were many reasons, aside from work and worship, for Londoners to be out and about.

A large number of London's almost half-a-million inhabitants were migrants from around the country who had brought with them a drive to better their lot. The Taswells were one such family. Merchants from the Isle of Wight, in 1660 they had moved to a substantial property in Bear Lane close to London's Custom House on the east side of the city.[18] The statistician John Graunt, himself the son of a migrant father, estimated that each London household consisted of roughly eight people: 'the Man, and his Wife, three Children, and three Servants, or Lodgers'.[19] As a typical merchant family, the Taswells probably conformed to this model. Headed by James and Elizabeth, they had at least two sons, and William, their second son, attended Westminster School on the other side of town. In Westminster, William Taswell may have unknowingly come into contact with another London family, the Mitchells. They lived in a house with five hearths and 'a little sorry garden'[20] in Wood Street. Headed by Miles and Anne, the Mitchell family also included at least two young adult sons and possibly a daughter that Anne had given birth to out of wedlock, thirty years previously.[21] As a family of book-sellers, information was their trade and for the past couple of years they had ploughed it well at Westminster Hall on the western side of the city.

As with many semi-public spaces, the ancient hall of Westminster – where nearly two decades earlier Charles I had been sentenced to death – had become a commercial hub packed with traders and shoppers, bartering for bargains and jostling for space. Approaching the hall on 7 March 1665, customers would first be greeted by the macabre sight of three heads skewered to spikes outside the entrance. They belonged to Oliver Cromwell and fellow regicides Henry Ireton and John Bradshaw who, five years earlier, had been exhumed from their tombs at Westminster Abbey on the orders of Charles II and 'executed' as traitors at Tyburn. Entering the main hall, customers would have found all manner of goods on sale, from clothing and books to wigs and buttons. The Mitchells' shop was noted in one of their publications as being 'the first shop in Westminster Hall'.[22] For company, they had their friends John and Elizabeth Howlett, who were haberdashers that had traded from Westminster Hall for at least twenty years. In fact, so strong was the bond between the two families that the eldest Mitchell son was betrothed to the Howletts' pretty daughter Elizabeth, or 'Betty' as she was known. Plans were in place for the couple, once wed, to move to a house in Thames Street, with the Mitchell boy taking on his father-in-law's trade rather than becoming a bookseller like his parents.

There were, of course, booksellers throughout London offering a multitude of printed works. John Playford sold music and dance books at the Temple; Henry Herrington sold plays and operas at the New Exchange; Peter Dring sold the works of cookery book writer Hannah Woolley next door to the Rose Tavern; and James Allestry sold works of science from the Royal Society at St Paul's Churchyard, including its new science journal *Philosophical Transactions*, printed for the first time the previous day. What marked the Mitchells' shop apart at Westminster Hall was its proximity to political power: it was the perfect place to pick up rumours and gossip from the movers and shakers of the city.

Alongside their books and pamphlets, the Mitchells probably sold the main weekly London newspaper, the *Intelligencer*. Smaller than modern newspapers, the *Intelligencer* ran to four or five pages and offered a round-up of events from across the country and the Continent. Since the return of the monarchy, a strict censorship had been imposed on the press under the management of Roger L'Estrange, but the newspaper still offered information for the casual reader. In the latest issue, customers could read about the murder of an English gentleman across the Channel, the capture of foreign merchant ships by a veteran Royalist in Portsmouth, and a great storm in France where there was 'little news at present, but disasters . . .'.[23] There were also reports that the Dutch fleet was rapidly expanding, and that it would be 'ready' by the end of the month.

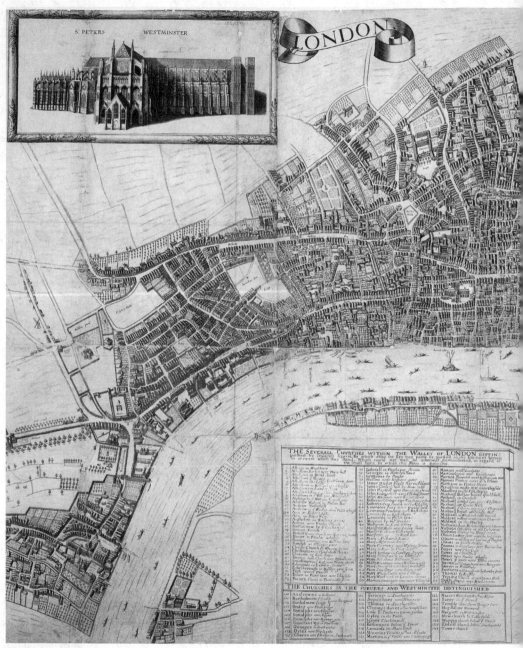

Richard Newcourt's map of London, 1658

Most of London would have known what was meant by 'ready', but those in any doubt could read the three-day-old notices pinned to the city's landmarks. They were all that remained of a grand, trumpeted procession that had swept through the capital the previous Saturday. Beginning at Whitehall gate at 10 a.m., the king's heralds, supported by sergeants-at-arms and eight trumpeters, had travelled along Cheapside before culminating at the Royal Exchange. Like the notices they left behind, the heralds had announced to the citizens of London that, for the second time in just over a decade, the English had declared war on the Dutch.[24]

It was a war that surprised few. Bound together by a shared Protestant religion in a largely Catholic continent, Anglo-Dutch relations were complex. Under Elizabeth I, the English had supported the Dutch in their revolt against Spanish Habsburg rule, which had resulted not only in the defeat of the Spanish Armada but in seven provinces of the Netherlands forming a free and independent Protestant state, the Dutch Republic. As the Habsburg Empire weakened, the Dutch merchant fleet grew into the largest in Europe, dominating trade along the Iberian coast and competing with the English in pursuit of former Spanish- and Portuguese-controlled trade posts. The resultant prosperity of the Dutch Republic, coupled with the splintering of competing Protestant factions either side of the Channel, stoked an Anglo-Dutch rivalry that shaped European relations throughout the mid- to late-seventeenth century. During the early years of Cromwell's Commonwealth in England, state-sanctioned privateering ensured this rivalry mutated into all-out naval war, with the First Anglo-Dutch War taking place between 1652 and 1654. Under the command of bullish Parliamentarian naval leaders such as Robert Blake, George Monck and John Lawson, English warships were victorious but their defeat of the Dutch was not decisive enough to stem the cause of tension: the tug-of-war for trade supremacy in the East and West Indies.

The fierce competition produced vicious literature that played on national stereotypes, with God and religion used to condemn the failings of each state: in 1664, an English pamphlet entitled *The English and Dutch affairs Displayed to the Life* argued that the recent deaths of thousands in Amsterdam due to plague was down to God's punitive will;[25] another, linked Dutch prosperity to 'the bloody and inhumane butcheries committed by them against us';[26] another still, entitled *The Dutch Boare Dissected, or a Description of Hogg-Land*, described the Dutchman as 'a Lusty, Fat, two Legged Cheese-Worm: A Creature that is so addicted to Eating Butter, Drinking fat Drink, and sliding, that all the World knows him for a slippery Fellow'.[27] For their part, Dutch anti-English literature centred on the idea that Britons were in league with the Devil following the regicide of Charles I. Imagery depicted the English with the tails of foxes, dragons and even devils.[28] In the Dutch poem *Nederlandtsche nyp-tang* (1652) the author claimed that, of the English:

> There false deceit I must tell
> and of course their descendency from Hell.[29]

Powerful factions in Holland were also fearful of the House of Orange, a formidable family of Dutch stadtholders – an elected position, essentially the Dutch Republic's head of state. Strategically planted with English seed when Charles II's nine-year-old sister married William II of Orange in 1641, in 1665 their offspring William was only fifteen years old and had been orphaned by the premature deaths of both his parents. His uncle Charles II was the closest link the teenager had to his beloved mother.

Yet for all the Anglo-Dutch hostility, there was also considerable cross-pollination. Many English Parliamentarians had fled to the Dutch Republic following the Restoration of Charles II, while Dutch merchants were among the numerous foreigners living in the metropolis of London. A particularly prolific Dutch family of goldsmiths and glass merchants headed by Johan Vandermarsh lived along Lime Street, within the city walls. Charles had spent time in the Netherlands during his exile, as had his brother James, and the king's ambitious Secretary of State, Lord Arlington, had recently married a Dutch woman. Artists from the Netherlands were highly regarded in England – with the death of the Flemish painter Anthony van Dyck, the Dutch-trained Peter Lely became the official royal painter; Dutch engineers specialising in the drainage of marshland had been sought out to transform the Norfolk broads; and even the chief coiner at the Royal Mint, John Roettiers, was of Dutch origin.

The path to the current war had started in April 1664, when the attentions of a committee organised by the House of Commons and chaired by Sir Thomas Clifford had shifted from investigating the nation's declining cloth industry to examining the deterioration of English trade in general. During the committee meetings, merchants were encouraged to voice their grievances against the Dutch. With companies venturing further afield for mastery of trade in gold, silver, sugar, tobacco, silks and spices, key complainants were the Levant Company, the East India Company, and the Royal Adventurers for Trade in Africa – who complained that the Dutch had taken possession of all the former Portuguese territories along the West African coast, inhibiting England's ability to trade.[30]

In fact, that same year, a forty-three-year-old Irish-born sea captain named Robert Holmes had been charged with facilitating the expansion of the newly formed Company of Royal Adventurers Trading into Africa. Founded on the belief that there were rich gold fields along the Gambia river, the state-backed company had regularly come into conflict with Dutch trading bases along the West African coast. Its primary goal was the acquisition of gold but it also had explicit orders to establish a trade in slaves, with the aim of acquiring 3,000 per year to sell to the West Indies. In his forty-gun flagship, the *Jersey*, Holmes led a taskforce of English vessels to capture the Dutch fortress of Carolusborg, on the northern part of the Gulf of Guinea. With him was a new spring-based pendulum watch, designed by the illustrious Dutch scientist and inventor Christiaan Huygens and refashioned by the Royal Society ready for the sea. It was hoped that the watch might enhance the accuracy of navigation. By his own admission, Holmes was a cunning man who looked 'his enemies in the face with as much love as his friends';[31] he was also a determined military leader. With the support of his loyal crew and aided by the latest naval weaponry and navigation equipment, it took Holmes eleven days to capture Carolusborg, which was renamed Cape Coast Castle under English control. The Dutch eventually managed to win back many of the other bases Holmes had taken, but they never again had control of Cape Coast Castle; a fortress that, over the next two centuries, morphed into the rotten heart of the British Transatlantic Slave Trade.

The Anglo-Dutch rivalry also played out across the Atlantic; New Amsterdam was (re)claimed in 1664 by the English and renamed New York (after the Duke of York), while Surinam was taken from the English by the Dutch in the same year. The opposing nations were evenly matched in their ambitions, their navies and their dogged confidence. As the Venetian ambassador in Paris warned,

> with both sides strong in the great number of their ships, well provided with troops and with officials on the fleet itself to distinguish the actions of captains in the very heat of action with reward and punishment, spurring the others on to valour and unparalleled determination, the scene cannot fail to be a very tragic one for both sides, the issue being left to the arbitrament of fortune.[32]

War could make many cripples, but it could also turn a profit for some. At the Navy Board offices in Seething Lane, an ambitious thirty-two-year-old clerk was finding that conflict could do wonders for a man's career. He was the son of a tailor, but the impending war had made him busier than usual and there was a growing possibility that his hard work and accounting skills might see him elevated to the position of Secretary of the Tangier

Committee, a powerful role with a substantial salary. On 7 March 1665, he sat with his back to the fire. He should have been working, but was troubled by a pain in his left testicle: he'd spent the previous night in agony with an ache in his groin and daylight had provided only mild relief. No doubt tired, he sat in his office until noon, but the pain returned. He blamed the heat from the fire and was set into such 'a great rage again' that he left the office and returned home to his wife, Elizabeth. Having undergone a risky operation in the late 1650s to remove bladder stones in his urinary tract, Samuel Pepys had a history of groin problems. Unable to focus on anything other than his severe discomfort, he spent the rest of the day lying in bed.

While he slept, thirty or so miles to the south-east the wheels of war turned. A small flotilla of ships was being readied at the key victualling dockyard of Chatham. It was to make the winding journey along the Medway to join the rest of the fleet at an anchorage called 'the Hope' close to Tilbury on the Thames. Among its number was one of the jewels of the Restoration navy, a 64-gun, second-rate frigate called the *London*. It wasn't the biggest ship of the fleet, but it was certainly one of the most prestigious, with 'a state-room much bigger' than that of the first-rate flagship the *Royal Charles*, though 'not so rich'. Built in 1656, it had formed part of the convoy that escorted Charles II from the Netherlands to England in 1660 – carrying the king's own brother and heir, James, Duke of York. A year later, it had transported the king's beloved young sister, Henrietta, to France to marry Louis XIV's brother, the Duke of Orleans.

Like most ships of the age, the *London* had three tall masts with large square sails and its watertight hull was likely coated with a mixture of resin made of 'deal, hair and lime' to prevent barnacles and wood-damaging 'ship-worm' taking hold.[33] At 37 metres long and 12 metres wide, the streamlined wooden vessel was typical of English seventeenth-century style. The long broadside had three decks, two tiers of which had a complete row of cannon ports, and the third had cannon ports filling half of the deck. It had a bulbous roundhouse at the rear, decorated with the gilded Stuart lion and unicorn, and glass windows facing out to sea and into the top deck.

The *London* was to be the flagship of experienced naval captain Sir John Lawson who was 25 miles away with the rest of the fleet, awaiting its safe arrival. Lawson was a complex man with money troubles, an upwardly mobile family and ambitious daughters. On several occasions he had tried but failed to remove himself from naval service. Born into a Scarborough – or possibly Hull – shipping family in around 1615, he had quickly risen through the ranks: he began as a merchant sailor and then, when the First Anglo-Dutch War broke out, became one of the many captains in the fleet. By the end of the war, he had been promoted to vice admiral. It was an impressive ascent for a man of his background, and one that could only really have happened in the quasi-meritocratic republican navy. But merit only took him so far. In the late 1650s, despite being by far the more experienced man, Lawson was overlooked for the role of Commander of the Navy in favour of the Earl of Sandwich. Lawson's dubious sectarian beliefs and his involvement in the Fifth Monarchists – a staunchly republican millenarian group formed during the interregnum that prophesied the End of Days – may have made him a risk not worth taking. Lawson had an attachment to the *London*, having commanded it during the famous 1660 convoy from the Netherlands with the king, and knowing it was to be his ship once more, he had manned the crew with many loyal men, family, and friends.

His ship was designed for a crew of around 300 men, but on this day records reveal that, curiously, women were on board too. Technically, women were banned from boarding navy vessels, but throughout the period sporadic references appear in the archives to their presence in the lead up to, and sometimes during, war. Given the length of the journey, it is possible that the ship was performing a kind of informal naval parade between Chatham and the rendezvous point along the Thames: the wives, daughters and sisters of the crew may have boarded to experience the sea before parting from their loved ones. It was not a long journey and at no point during the voyage would the ship be in the open sea. Bolstering this theory is a letter sent by one John Allin ten days later. Writing from Southwark to his friend in Rye, he revealed that the ship contained not only men and women, but 'children together' too. As teenage sailors were very common within the fleet (the Earl of Sandwich took his fifteen-year-old son on his campaigns) the term 'children' probably referred to the very young, almost certainly of a pre-teen age. There would be no reason to have very young children on a warship, unless they were with family.

Preparations at Chatham had not been without difficulty. A couple of weeks earlier, orders had been made for some hoys (small carrier ships) to transport ballast to the *London*, but en route one of the vessels had been stopped at Deptford and 'all her men pressed away'[34] (since 1664, the Navy had adopted a system of enforced subscription, known as 'impressment'; seamen on board merchant vessels were often targeted). When a delivery of 5,000 hammocks arrived at the dockyard, to provide somewhere for crew on the various ships to sleep, many were found to be of 'bad' quality, while timber needed for repairing ships and the building of new ones had been slow to arrive from Sherwood Forest, because the sailors tasked with transporting it to the various dockyards had been scared to take to the sea in case they too were 'pressed'. Nevertheless, on 7 March 1665, the *London* was deemed to be ready to join the fleet. As it left the dockyard, it was packed with supplies: leather boots, clothing, candles, food, bedding, medical equipment and beer and water barrels filled the storerooms in the lower decks. The vessel was also armed with brass ordnance and plenty of gunpowder.

On entering the ship, passengers would have found themselves in the middle of the three decks close to the Great Cabin, a common space used for music, drinking and socialising during voyages. Directly above, was the assembly room, where the officers dined and held councils of war. The quarterdeck was above this, with the far end roofed by the 'poop', and within this space the most senior members of crew had their cabins, with windows looking out to sea. It was a cold day, but if the passengers had looked out as the *London* sailed along the Medway, they would have seen flat agricultural fields dotted with farmhouses, and as the ship hooked around St Mary's Island they would have viewed an open expanse of water littered with small islands. With plenty of twists and turns, the Medway was a tricky estuary to navigate, forming an almost impenetrable avenue into the south-east of England. Only a year before, a bill had been passed by Charles II to make the River Medway, and other important waterways, more 'navigable'.[35] Yet, the *London* sailed seamlessly along.

As the ship approached the Nore (a sandbank used for anchoring at the mouth of the Thames estuary), something went dreadfully wrong. The cause is debated to this day, but fresh archaeological evidence suggests a likely scenario. As the *London* continued its journey towards the Thames, deep inside the ship's magazine (where the ship's artillery was stored), gunners began the process of preparing the cartridges and cannons that would be used in battle. Like many ships of this time, the magazine included cartridges that would be re-used. These second-hand cartridges often contained traces of old gunpowder and cotton that could become highly combustible if mixed with fresh gunpowder; needing only the smallest amount of friction to explode into fire. Evidence suggests that the ship's gunners were in the process of packing the cartridges into the cannons when the contents of one of the half-filled cannon barrels sparked, igniting the ship's magazine. This sent fire careering through the hold where the rest of the ship's gunpowder suddenly exploded.[36]

Travellers on a small boat about half a league away watched the devastation unfold, witnessing the ship's almost total destruction as the force of the fire tore through the huge vessel. One blast propelled the front half of the ship westwards, destroying its central part and pushing the hull, filled with disused cannons as ballast, down into the water. Nothing except part of the hull and the stern was left.[37] There are no records of those last few moments on the ship, but of the 350 people on board, as Pepys later wrote, only 'about 24 [men] and a woman that were in the round house and coach saved; the rest, being above 300, drowned'.[38]

News of the explosion travelled fast, although details were lacking at first. Writing that day to Lord Arlington (Secretary of State), William Coventry (Commissioner of the Navy), informed him how 'A ship hath blowne up below the Hope what kind of ship I cannot tell but it is supposed one bound to the Barbadoes'.[39] The next day, the eye-witness on the carrier boat delivered an account of what he had seen to an official at Dover, who immediately wrote to Arlington's secretary Joseph Williamson: '[the] brave ship London is blowne upp but how god knows, [there is] . . . nothing left but part of the Hull, & stearn'.[40] At his office, Pepys – somewhat recovered after passing 'two stones' the previous day – also received news of the disaster. Recording in his diary:

> This morning is brought me to the office the sad newes of 'The London', in which Sir J. Lawson's men were all bringing her from Chatham to the Hope, and thence he was to go to sea in her; but a little a' this side the bouy of the Nower, she suddenly blew up . . . the ship breaking all to pieces, with 80 pieces of brass ordnance. She lies sunk, with her round-house above water. Sir J. Lawson hath a great loss in this of so many good chosen men, and many relations among them.[41]

From Pepys, we also discover that reports were quick to spread. When he visited the Exchange later that same day, he found that the news had been 'taken very much to heart' and it wasn't long before plans were put in place for the city to give the king a new ship to replace the *London*.[42]

The more pressing matter was the survivors. This fell to one of the four commissioners responsible for the care of wounded seamen and prisoners of war, John Evelyn. Evelyn lived in a grand house at Sayes Court, near to Deptford dockyard, with his wife, Mary, and their ten-year-old son, also called John. There had been other children – four, in fact – but three had died before their first birthday and another had only lived until his fifth. On 9 March, Evelyn 'went to receive the poor creatures that were saved out of the London frigate, blown up by accident, with above 200 men'.[43]

By 10 March, rumours circulated in the coffee houses of London that the ship had blown up because the navy had used cheap gunpowder from sellers outside the capital, that was '20s cheaper than the powder sold in London'.[44] It was also on this day that word of the disaster began to be spread by foreign ambassadors, with the Dutch ambassador in London, Michiel van Gogh, writing that 'The London, prepared for Vice-Admiral Lawson, was blown up while sailing up the river, and only 19 out of the crew of 351 saved'. Besides the obvious tragedy, it was a real financial loss: brass ordnance was expensive, plus the ship had been fully stocked with supplies. On 11 March, Sir William Batten and Sir J. Minnes, who had been to survey the wreck, returned to London claiming that 'the guns may be got, but the hull of her will be wholly lost'.[45]

Over the course of the next couple of months, John Evelyn took charge of organising the care of 'the poor orphans and widows made by this bloody beginning . . . whose husbands and relations', he wrote, 'perished in the London frigate, of which there were fifty widows, and forty-five of them with child'.[46] Sir John Lawson, who had lost a number of his kin, offered recommendations regarding the most in need. Before the Second Anglo-Dutch War had even started, it had been baptised in fire and death.

To the pamphleteer Thomas Greene the destruction of the *London* marked the beginning of a series of terrible events indicating God's displeasure with the people of London:

Oh my heart hath been in sorrow for thee, and a burthen hath layn upon me as concerning thee, ever since the Lord began to manifest his displeasure against thee, even ever since the Ship called the London was blown up where more then 200 persons were torn to pieces, whose Graves were in the sea; this then was the cry of my heart; saying, think yee they were greater sinners above all men?[47]

2

Outbreak

Wherein could this flea guilty be,
Except in that drop which it sucked from thee?
John Donne, 'The Flea'[1]

AFTER THE DEATH of their host, fleas have around three days to find a new source of blood. After that point, they will starve. If a flea carries *Yersinia pestis*,[2] a bacterium that blocks the valve to the stomach, the need to feed intensifies. Only through the flea's persistent efforts to feed will the bacterium become dislodged, after which it is spewed into the bite wound. While the flea's belly fills with fresh blood, the bacterium infiltrates the new host's bloodstream, multiplying and injecting toxins into every cell.[3] On board a ship, fleas might cling to cotton or silk bales until another living body, usually a black rat, can be found. In this way, jumping from host to host, the parasite can travel across waters; across from, say, the Netherlands to England.

In the winter of 1664, a cluster of isolated and unusual deaths occurred in the English port of Yarmouth. They coincided with a spectacular 'blazing light' that scratched a line across the sky. It was the brightest comet seen for decades, visible for several days across western Europe, and many observers, including the king and members of the Royal Society, wondered what it could mean; in the seventeenth century comets were thought to be portentous symbols of doom. Then, during the Christmas holidays, a London physician named Nathanial Hodges was called to a patient with 'two risings about the size of a nutmeg . . . one on each thigh', encircled with what he described as a 'black hue'. In the first week of January 1665, the weekly Bills of Mortality – drawn together by parish clerks and sold for a penny – revealed the death of a person in the parish of St Giles in the Fields, London. The 'Bills' as they were often called detailed not only the number of dead the preceding week, but their cause of death too. The death in St Giles in the Fields was curious; it was a woman and her body showed the symptoms of a much-feared contagion. Unknown to the deceased and everyone else, her journey to the grave had begun with a bite from a flea carrying *Yersinia pestis*. The Black Death had returned to London.

The visit of plague in 1665 should not have come as a surprise. Plague was endemic in England, with a small number of cases occurring around the country almost every year. As Dr Hodges noted: 'It was a received notion amongst the common people that the plague visited England once in Twenty Years . . . as if after a certain interval, by some inevitable necessity, it must return again.'[4]

In truth it had been almost thirty years since the last large-scale epidemic of plague in London, but significant outbreaks had occurred throughout the seventeenth century. In 1603, plague struck London immediately after the death of Queen Elizabeth I, killing over 30,000 people. In 1625, following the death of James I, another outbreak wiped out just over 20 per cent of London's population. In terms of the proportion of the population killed, this was the last truly dreadful plague year in the capital, but there were further epidemics in 1630 and 1636. By 1665, for many of London's inhabitants, a major epidemic was just outside the realms of living memory.

Bubonic plague was, and remains, a disease unrivalled in its capacity to dehumanise its victims. It destroys the body by infecting the lymphatic system, causing fever and chills, headaches, weakness, seizures, vomiting, diarrhoea and extreme muscle pain. Initially, victims develop a rash and become lethargic but are unable to sleep due to extreme internal and external pain. As the fever sets in, speech and coordination fail, causing victims to resemble drunks. The swelling lymphatic glands form the buboes in the groin, armpits or neck (and sometimes at the site of the flea bite). Pressure from these buboes causes bleeding underneath the skin, turning the area a dark blue or black – hence 'the Black Death'. Finally, red spots, known as 'tokens', appear when the victim is close to death.

Unlike many other diseases that tended to affect the weakest in society, Thomas Vincent, a puritan preacher, believed that the plague spared 'no order, age, or sex'. He thought that the vicious arrow of plague 'pointed to rich and poor, to high and low'. But he was wrong. In reality, plague was a disease of the poor and it was those living in the poorest areas of London, in highly concentrated ramshackle tenements, full of tenants and families, and those with-out the means to leave the capital, that generally died.[5] Mortality rates were high – estimates are between 70 per cent and 80 per cent – and little had changed in prevention or treatment since it had first arrived in England three hundred years earlier. Locked into cen-turies of flawed medicine, there was no prospect of a cure.

In the seventeenth century, medical practice rested upon age-old Galenic theories. This posited that the body became ill due to an imbalance of the four humours: black bile, yellow bile, blood and phlegm. For this reason, treatments involved balancing out the humours – inducing sweat or vomit, or letting blood. A contagion like plague was believed to be spread through *miasma*, or 'bad air', so preventative measures rested on 'purifying' the air with aromatic bonfires and pleasant scents. It would take another 250 years for the biological nature of the disease to begin to be understood, and even now discussion continues regarding the different strains of the disease. Historic epidemics appear to have been much more virulent than modern plague, leading some to posit that human fleas and body lice may have also played a sig-nificant role as vectors of the disease during the early modern period. In humans, bubonic plague is typically caused by a bite from infected fleas that infest *Rattus rattus*, or the black rat.

What *was* known at the time was that outbreaks in England were usually preceded by outbreaks on the Continent. From as early as 1663, the presence of plague in the major trading ports of Amsterdam and Hamburg caused enough concern within the Privy Council for a plan to be developed to prevent it reaching British shores. At the recommendation of the Lord Mayor of London, Sir John Lawrence, a quarantine unit was established at Canvey Island, at the mouth of the Thames estuary, to isolate any infected ships and crew before they could approach England. Despite initial success – in 1664, there were 24,000 plague deaths in Amsterdam compared with just a handful in England – plague was a force too great for seventeenth-century border control. Inevitably, the contagion entered England.

Late in 1664, there were rumours that a group of infected Frenchmen had carried plague from Westminster to the City of London, but it is just as likely that it arrived in several waves from infected Dutch ports. This was made all the easier in March 1665 when war between the English and the Dutch was declared, and offshore quarantine measures relaxed. In his memoir from the period, Dr Nathaniel Hodges argued that it: 'was imported to us from Holland, in packs of Merchendize; and if anyone pleases to trace it further . . . it came thither from Turkey in Bails of Cotton, which is a strange Preserver of the Pestilential Steams'.[6]

In any case, the first official plague fatality of 1665 in London did not cause widespread alarm. St Giles in the Fields was a poverty-stricken area to the west of the city. Named after the patron saint of lepers, the suburban parish was built on the site of a long-gone medieval leper hospital and was a good distance from both the River Thames and London's mercantile heart-land. By 1665, it had become a cosmopolitan place, home to a substantial French population (including Samuel Pepys's mother-and father-in-law), and contained well over a thousand dwell-ings.[7] The largest of London's outer parishes, it was a mix of poverty and prosperity and stretched from Lincoln's Inn Fields in the east to Charing Cross in the west. The poorest inhabitants lived in timber tenements in Cole Yard, Cross Lane and the alleys and lanes surrounding a drinking haunt named the Crown Tavern. The richest residents – including the president of the Royal Society, William Brouncker – lived in grand brick houses along Great Queen Street and the blossoming theatre district of Drury Lane.

In places like St Giles in the Fields, the existence of the odd plague death on the Bills of Mortality every now and then was not unusual. As long as cases remained at a low level, there was usually no cause for concern. In this spirit, the January plague fatality was brushed aside as an isolated case. But then, in February, the parish witnessed its second plague fatality and the Bills of Mortality revealed a steady increase in the number of deaths overall. This included cases of 'spotted fever' (now known as typhus), an infectious disease spread by body lice with very similar symptoms to plague. Nathaniel Hodges, who lived within the city walls, claimed that as soon as rumours of a possible contagion reached 'the common people . . . every one predicted its future Devastations, and they terrified each other with Remembrances of a former Pestilence'.[8] Writing some years after the event, Daniel Defoe, who was only a young boy at the time seems to have based his account on a combination of research and the second-hand testimony of older relatives, claimed that this second death 'possessed the heads of the people very much' with very few caring 'to go through Drury Lane, or the other streets suspected, unless they had extraordinary business that obliged them to it'. In reality, however, one of the area's most famous businesses, the King's Playhouse, was busier than ever.

Saddling Drury Lane and Bridges Street, the King's Playhouse fell just outside the parish of St Giles in the Fields and into the adjoining parish of St Clement Danes. Opened in 1663, the grand three-tiered theatre was a defining symbol of Restoration London and home to the King's Company of Players. Set back from the street, the theatre was described as being 'very large' by one commentator, and reached by a narrow passageway that led into the main arena. Space was in short supply, and while gentlemen and their wives mingled in the boxes, the rising 'middling sort' jostled in the crowded pit as pretty young girls sold oranges. It was an impressive place, but not perfect. Pepys found the boxes to be too far from the stage and the roof,[9] topped with a cupola, often let in rain, leaving the seven-hundred-strong audience at the mercy of bad weather. To perform in such a space required nerves of steel, and the theatre swallowed up and spat out many a would-be actor.

It was in the King's Playhouse, under the guardianship of the ambitious Thomas Killigrew, that many of the finest performers of the age cut their teeth. In March 1665, it is possible that one such performer made her debut.[10] Still in her early teens, Nell Gwynn knew the playhouse well, but not as an actress. Having spent most of her childhood in a Covent Garden brothel with her alcoholic mother and older sister, at around twelve years old she had become an orange seller in the theatres of London and had moved into rooms at the Cock and Pie Tavern, within the parish of St Giles in the Fields. Had Nell been born in a different place or a generation earlier, her life would have likely mirrored her mother's, but the return of Charles II brought with it dramatic changes. Not only were theatres reopened, but women were officially allowed to perform on the public stage in England for the first time, and they proved to be a major commercial draw. With a pretty face, a tenacious personality and a lively wit, Nell was custom-made for this new public arena. At some point, perhaps while selling oranges, she caught the attention of Killigrew.

So it was that only a few weeks after the second case of plague, Nell is likely to have taken to the stage for the first time as Cydaria in John Dryden's dark epic *The Indian Emperour*. She was fourteen and her leading man was her real-life lover, thirty-nine-year-old Charles Hart. It was a serious role and an unprecedented leap for someone of Nell's background, let alone her tender age. She was not the first actress on the English stage – that accolade is thought to go to Anne Marshall, who played Desdemona in an adaptation of Shakespeare's *Othello* in November 1660 – but she would become one of its brightest. To act was a vocation that brought with it unprecedented social progression, but also unwanted attention. Gentlemen were known to enter the 'tiring rooms' backstage following performances to ogle at the actresses while they dressed. On one occasion, a performer named Rebecca Marshall (Anne Marshall's younger sister) was 'way-laid and attacked by a ruffian, on her way home from the playhouse' after rebuffing the advances of one Sir Hugh Middleton.[11] Sadly, there is no record of how Nell's first performance fared, but by 3 April she was sufficiently well known for Samuel Pepys to recognise her in the audience at the Duke's Playhouse.

Managed by William Davenant, the Duke's Playhouse was a former tennis court that had been converted into a theatre at Lincoln's Inn Fields, within the parish of St Giles in the Fields. Pepys was there with his wife to watch actor Thomas Betterton in the tragedy *Mustapha*, a new play about a flawed ruler with a weakness for the 'fairer sex'. Nell was joined by Rebecca Marshall who also worked for Killigrew's company. Yet by far the most esteemed member of the audience that afternoon was King Charles himself. The king regularly attended the theatre in public, and on this occasion he was accompanied by his twenty-four-year-old mistress, Lady Castlemaine. At the time, she was around a month pregnant with their fourth illegitimate child. Though they didn't know it, the eclectic group was in one of the most perilous parishes in all of England. In fact, within days, a young girl was to die of plague a mere ten minutes' walk from where they had been watching the play.[12]

Throughout the spring, the playhouses acted like a magnet, drawing daily swathes of Londoners into the epicentre of the outbreak. All the while the infection continued to take hold. How much the king knew of the situation in the contaminated parish of St Giles in the Fields is not clear, but on 15 April he travelled to the College of Physicians on Paternastor Row. Among other things, he is recorded as 'enquiring into the seat and causes of infectious diseases' and the 'means and methods of preserving and advancing the health of his subjects'.[13]

When the Bills of Mortality were released on 24th April, they revealed two further plague deaths in St Giles in the Fields. Quarantine measures were swiftly introduced and a number of residences were 'shut up'. In keeping with established protocol, a red cross was painted outside the premises and a paper note, reading 'Lord have mercy on our souls', was fixed to the door. Residents of one particular house, described as being near to 'the sign of the ship [inn]', took issue with the enforced isolation and removed the sign and opened their door in what was reported to be 'a riotous manner'. They then went 'abroad into the street promiscuously, with others'.[14] It was a patent breach of law and order, and on 28 April the king was briefed about the disturbance during a council meeting at Whitehall. He ordered that the offenders suffer the severest punishments that 'the right of the law will allow'.

Though the Bills of Mortality didn't yet show it, suspicions were growing that more than one parish was infected. Notes from the king's council meeting state: 'Plague has broken out and Vehemently suspected to be in some houses within the parish of Saint Giles in the Fields and other out parishes'.[15] A decision was made to create pesthouses outside the city to keep anyone infected away from the populace. Not much is known about London's pesthouses at this time, but records suggest there was a permanent timber building for the housing of those infected with contagion close to Old Street, to the north of the city. Were the king and his council deliberately taking care 'to keep it as much from the knowledge of the public as possible', as Daniel Defoe would later argue? Or did they think the situation could be contained? Perhaps both. It seems, however, that at this point only a few were privy to the full scale of the threat.

Close to the council chamber that same day, but seemingly oblivious to the escalating situation, was Pepys. As the newly created Treasurer of the Tangier Committee, his workload had increased once more. Today, he was waiting at court to see if a complaint he had put forward regarding some unfit watermen who had been put on board victualling ships had been read out. With many of his colleagues engaged at sea or elsewhere, Pepys would often find himself called upon by name to discuss 'Navy business' with the king. This new familiarity with the monarch had initially unsettled Pepys, putting him off travelling to Whitehall unless he was 'ready to give good answers'. As the council session closed, the king emerged from the chamber and informed Pepys personally that his complaint had been read. Writing in his diary that night, he noted that the king now knew him so well that 'he never sees me but he speaks to me'.[16]

Two days later, a new concern entered his diary. For the first time that year he wrote how there were: 'great fears of the sickness in the city, two or three houses boarded up'.[17] He was referring to houses in St Giles in the Fields, but it wasn't long before the Bills of Mortality revealed fatalities in other out-parishes too. In the first week of May, three more deaths in St Giles in the Fields were accompanied by deaths in the bordering parishes of St Andrew Holborn and St Clement Danes. From its crucible in the west, London's plague scurried eastwards through dirty streets and open sewers to the packed and squalid out-parishes that surrounded the walls, before finally creeping into the City of London.

On 9 May, the Bills of Mortality revealed a single plague death inside the city walls. It had occurred in Bearbinder Alley, in the parish of St Mary Woolchurch Haw, within walking distance of Pepys's home in Seething Lane. The victim was rumoured, once again, to be a Frenchman, connected to the earlier cases in St Giles in the Fields, who had fled into the city for safety. Once inside the city walls, established public health systems were immediately brought into effect by the Lord Mayor, John Lawrence. On an upward career trajectory, Lawrence, a London merchant and member of the Worshipful Company of Haberdashers was elected alderman in the tiny ward of Queenhithe, south of St Paul's Cathedral, in 1658. By the time he was elected Lord Mayor, he also held the title of Master of the Haberdashers. A father to several daughters, Lawrence was a strong personality, supported by a coterie of loyal followers and plague gave him the perfect opportunity to flex his powers.

Under his instruction, aromatic bonfires were erected throughout the city to purify the air, and on 11 May he ordered that the streets of all parishes 'be watered, swept and cleansed of all manner of dirt, filth and rubbish'. London had an ongoing problem with filth caused by exposed sewage, and only a month before the king had ordered Lawrence and the city aldermen to conduct a strict review of all sewers 'to preserve that great and populous city from fire and other accidents'.[18] Concurrently, the College of Physicians was instructed to consult previous plague guidelines in order to issue an up-to-date pamphlet of medicinal advice for the public. For a short time, it must have seemed as though the plague had abated. Almost as soon as the orders were issued, the number of fatalities dropped – from nine cases one week to three the next, with none inside the walls.

At Gresham College, the Royal Society had taken the precaution of warning readers of their journal, *Philosophical Transactions*, that the increase in plague might bring interruptions to normal production of the journal and public meetings.[19] Since 1663 the Royal Society had used Gresham College in Bishopsgate as its de facto headquarters – conducting experiments and presenting lectures and debates there – and meetings continued throughout the month of May. It was a broad church; a mix of gentlemen, nobility and ambitious sons of drapers, tailors and the like. Among their number was Robert Hooke, who was fast becoming the society's fledgling star.

Hooke lived within Gresham College itself and at just twenty-nine years of age, he had already achieved more than most in a lifetime. Beginning as an apprentice artist under Peter Lely, he had progressed to Oxford where he had worked under the renowned scientist Robert Boyle on the development of an air pump. He had also discovered the law of elasticity, a law that would later become known simply as 'Hooke's Law' and in 1662 he became the Royal Society's Curator of Experiments (the first professional research scientist) where he built a Gregorian reflecting telescope and made numerous astronomical discoveries.

For the last couple of years, he had been quietly working on a new project using compound microscopes. Examining thirty-nine carefully chosen and minute specimens at close range, he had worked tirelessly to create exquisitely detailed anatomical illustrations, accompanied by explanatory text. While examining cork and plants, Hooke noticed honeycomb-like chambers within the specimens. He decided to call them 'cells' after the Latin word *cella*, meaning 'small room'; it was the first use of the word in this way. The project had seen Hooke detail threads of silk, the head of a pin and even snowflakes, but by far the most impressive illustration of all was his 18-inch fold-out image of a magnified flea. In this spectacular image Hooke transformed a creature that was 'normally known only as a speck that bites' into something that was 'made familiar in every detail'. Hooke certainly seemed entranced by the flea when he wrote:

> . . . as for the beauty of it, the Microscope manifests it to be all over adorn'd with a curiously polish'd suit of sable Armour, neatly jointed, and beset with multitudes of sharp pinns, shap'd almost like Porcupine's Quills, or bright conical Steel-bodkins; the head is on either side beautify'd with a quick and round black eye, behind each of which also appears a small cavity, in which he seems to move to and fro a certain thin film beset with many small transparent hairs, which probably may be his ears; in the forepart of his head, between the two fore-leggs, he has two small long jointed feelers, or rather smellers . . .[20]

The book – named *Micrographia: or Some Physiological Descriptions of Minute Bodies Made by Magnifying Glasses with Observations and Inquiries Thereupon* – was yet to be widely published, but the Royal Society was far from ignorant of its significance. Copies of the text had been circulating as unbound folios since before Christmas. And in April the Royal Society had issued an assessment of the work within *Philosophical Transactions*, claiming that it would 'excite and quicken the Philosophical heads to very noble contemplations'.[21] Pepys, who had read it in January, thought it to be 'the most ingenious book that ever I read in my life'.[22] He was right to be impressed. It was a pioneering work in the field of microscopy, and the author's skilled artistry and scientific rigour had produced a book unlike any written before. While Hooke basked in the glory of his magnum opus, the tiny parasitical creature of 'strength and beauty' that had so amazed him was laying the groundwork for the worst outbreak of plague to hit London since the Black Death.

Only three years earlier, Hooke's peer, the statistician John Graunt, had written a much commended treatise on the pattern of historic plague outbreaks. He had asserted that in times of plague, the Bills of Mortality were closely followed by the rich so that they 'might judge of the necessity of their removall'.[23] Anyone reading the Bills on the 23 May would have had good reason to be concerned. Far from confirming a fall in the number of cases, they showed fourteen new plague fatalities and a marked increase in the number of fatalities caused by 'spotted fever'. Indeed, the deaths of Rebecca and Sarah Flowers, daughters of a Cripplegate wiredrawer named William Flowers, were recorded as such. Interestingly, the sisters were not buried in their local parish church, but taken to consecrated land outside the walls used in times of plague. Whispers of a potential epidemic started to travel across the English Channel. Since 1663, the Venetian ambassador in Paris, Alvise Sagredo, had received regular dispatches from an anonymous informer in London. Writing to Sagredo at the end of May, the informer divulged: '. . . the plague is beginning to increase in this city. The mortality bills admit that fourteen have died of it this week, but some physicians say that three times that number have perished of that disease these last eight days.'

Yet even as the contagion began its steady progession, the public playhouses remained open. Although the cast is unknown, during the middle of May the King's Playhouse put on a production of *Love's Mistress, or the Queen's Mask* by Thomas Heywood. Samuel Pepys attended on his own and thought the play to have 'good variety in it, but no or little fancy'.[24] Away from the stage, but no less dramatic, was another distraction for those drawn to gossip. A young earl had decided to kidnap a wealthy heiress. John Wilmot, the 2nd Earl of Rochester, was days away from his eighteenth birthday when on 26 May he made an audacious attempt to seduce fourteen-year-old Elizabeth Malet and make her his wife. Rochester's father, the 1st Earl of Rochester, had been a distinguished Royalist general during the Civil Wars. However, he had died in debt in 1658, leaving his son a title, but little else. Reliant on subsidies from the king, the young Rochester must have seen the heiress as an invaluable opportunity. Indeed, on several occasions the king had encouraged Miss Malet to take Rochester's hand in marriage, but to no avail.

On the night of the incident Sir Francis Hawley chaperoned the young heiress as she returned to her lodgings by coach, following a dinner at Whitehall. On reaching Charing Cross, their coach was seized by armed 'horse and foot men' and Miss Malet was snatched and bundled into a separate coach. Two women, ready to receive the young girl, carried her away. Rochester, who had orchestrated the enterprise, followed the carriage, only to be apprehended at Uxbridge. The king was livid and immediately issued a warrant for his arrest. Malet was quickly discovered and returned to her family. Despite being clearly fond of Rochester, who was only a couple of years older than his first (illegitimate) son, the king could not condone such reckless behaviour and sent the young earl to the Tower.

★

On 3 June, the king's attention swung eastwards: away from London, away from Rochester and his petty misdemeanours and towards a stretch of sea forty miles off the coast of Lowestoft. The English fleet of 88 ships faced a Dutch fleet of 109 ships in the first great clash of the Second Anglo-Dutch War. Londoners could do nothing but wait and listen. Pepys recalled that, 'all this day by all people upon the River, and almost everywhere else hereabout were heard the guns, our two fleets for certain being engaged'.[25] Dryden described how 'Everyone went following the sound as his fancy led him; and, leaving the town almost empty, Some took to the River, others down it, all seeking the noise in the depth of silence'.[26] Hearing the gunfire and anticipating the casualties, Evelyn instructed his officers to be ready to receive the wounded prisoners.[27] Of course, in London, miles away from the action, there was no way of knowing how the battle was progressing.

What they were hearing was the final leg of a two-day stand-off. Desperate to prevent a blockade of their ports, the Dutch had been ordered to attack the English during a period of favourable winds. On 1 June, the opposing fleets were in each other's sights, but for some reason the Dutch hesitated in their attack. By 3 June, the winds changed, putting the English in an advantageous position. After a few hours of manoeuvring, the first cannons were fired at 10 a.m. and continued for eight hours. From the three-decked and 80-gunned flagship *Royal Charles*, the Lord High Admiral, the Duke of York, commanded an English fleet packed with aristocracy: Prince Rupert of the Rhine, the Earl of Sandwich, the Duke of Monmouth, the Duke of Buckingham, Sir Charles Berkeley, Lord Muskerry, the Earl of Burlington's son, Richard Boyle, and Lord Buckhurst. The fierce battle culminated in a bloody duel between the flagships the *Royal Charles* and the *Eendracht*. At noon, the *Royal Charles* was hit by a chain-shot on the quarterdeck and Berkeley, Muskerry and Boyle were killed in one go next to the Duke of York; 'their blood and brains flying in the Duke's face'. Later, the poet Andrew Marvell satirised the action:

> His [Berkeley's] shattered head the fearless duke distains
> And gave the last-first proof that he had brains.[28]

Rear-admiral Robert Sansum was also killed, leaving a crucial flag office vacant. Captain Robert Holmes was proposed, but in the heat of battle the Duke of York promoted Captain John Harman instead. It was a slight Holmes did not forget. Finally, the *Royal Charles* sank its opposite number when a huge, and possibly accidental, explosion destroyed the *Eendracht*. So loud was the blast that in The Hague houses reportedly shook and windows blew open. All but five of the 409 men on board the *Eendracht* were killed, including the Dutch commander Obdem. Their flagship destroyed, the Dutch fleet retreated. The Duke of York could, and perhaps should, have pursued the beaten fleet, but for some reason he decided not to. The diarist John Evelyn believed that if the duke had chased the Dutch fleet, the victory 'might have been a complete one, and at once ended the war . . . but the cowardice of some, or treachery, or both, frustrated that'.[29] The battle was claimed as a victory for the English and a personal triumph for the king's brother and heir. The city celebrated with bells and bonfires.

Details of the battle were slow to emerge. After the blasts, Pepys wrote how 'all our hearts [are] full of concernment for the Duke'.[30] In a rather honest account, the *Intelligencer* reported:

> The Rumours of This Town have been so wild and various concerning the particulars of the late Battle, betwixt His Majesties Fleet, and the Hollanders, that there is scarce any place left for Truth, the People having been so wonted to Fables.[31]

The most significant English scalp was that of Sir John Lawson. An injury sustained to his knee turned gangrenous and sent him to the grave a couple of weeks after the battle. His body was transported from Greenwich and buried without ceremony a few days later in the church of St Dunstan-in-the-East, London, next to the grave of his daughter Abigail. London was in the grip of the Great Plague so the burial took place at night, only the navy officials who carried his coffin were present.

In the Tower, Rochester was in a perfect position to hear the bombardment as it echoed down the River Thames. To the king, the question of how to turn this rebellious youth into a respectable man may have found its answer in the blasts of naval gunfire, and, three weeks after being arrested, he was quietly permitted to return to Whitehall. The young earl's return to the palace, however, was to be brief. Mathematician Sir William Petty had once mused that an epidemic had only begun when the weekly death toll had surpassed 100. On 13 June exactly that happened, the number of plague dead jumped from 43 in one week to 112 the next. Then on 20 June, this figure soared to 168 plague deaths in a week. The king and court, followed by a handful of playwrights and actors, evacuated the city.

The Puritan preacher Thomas Vincent quietly observed the rising panic in his city. He noted how Londoners avoided 'new roses and other sweet flowers' in case their 'sweet smell' attracted the infection. He saw trade slow down and people become wary of talking to one another. He wrote: 'the lords and gentry retire into their countries; there remote houses are prepared, goods removed . . . few ruffling gallants walk the streets; few spotted ladies are to be seen at windows'. This was not an overreaction. On 27 June, the Bills of Mortality revealed the number of plague dead had shot up again, to 267. Twenty parishes were infected, including four inside the city walls.

Among those to evacuate was John Milton, who had spent a good portion of the last five years in hiding. He fled to the Buckinghamshire countryside. John Dryden also left the city and retreated to Wiltshire. Many merchants left, including the bakers, brewers and butchers that kept London fed. Towards the end of

July, Miles and Anne Mitchell, the booksellers at Westminster Hall, evacuated the city with their family and a pint of wine given to them by Pepys. At some point during the summer, plague claimed the life of their older son, leaving Betty Howlett without a fiancé. The master of Westminster School, at first moved his pupils to buildings in Chiswick but plague followed so he instructed his pupils, including twelve-year-old William Taswell, to return to their respective homes. Taswell joined his family in Greenwich where his father was forced to send two of their maids to the pesthouse.[32]

An estimated 30,000 people left the city during the first fortnight of July, and thousands more followed soon after. Pepys sent his mother to Woolwich at the end of June, with his wife following on 5 July. Parliament was prorogued and the Exchequer moved out of London to the royal residence of Nonsuch Palace in Surrey. Of the Royal Society, Robert Hooke, John Wilkins and William Petty evacuated to the country estate of Durdans in Epsom in early August. Only the society's president, Lord Brouncker, and its secretary, Henry Oldenburg, remained behind.

The most infamous evacuation of all was that of London's physicians. Most of the College of Physicians fled, including its president Sir Edward Alston. They did so for a variety of reasons, panic doubtless being one, but there was clearly a financial incentive drawing them towards the homes of the fearful and wealthy. Dr Jonathan Goddard, the son of a Deptford shipbuilder, defended 'his and his fellow physicians going out of towne in the plague-time' because 'their particular patients were most gone out of towne, and they left at liberty'.[33] In fact, so few physicians remained that the college was raided by opportunistic thieves, who made off with a chest full of gold coins as well as other treasures, including a silver fruit dish owned by the queen's physician Sir Francis Prujean. The few that lingered, including Dr Nathaniel Hodges and Pepys's personal physician Dr Alexander Burnett, faced an impossible task. The mass exodus of the capital is one of the most striking moments of the plague in 1665. As the highways out of London 'thronged' with passengers, coaches and goods, they left the poorest without food or medicine and at the mercy of fate. As Thomas Vincent put it: 'the grave is now opening its mouth to receive their bodies, and hell opening its mouth to receive their souls'.[34]

In this skeletal city, Sir John Lawrence was the most senior official remaining, supported by a handful of aldermen. But the Lord Mayor's jurisdiction did not cover many of the suburban out parishes that were most severely affected by plague. Of the nobility, George Monck, Duke of Albemarle, remained at the Cockpit, at Whitehall Palace. Monck was a towering mid-seventeenth-century figure: a soldier on the Royalist side during the Civil Wars, he had been given military control of Scotland during the Protectorate under Oliver Cromwell, before orchestrating the Restoration of Charles II. Known to his contemporaries as 'the General' he was officially the Captain General of Charles II's land army and controlled a band of officers known as the Lord General's Regiment of Foot Guards. He was supported by his friend William, 1st Earl of Craven, who remained at his house in Drury Lane. Like Monck, Craven was a seasoned military leader (unlike Monck, he had also once enjoyed a love affair with Prince Rupert of the Rhine's mother, Elizabeth, the Queen of Bohemia). Of the tiny handful of physicians who remained behind, Dr Nathaniel Hodges and Dr Witherley were put in charge of plague prevention within the City of London and the liberties (parishes outside the walls that fell within the City of London's jurisdiction), supported by two more physicians who would be paid out of funds raised by charitable donations. They were woefully overstretched. Pepys chose to remain in the city at the Navy Board offices, but made regular visits to his wife in Woolwich.

City-wide Plague Orders, issued during times of epidemic since the turn of the century, were swiftly brought into effect. Lifted almost completely from the Plague Orders of 1646, they stipulated that no clothes or bedding were to be removed from the houses of the infected, no family or friends were to witness the burial of the plague dead and no one was to leave an infected house, unless they were taken to one of at least five pesthouses that had been created around the city. The dead were to be buried in darkness and each parish was to appoint 'examiners' to keep a record of all sickness in their parish. Each infected house was to be guarded by two 'watchmen': one for the daylight hours of 6 a.m. to 10 p.m. and the other for the remaining hours at night. They were to ensure no one entered or exited the house. The most revolting task fell to the 'searchers', women of 'honest reputation' who were to examine the dead and report 'to the utmost of their knowledge' whether they had died of plague.

As London entered July, the days swelled with sunlight and the capital experienced 'the most extraordinary hot'. Lawrence drew up a mayoral proclamation, ordering all the city's aldermen to remain in the capital, forbidding the singing of ballads and selling of goods in the streets, instructing residents to remove the dogs and cats lying dead in the streets and closing all schools. The death toll for the first week of the month was 470, with thirty-three parishes infected. Visiting the city during this time, Cambridge scholar Samuel Terne noted how most people still went readily about their business, only avoiding the heavily infected areas such as St Giles in the Fields. There, he described, 'they have a Bellman with a cart; there dye so many that the bell would hardly ever leave ringing and so they ring not at all'. The number of plague dead rose to over 1,000 in the week of 11–18 July, with the final week seeing 1,843 deaths. The Plague Orders that had been brought into effect at the beginning of the month seemed to have made no difference at all, with the contagion spreading itself 'beyond all hopes of abatement'.[35]

Just outside the historic city walls, a lonely woman wept as she walked towards the New Churchyard next to Bethlem Hospital, carrying a tiny coffin under her arm. Nearby, Thomas Vincent watched. He judged her to be the mother of the child inside the coffin; and alone because all of her family had died. She must

43

surely have had to coffin up her own offspring, he mused, and would be forced to bury her last remaining child with her own hands. Wrapped in the immediate sphere of her reality, the woman paid little attention to Vincent, and remained oblivious to the posterity this brief encounter would bestow on her. For a month, scarcely a day had gone by when Vincent hadn't heard about the death of someone he once knew, but the sight of this pitiful woman moved him enough to write about it in his blistering account of the plague, elevating her fleeting slice of grief into recorded history.

While the woman's eventual fate is unknown, what we do know is that her approach to the New Churchyard would have presented scenes of horror. By 1665, the graveyard was far from 'new'. Originally set up in 1569 as consecrated land to be used by neighbouring parishes in times of need, the plague had pushed it into a profound crisis. It was stretched to capacity and heavy with the 'noisome stenches arising from the great number of dead'. Across the capital, churchyards were 'stuffed so full with corpses, that they are in many places swell'd two or three feet higher than they were before'. As more people died, new ground had to be broken up to inter the dead. Individual burials gave way to mass pits containing dozens of plague-riddled corpses. Men, women and children, wrapped in the linen they had died in, were packed into the earth 'thirty or forty together'.

The bodies tumbling into the earth of the New Churchyard near Moorfields came from across London. Parish records reveal the sad sequence of events that saw many families separated in life, only to be reunited a few days later in death. Ordinarily men in Restoration London tended to die more frequently than women (at a ratio of roughly 10:9). During this epidemic, however, the ratio not only equalled out, but the number of women dying actually surpassed that of men (at a ratio of 10:9.9).[36] In Pepys's own parish, William Ramsey, an almsman at the Draper's Company, buried his daughter Elizabeth on 23 July, his other daughter Mary on 24 July, and a young boy of his household on

25 July.[37] Walter Young, from the parish of St Peter Cornhill, buried his daughter Temperance on 12 July, another daughter, Martha, on 17 July, a third daughter, Elizabeth, on 21 July, and a fourth daughter, Mary, on 1 August. Robert Freestone was buried with his wife, Martha, on 5 August. When Thomas Howle died on 29 July, his wife, Mary, joined him a few days later.

In death, masters and servants and parents and children were equalled. A carpenter named William Frond was buried the day after his servant Ann. Thomas Roo, from the parish of St Mildred Poultry, was buried with his son Peter Roo on 25 August. In just over two weeks, William Greenop from the parish of St Olave, Silver Street, buried three daughters, one son and his wife.[38] Many that were last to be buried from a family were recorded in the register by just their surname, some as 'noone'. Archaeological evidence suggests that an effort was made to bury the dead in an east–west position and, far from being buried naked, they were wrapped in burial shrouds, probably their bedclothes, before being interred. When a young girl named Mary Godfrey perished in the parish of St Giles without Cripplegate, her loved ones commissioned a gravestone to mark her place of burial in the New Churchyard.[39] The bereft faced difficult times. Elizabeth Lingar, a widow, lost two daughters to the plague and was registered in the Hearth Tax records a year later at the same address, needing poor relief.[40]

It was the smell that Londoners feared more than the spectacle. If infected 'bad' air could be smelled, the plague could be caught. Given the stench caused by the decaying corpses in the New Churchyard, locals were keen to cover them with earth quickly, but how much should they use? How deep should they dig? Daniel Defoe described how the pit in his parish of Aldgate was 'about forty feet in length, and about fifteen or sixteen feet broad' and 'it was said they dug it near twenty feet deep afterwards in one part of it, till they could go no deeper for water'.[41] New Churchyard was one of the busiest plague pits in London, and bodies lay waiting to be buried in full view of those who cared to look. Pepys was drawn to the ghoulish spectacle when he travelled to adjoining Moorfields at the end of August 'to see (God forbid my presumption!) whether I could see any dead corps going to the grave; but, as God would have it, did not'. His macabre trip was not fruitless, however, as around Moorfields he noted how 'every body's looks, and discourse in the street is of death, and nothing else, and few people going up and down, that the towne is like a place distressed and forsaken'. So full did it become that the keeper of the graveyard was eventually ordered to stop making pits.

Thomas Vincent was thirty-one years old and lived close to the New Churchyard in a small residence in Hoxton with two other men, three youths, an old woman and a maid. In a city of lodgers and tenants, it was a family of sorts. Educated at Oxford, Vincent had, until 1662, been a minister of the Church of England, but the Act of Uniformity – which required all Church of England ministers to adhere to the Book of Common Prayer – had resulted in the ejection of 2,000 Puritan ministers, including Vincent. The so-called 'Five Mile Act', introduced in 1665, forbade any clergy from living within five miles of a parish from which they had been expelled, unless they swore an oath to obey the king and accept the Book of Common Prayer. Vincent was clearly running foul of the law, which carried a £40 fine. But he argued that in times of great need the laws of God should prevail over the laws of man, and he continued to preach illegally to the destitute, witnessing first-hand the escalating situation. Summoning apocalyptic imagery, he wrote:

Now the cloud is very black, and the storm comes down upon us very sharp. Now death rides triumphantly on his pale horse through our streets, and breaks into every house almost where any inhabitants are to be found.

The weekly Bills of Mortality ratified suspicions. The epidemic had got worse. July had peaked with a total of 2,010 recorded plague deaths in one week, but this escalated to a total of 6,102 recorded plague deaths during the worst week of August, with the overwhelming majority occurring outside the city walls. The situation was probably even worse than the Bills of Mortality let on – Quakers, Jews and other minority religious groups were not listed in the official record of burials, and some of the largest parishes seem to have given up detailing individual burials in the parish register in favour of 'running totals' that were fed into the weekly Bills of Mortality.[42] In addition, there seems to have been a deliberate attempt to downplay the scale of the epidemic. Towards the end of the month, Pepys was in conversation with the parish clerk of St Olave Hart Street, who revealed that the number of plague dead in his parish was not only increasing, but being consciously underplayed. Pepys records him as saying 'there died nine this week, though I have returned but six'. Drawing on previous plague epidemics, Pepys's near neighbour John Graunt, had supposed that during plague time 'a quarter part more dies of that Disease than are set down'.[43] There were also accusations that the searchers, being 'old and simple' or 'ancient' women, did not know what they were looking for when assessing dead bodies.[44]

Official communication with the world outside the capital was sustained in large part by the work of the chief clerk at the General Letter Office, James Hickes, and his colleagues, who kept their offices on Threadneedle Street within the city walls, 'so fumed, morning and night' that they were hardly able to see each other. Writing to Joseph Williamson, he declared that, 'had the contagion been catching by letters, they had been dead long ago', and expressed his hope that they might be 'preserved in their important public work from the stroke of the destroying angel'.[45] There were fears that the contagion could be caught just by touching the letters of those from infected places, so Hickes had devised a system of airing mail over vinegar before sending it further.

With 'no rattling coaches, no prancing horses, no calling customers, no offering wares', London was still and solemn. Grass had started to grow on the deserted streets and Roger L'Estrange was not alone in noticing how the poor 'suffer for want of bread' and sustenance. Many starved, or were forced to steal, beg or both, due to the swathes of brewers and bakers that had shut up shop. Those who remained kept themselves indoors, venturing out only when necessary. During a trip to Holborn, the protagonist of Daniel Defoe's account of the plague saw people break the established tradition of jostling for the wall to walk in the *middle* of the road. So acute was the fear of contamination from infected houses.

The unnatural silence of the metropolis was broken only by the groans of the dying and the calls of the 'dead carts'. In Paris, the Venetian envoy Alvise Sagredo received word from his English informer that 'they take carts through the streets crying "Bring out your dead, bring out your dead" and when the carts are full they take the bodies to be buried'.[46] There wasn't enough night to inter the dead under cover of darkness so the revolting task continued through dawn and into the day – as Pepys noted, parishioners were 'fain to carry the dead to be buried by daylight, the nights not sufficing to do it in'.[47]

There were so many infected that in some areas plague-visited houses were no longer shut up. The healthy were never far from the sick. In Southwark, an area hit particularly hard, an apothecary named John Allin wrote about being 'troubled by the approach of the sicknesse nearer every weeke, and at a new burying place which they have made neer us'. In early August, Pepys took a trip across London and was told the sad story of a man familiar to him, an ale-seller named Will, whose wife and three children had all died 'I think, in a day'. The closeness of the horror made Pepys decide to limit his journeying across the capital. Apothecary William Boghurst, who had set up shop in the White Hart pub on Drury Lane, noted how, rather than spreading from one place 'further and further', the infection 'fell upon several places of city and suburbs like rain'.[48] There was no way of guessing who, or where, would be hit next.

In this climate of fear, a range of preventative medicines and remedies were recommended. Dr Thomas Cocke advised the poor to force themselves to vomit if they suspected plague and to have a 'hot posset drink'. He then suggested they 'wash their mouth and hands with warm water and vinegar'. Like many who could afford it, Pepys chewed tobacco. Others turned to amulets and charms. Writing to her nephew who still remained in the city, one Lady Isham advised him to 'ware a quill as is filed up with quicksilver and sealed up with hard waxe & soed up in a silke thinge with string to ware about your neck'.[49] On one occasion there were rumours of a mineral-based medicine developed in France that could cure the plague. Many physicians were hopeful when samples were sent over, but found the 'cure' only worked to send 'patients into their last sleep' faster.[50] Some thought that the consumption of 'unwholsom meat (by reason of the great Rot among Sheep) eaten by the Poor last Year' may have caused contagion.[51] It was claimed that the nurses, usually women who had survived plague and therefore thought to be immune, recommended consuming human excrement as an antidote and encouraged the drinking of urine. In search of a remedy, one man who had found a carbuncle a little below his elbow applied a plaster to it. It turned gangrenous and scarification was needed, but the surgeon cut into a large vein and the man bled to death within three hours.

There was no harmony between those who treated the sick. Each family was supposed to be under the care of a nurse who would tend to their needs, but they were not always trustworthy characters. The physician Nathaniel Hodges lamented how 'these wretches, out of greediness to plunder the dead, would strangle their patients and charge it to the distemper in their throats'. They were accused of 'secretly convey[ing] the pestilent taint from sores of the infected to those who were well'.[52] On one occasion, a nurse reportedly fell down dead under the burden of goods stolen from a house full of plague dead. Quack doctors didn't miss the opportunity to make money from the ills of the time – one enterprising young man commissioned a paper advertisement that listed all the people he had 'cured' from plague with a miracle powder he had recently acquired, including four milk women in Covent Garden and 'Rich. Pearce, his wife and his nurse' on Bridges Street – but even qualified physicians were accused of being ready to take money but unable to offer a cure.[53]

At the time of the plague Dr Nathaniel Hodges was in his mid-thirties. The son of a Kensington vicar, he was born in London and attended Westminster School before heading to Cambridge in 1646, then transferring to Christ Church, Oxford. He qualified as a physician in 1659 and became a member of the College of Physicians in the same year, taking up residence in the parish of Walbrook. Clearly talented, while he did not challenge accepted medicine, he did put a great deal of weight on observation and real experience. Hodges meticulously noted the symptoms of plague as he witnessed them, commenting on the 'rancid brackishness' of victims' vomit and the 'frothy and fermentative nature of what was ejected by stool'.[54] On one occasion he noted how the plague tokens were 'not easily distinguishable from a Flea-Bite'.[55] He rejected some treatments accepted by his contemporaries, such as powder from a unicorn's horn and even bloodletting, which he said he 'should pass it by as fatal' and also acknowledged that the 'moderate breezes' of the summer should have been enough to 'prevent the air's stagnation and corruption'.[56]

When he visited infected patients he ordered that they be put straight to bed and covered in woollen blankets to encourage sweating. Fires were made using juniper, fir, oak, elm and chestnut, but not coal – this he deemed to be impure. The infected were not allowed to change their clothes in case dampness from clean clothes unsettled them. He recommended a diet of 'bread soaked in wine, poached eggs, juice of citrons, pomegranates, or elder vinegar, as well as chicken broths, gellies and wines'.[57] Naturally, the very poor could not afford such a range of food and many died in 'extreme languishing misery'.

Those close to death often suffered a kind of madness. Some attempted to relieve their situation by getting out of their beds in 'a frenzy' and 'leaping about their rooms: others crying and roaring out of their windows'.[58] Some sufferers, in a state of delirium, limped into the streets, almost naked and exposing their sores. One poor man burned himself to death after finding himself sick and alone. In August, Thomas Vincent witnessed a man staggering towards a railed barrier on the corner of Artillery Wall, close to where the Artillery Company (the forerunners of the Royal Marines) trained. The man bashed his own face against the rails with such ferocity that blood gushed out, prompting Vincent to rush over. He found the man lying with his face over the rails, bleeding on the ground. Leaving him, perhaps to get help, Vincent returned a little later to find the man several yards away, lying on his back under a tree in Moorfields. Vincent attempted to speak to him, but the only sound he heard was a 'rattling' from the man's throat. Half an hour later, the man had died.

At the end of August, Pepys was told that his physician, Dr Alexander Burnett, had died of plague. Pepys found it to be a strange turn of events given how long ago the physician's servant had died of the contagion and that, as he wrote in his diary, 'his house [had been] this month open again'. Unknown to the diarist, along with a handful of other physicians 'some surgeons, apothecaries, and Johnson the Chemist', Burnett had recently 'opened up a dead corpse that was full of tokens'.[59] Many died after the foolhardy and unauthorised dissection, which suggests a presence of pneumonic plague – which can be transferred from human to human through breath and body matter. Another physician to die from plague was Dr Conyers, 'whose goodness and humanity claim[ed] an honourable remembrance with all who survive[d] him'.[60]

Some were luckier. Dr Hodges, who remained in the city throughout the epidemic, became sick twice during this period but managed to avoid the plague, despite coming into contact with it regularly. Detailing his daily routine, he describes taking a medicinal nutmeg electuary every day immediately after rising – interestingly, nutmeg is now known to be a natural flea-repellent. Then he dealt with any private matters, before entering the large room of his residence where crowds of citizens awaited him with all manner of conditions to be inspected – from uncured ulcers to the first symptoms of seizure. When he had discharged the crowd, he breakfasted and then visited the sick in their own houses.

Hodges followed a strict routine when entering the homes of the infected – first burning some 'proper thing upon coals' and then keeping a lozenge in his mouth while he examined patients. He didn't use hot ingredients like ginger as he believed they would inflame the tonsils and endanger the lungs. He also took care not to go into rooms of the sick if he had been sweating or was short of breath. Returning home for dinner, he drank a glass of sack infused with walnut (another known flea repellent) to 'warm the spirits', and ate meat and pickles. After his dinner, more people came for advice. Once they had been dispatched, he again visited houses until 8 or 9 p.m. at night. Hodges would drink more sack before bed to help him sleep and breathe easy 'through the pores all night'. If he ever felt the beginnings of the sickness upon him, he drank sack.

Away from the medical professions, rules were in place to try to prevent the contagion spreading. All public activities excepting worship were banned. However, outside the city walls, in Westminster, a lute-master called Mr Caesar reported 'bold people [going] . . . in sport to one another's burials' despite the risk of contagion. Mr Caesar also claimed to have seen sick people breathing out of their windows into the faces of healthy people passing by.[61] Near to the Exchange, a coffee house remained open 'all the plague time'.[62] Licensed and unlicensed ministers, like Vincent, preached to congregations fearful that they were being punished by God for some great and unholy deviance. In some instances, so many people crammed into the churches that Vincent had to climb over pews just to get to the pulpit. Addressing the assemblies, he found 'eager looks; such greedy attention, as if every word would be eaten, which dropt from the mouths of ministers'. He mused that 'if you ever saw a drowning man catch at a rope, you may guess how eagerly many people did catch at the word . . .'

Many hoped that the end of summer would bring a decrease in the number of dead, but it got worse. At the beginning of September, a sad incident occurred on Gracechurch Street, in the centre of the City of London. After losing all except one of their children to plague, a respected saddler and his wife were shut up in their house. Desperate for their remaining child to have a chance at life, they reportedly handed it 'stark-naked into the arms of a friend' who dressed it in fresh clothes and carried it to Greenwich. The friend was apprehended, but eventually allowed to keep and look after the orphaned youngster.[63] During the third week of September, the Bills of Mortality shot up to 7,165 in just one week. It was the peak of the epidemic, and of the 130 parishes in London only four remained uninfected. By far the worst-hit parishes were those outside the city walls, with St Boltoph's Aldgate, St Sepulchre without Newgate, Stepney parish, St Saviour's Southwark and St Olave's Southwark suffering the highest fatalities. Within the walls, the worst hit areas were St Andrew by the Wardrobe, St Ann Blackfriars, Christ Church Newgate Street and St Stephen Coleman Street.

Even during the height of plague a few brave souls made the journey into London. During September, the schoolboy William Taswell was tasked with carrying letters from his family's temporary residence in Greenwich to the capital. Armed with aromatic herbs that his father believed would protect him from plague and a bag of food and Spanish wine from his mother, the young boy reluctantly journeyed to town. He found a place of horror: people in the throes of plague, others lamed by the swelling buboes in their groins; a few cried out to him for help while bodies were carried on carts to be buried. As he explained, 'nothing but death stared me in the face'. He delivered his first letter to one Mrs Harrison who he found to be the only survivor of her family of seven children. The next was for his family's long-time servant and his childhood carer, a woman called Johanna. She was managing their house in Bear Lane while the family remained in exile. As soon as she saw Taswell she wrapped her arms around him and declared, 'My dear boy, how do you do?' Taswell was pleased to see her, but keen to return to his parents in Greenwich. He left her and shortly afterwards Johanna caught the plague but luckily managed to recover.[64]

Offering a glimpse of what life was like for those 'shut up' in their houses, Thomas Clarke's testimony is a troubling read. He was put under quarantine for three months in total – losing two of his children and witnessing three others become sick. Unlike others, Clarke's house wasn't padlocked and he didn't have a guard outside his door. Instead, he was left to 'his own discretion', not daring to transgress in case he offended his neighbours. His rare piece of testimony, described by Clarke as being 'the sobs and groans of an afflicted man', heaves with sorrow and loneliness. He describes being largely abandoned by neighbours and friends; nobody asked 'how do ye?' or shared in his conversation. Even within the house, loneliness abounded. Those infected – whether adult or child – were secluded. Clarke recalled how, on one occasion, a neighbour supplied him with keys to fit 'in every door', presumably an attempt to keep the sick and the healthy in separate areas of the house. As he confessed, during times of plague love was present, but 'fear is a stronger passion' and so:

> The Daughter dareth not approach the Mother,
> Nor dares one Brother to come at another.
> The father may not his own child come near
> Nor may the child the parents for fear.
> The Mother doth bewail her child at a distance,
> The child oft wants the Mother's strong assistance.[65]

Clarke was a man who enjoyed the company of others and found this unnatural but necessary separation to be enough 'to sink the spirit, make the heart to bleed'. His sorrow was compounded by the denial of funeral rites to the plague dead – their bodies were thrown into carts 'much like offenders, t'execution place'.[66]

In Walbrook, Dr Hodges saw the damage that strict quarantine could do. On one occasion, he attended a young girl who had broken free from a shut-up house. He recorded how she was 'full of sadness and consternation' because all the rest of her family were dead. Showing the doctor what she thought to be a plague token on her leg, the young girl was relieved to find that it was actually just a wart, and that she did not have the plague. Hodges knew that by locking the sick and the well together, entire households would become infected. The very measures in place to prevent the spread of plague, he thought, put the healthy in severe danger and he noted how the dismay of those separated in such a way from society was 'inexpressible'. He deemed the marking of doors as hazardous, explaining that he 'verily believe that many who were lost might now have been alive had not the tragical mark upon their doors drove proper assistance from them'. He was not alone in his criticism; the apothecary William Boghurst found quarantine to have been 'enough tried and always found ineffectual'.[67] Dr Hodges suggested that if plague were to return again, proper accommodation outside the city should be created for those 'not yet touched in infected families'. The sick, he argued, should be sent to separate apartments.[68]

In September, Thomas Vincent's residence was finally hit by the contagion. It began with the infection of a neighbouring family. Then, one Monday, while Vincent was out seeing a friend in the city, the maid started to tremble and took ill. By Thursday she was full of 'tokens' and dead. The next day, one of the youths, 'a sweet and hopeful' boy, noticed a swelling in his groin which swiftly escalated. He declared that he wanted to live 'till fire and faggot', but he was dead by Sunday. That same day, another boy became sick and was dead the following Wednesday. The second boy's master fell sick on the Thursday but, although his body was 'full of spots', he recovered. There was much sadness in Vincent's household for the lost, and the mother of the first youth grieved particularly hard for her son. This was something that Vincent didn't approve of – it was God's will, after all.[69]

The scale of the loss and its emotional toll on the living is best demonstrated in Pepys's diary entry on 14 September:

> To hear that poor Payne, my waiter, hath buried a child, and is dying himself. To hear that a labourer I sent but the other day to Dagenhams, to know how they did there, is dead of the plague; and that one of my own watermen, that carried me daily, fell sick as soon as he had landed me on Friday morning last, when I had been all night upon the water (and I believe he did get his infection that day at Brainford), and is now dead of the plague . . . that Mr. Sidney Montague is sick of a desperate fever at my Lady Carteret's, at Scott's-Hall. To hear that Mr. Lewes hath another daughter sick. And, lastly, that both my servants, W. Hewer and Tom Edwards, have lost their fathers, both in St. Sepulchre's parish, of the plague this week, do put me into great apprehensions of melancholy, and with good reason.[70]

Then, finally, the plague began gradually to subside. It is estimated that 100,000 people lost their lives to plague in London. A significant portion had also suffered and recovered, and almost everyone in London knew someone who had perished. As the contagion continued to abate, late October and November saw people returning to the capital.

It was but a temporary respite.

3

The Turning Tide

His cousin Montagu (by court disaster
Dwindled into the wooden horse's master) . . .
Then Teddy, finding the Dane would not,
Sends in six captains bravely to be shot.

Andrew Marvell,
'The Second Advice to a Painter'[1]

North Sea

IT WAS A strange pact to make. As their ship sailed ever further from England, the teenage Earl of Rochester urged his friends Mr Windham and Edward Montagu to enter into an agreement with him. If any one of them should die during their mission, they were to return to the others in spirit form to prove that there was a 'future state'. Montagu, full of foreboding and convinced he would not return alive, rejected the offer, but Windham – who was around the same age as Rochester – agreed.

It was July 1665 and while London battled plague, the companions were three of many so-called 'Gentlemen volunteers' to have escaped the pestilence by joining the Earl of Sandwich's fleet on what was believed to be a low-risk high-gain mission.[2] Sandwich was one of a number of men whose non-partisan character had enabled his seamless transition from loyal Cromwellian to trustworthy Royalist, and was a strong military leader who had been given active command of the fleet following the Duke of York's

57

near death encounter at the Battle of Lowestoft. For months, a network of English diplomats and spies had been gathering intelligence in The Hague and orchestrating diplomatic deals in Copenhagen, in an effort to strike the Dutch a killer blow. From The Hague, George Downing had sent news that not only was a convoy of extremely valuable Dutch East India vessels on its return, but there was also word that a fleet of ships from Guinea, helmed by the Dutch admiral Michiel de Ruyter, would soon be arriving. Sandwich's mission was to track down, blockade and then raid the returning Dutch merchant vessels. If successful, English gains would devastate the Dutch, perhaps irreparably, and fund the entire English war effort.

Crucial to the plan was the assistance of the Danish king, Frederick III, who ruled over both Denmark and Norway. Since the outbreak of the war, returning Dutch vessels had avoided the English Channel, instead making their way home by sailing around Scotland and heading south, often anchoring at neutral Nordic ports en route. It was near to one of these neutral ports that the English wanted to ambush its enemy. From as early as 1664, Sir Gilbert Talbot, the English envoy in Copenhagen, had been leading secret negotiations with the Danish king in an effort to persuade him to betray his trade agreement with the Dutch and support an English attack. Heavily in debt to the Dutch, the Danes would be rewarded with a share of the anticipated plunder and the promise of English naval assistance, should the Dutch retaliate. If the Danes agreed, the new alliance had the potential to cut the Dutch off from the Baltic – effectively blocking them in. To the cash-strapped Charles II, it was an intoxicating possibility.

After months of wavering, the unexpected English victory at Lowestoft changed everything for the Danes. Indeed, it had taken many foreign observers by surprise and with the boost in English morale came Frederick III's agreement with the English. When Sandwich set sail, Talbot, who had masterminded the whole operation, was still negotiating terms with the Danish king, so key details of exactly how the Danes would be involved were not finalised. Despite this backdrop of uncertainty, the English fleet set out on its voyage.

Even by seventeenth-century standards, conditions for the crew were not easy. Speaking months later, Sandwich told Pepys that 'no fleete was ever set to sea in so ill condition of provision'.[3] He had good reason to be frustrated. One of the great weaknesses of the English navy during this time was that, with the exception of a small harbour at Bridlington, there was a limited number of places for the fleet to anchor and be fully resupplied north of Harwich and Sole Bay. Indeed, naval combat around the British Isles was almost exclusively concentrated along the English Channel, or the lower half of the North Sea. Sailing so far north – as Sandwich was doing – meant that the fleet was pushed to the absolute limit of its logistical capabilities,[4] and to exacerbate the problem, many established victualling tenders had to be cancelled because they came from places associated with plague. There was a real shortage of casks for water and beer due to the disappearance of many London coopers, and concerns that clothes carried 'miasma' meant that proper clothing was in short supply, leaving many seamen appallingly ill-equipped for the harsh winds and weather of the North Sea.[5] On top of this, the majority of the fleet's crew had not been granted shore leave since the Battle of Lowestoft over a month ago. Fear of plague had kept them in a state of de facto quarantine.

Healthy young recruits were always welcome and Rochester joined the fleet a month after Lowestoft, along with a 'Lieutenant O'Brien and a French gentlemen', near Flamborough Head, just south of Scarborough. Rochester had been travelling with Sir Thomas Allin's small flotilla and was reportedly 'very earnest to go away to the fleet'. So on 12 July, Allin sent him with a small ketch and the warship, the *Success*, to join the fleet.[6] On 15 July, Sandwich noted in his diary that, 'My Lord Rochester came . . . to remain on my ship for the voyage.'[7] At King Charles's request, Rochester was placed under the admiral's direct care and given a cabin of his own on the fifty-year-old, 90-gun flagship, the *Prince Royal*. The imposing vessel was one of the most powerful ships in the English navy. Remodelled and refined over the decades, it was built under James I, had seen action under Oliver Cromwell during the First Anglo-Dutch War, and had recently taken part in the Battle of Lowestoft. Sandwich, whose fifteen-year-old son, Sydney, was also on board, said he had accommodated Rochester 'as best I can'. Montagu joined the fleet a day later: he had travelled from Sole Bay on the 60-gun, third-rate frigate *Swiftsure*.[8] On 17 July, Sandwich made a list of all the ships that had joined his fleet and set sail for 'the Naze of Norway'.[9] A notable absence from Sandwich's fleet was Captain Robert Holmes who had been so offended at being over-looked for promotion to flag officer during Lowestoft that he had resigned his navy commission.

The North Sea is a tricky expanse of water to navigate. The current moves in an anticlockwise pattern. It has dangerous shoals, unpredictable weather and heavy winds that often turn into gales or storms. In the seventeenth century, a moment of distraction could send even the most experienced sailor miles off course or crashing into the northern rocks. This was the age of sailing – utilising the wind and finding the 'weather gage' (an advantageous state whereby a ship had the wind behind its sails; in battles this could also mean a better positioning for engaging an enemy ship) was of utmost importance as it could determine the victor of a battle. Yet, new research has revealed that, in 1665, a deep shift was happening, one that none of the fleet could have predicted. Since 1560, the world had been experiencing a mini ice age, which had been interrupted since 1629 by a milder climate and westerly winds. In 1662, however, the weather once again started to change, with easterly winds steadily increasing and the jetstream pushing further south.[10] In crude terms, this meant that during the First Anglo-Dutch War, led by Cromwell, conditions had often helped the English warships 'set the terms' of battles, but in 1665 the persistent cold, easterly winds would often lend an advantage to the Dutch.[11]

Under the harsh conditions at sea, friendships were quickly formed. It is possible that Rochester already knew Windham as he'd been at Oxford with his brother Thomas. Whether he was acquainted with Montagu before the trip is less certain, but what is certain is that the two had an awful lot in common. While the young earl's attempt to kidnap Elizabeth Malet had annoyed the king, Montagu had done something far worse. Born into privilege, and as Sandwich's cousin, Montagu had a link to a respected name and all the opportunity that this allowed. Although he was at least ten years younger than his cousin, Montagu had been the one to encourage Sandwich to endorse the Royalist cause leading up to the Restoration – a point he well remembered – and in 1662 he'd travelled with his older cousin to Lisbon to collect Charles II's prospective bride, Catherine of Braganza.

Despite her twenty-three years, Catherine had lived a very sheltered life. During the return voyage, Montagu won her confidence and shortly after arriving back in England, he was made the queen's Master of Horse. Montagu was not a man to engender the goodwill of his peers; he offended many courtiers, ran up debts (not unusual in that time and place), and seemed to harbour ambitions in the new queen's household. In May 1664, however, he crossed a line. Catherine was a pious woman who quickly found herself surrounded by the capricious wit and beauty of Charles's many mistresses, bearing witness to the birth of a succession of royal bastards. It is clear that she loved Charles though, and when she fell seriously ill in 1663 she sobbed and apologised to him for being a bad wife. If Charles was not in love with her, he held her in deep regard and became very protective of her.

In early 1664, Pepys noted how Montagu had 'more of [the queen's] eare than any body else, and would be with her talking alone two or three hours together'. In jest, he added that 'the Lords about the King' would tell Charles that 'he must have a care of his wife . . . for she hath now the gallant'.[12] While alone with Catherine one day, Montagu stroked her hand. It was a dangerous play for power and an overt act of intimacy that carried substantial risks. While this was not the court of Henry VIII, doubts about the queen's fidelity still had the power to under-mine the legitimacy of the Stuart dynasty. What had been going through Montagu's mind, one can only guess. Later, Catherine innocently asked her husband what it meant when a man stroked a woman's hand and told him what had happened. The 'Merry Monarch' was not amused. Montagu was ejected from court.

There is no question that this trip would provide both Rochester and Montagu with the opportunity to claw their way back into the king's favour, but there was doubtless a treasure-lust motivating them too. Privateering ran deep in the English psyche, and was legally sanctioned throughout the seventeenth century. Indeed, merchant syndicates from the port cities of London, Dover, and Bristol invested in privateering schemes, as did many war widows whose husbands had died at the hands of the Dutch – even Pepys invested in a scheme to send out the privateering ship *Flying Greyhound*.[13] For men at sea, prizes were only possible for the upper echelons of the crew. The average seaman would not have benefited significantly from captured vessels but officers and gentlemen volunteers like Montagu and Rochester could. In his correspondence, Rochester describes how he and his compan-ions were 'full of hopes and expectation' and planning how to split the predicted prizes. Rochester was seeking 'shirts and gould', while others chose spices, silks and diamonds.[14]

As the fleet travelled further north, its crew heard several rumours from passing boats regarding the whereabouts of de Ruyter and the Dutch East India Company fleet,[15] but none of them proved to be true. By 22 July, the crew had started to catch fresh cod and ling in the chilly waters. It was just as well as stocks were running low and – worst of all – beer was only days away from being rationed. Then, on 23 July, Sandwich received the disappointing news that de Ruyter's fleet had made it back to the Dutch Republic, but also that there was a significant number of Dutch ships at the Norwegian port of Bergen. On 30 July, Sandwich held a council of war aboard the *Prince Royal*, where a plan was formulated. Bergen was a tricky place to anchor, and unsuited to large warships, so Sandwich decided that a 22-strong squadron of fourth- and fifth-rate frigates and 3 fireships should be dispatched under the command of Rear Admiral Sir Thomas Teddeman, with the statesman Sir Thomas Clifford on board to negotiate terms with the governor of Bergen. A thirty-four-year-old father of two young sons and at least five daughters, Devon-born Clifford came from a modest family of landowners and was the MP for Totnes. He was the protégé of the Secretary of State, Lord Arlington, and possessed a superior and incisive intellect. As with many younger statesmen, the war with the Dutch presented an unparalleled opportunity to prove himself in the arena of state affairs.

Teddeman and Clifford were to travel on the largest of these smaller vessels, the eleven-year-old, 60-gun warship, the *Revenge*. The council agreed that the shortage in food rations (it was estimated that they only had a three-week supply remaining) meant that they would either need to launch the mission straight away or 'nothing could be attempted'.[16] Splitting the fleet was a bold and potentially risky move, and Sir William Penn was noted as being initially against it. Further intelligence arrived, however, that changed his mind: it was reported that ten cargo-rich Dutch East India Company ships were also approaching the port.

After weeks at sea, Rochester didn't want to miss out on any of the action. He went straight to Sandwich and asked for leave to join Teddeman on the *Revenge*, claiming that 'it was not fit for mee to see any occasion of service to the King without offering my self'. His request was granted and he, Sandwich's young son Sydney, John Windham and Edward Montagu joined Teddeman's flagship. The squadron set sail at six that evening, leaving the rest of the fleet, under Sandwich, waiting outside the scattered islands surrounding the mainland. A strong gale pushed Teddeman's ships as they cleaved their way through the perilous waves of the North Sea. They stayed overnight at Cruchfort, sailing on to Bergen at noon the next day. Rochester was told by a hardened sailor that 'the danger of the rocks . . . was greater than ever was seene by any of them'.[17] Ever northwards they travelled.

England

He closed his eyes, looking into the blackness and allowing the 'fantasie of seeing' to develop. There first appeared a blue spot, which grew lighter and lighter until it became 'white & bright'. Then red, yellow, green, blue and purple circles surrounded it, all of which were contained by a dark green or red colour. The image then turned blue and red. When he finally opened his eyes, it was as though he had been looking directly at the sun. Light objects appeared red and dark objects looked blue.[18]

He jotted his observations down in a well-thumbed notebook, which he'd named *Quaestiones Quaedam Philosophicae* (*Certain Philosophical Questions*). It was crammed with his thoughts on light, sound, the natural world and human emotion. On the book's title page he'd scrawled the maxim 'Plato is my friend, Aristotle is my friend, but my best friend is truth'.[19] The young man was studying at Cambridge and while he'd not particularly distinguished himself in the eyes of his university tutors, who endorsed a classical curriculum rooted in the works of Galen, Plato and Aristotle, he had been quietly and meticulously expanding his mind in other ways. In private study, he'd devoured the writings of Descartes, Hobbes, Galileo, Kepler and Boyle, and teased apart their work to develop his own theories and pose new questions. Isaac Newton was twenty-three years old and had led this dual life – part independent thinker, part obedient scholar – at Trinity College, Cambridge, for the past four years.

Over the course of the century, Trinity College had boasted some of England's leading thinkers in natural philosophy and mathematics. Only a generation before, it had produced the naturalists John Ray and Francis Willughby. A few decades earlier, the great Renaissance thinker Sir Francis Bacon had transformed scientific theory within its cloistered walls, and Newton's own adviser Isaac Barrow was a leading thinker in mathematics and calculus. Founded by Henry VIII in 1546, Trinity was one of the largest colleges in Cambridge. The building complex consisted of an imposing Great Court, thought to be the largest contained space in Europe, a newly built hall, and a series of residential buildings. It was here that Newton shared a room with John Wickins, whom he had befriended in 1663.

In the mid-1660s, the college was under the mastership of the fifty-two-year-old Royalist, scholar and preacher John Pearson. He was supported by tutors and fellows such as Isaac Barrows and James Duport. Newton had already completed his bachelor's degree and was due to embark on further studies when the threat of plague escalated. As a city of considerable size and importance, the residents of Cambridge had reason to be fearful; the last substantial outbreak in the city had occurred in 1630 and was still in living memory for the university's older dons. At some point in early summer, Newton left the city and returned to his family home of Woolsthorpe Manor, Lincolnshire, adding his name to the vast number of men, women and children moving around England to escape the contagion. The exile would be the most academically fruitful period of his life.

Like a drop of ink on blotting paper, once plague had marked London it was always going to spread further afield. As panicked Londoners made their exodus, the contagion followed them. It was carried along the highways, taking sinuous routes into neigh-bouring towns and villages. Horror stories abound: many died in fields or farmland before they found refuge, while locals, fearful of catching the contagion, left the exposed rotting corpses as prey for dogs and crows.[20] Just outside Dorchester in Dorset, an infected man spent his final days in a 'poor hovel' on a farm. Unwilling to handle his corpse, the people of Dorchester boarded up the structure and tossed it all into a deep pit.[21] Two miles outside Southampton, the bodies of a man, woman and child lay in the open fields. The woman, presumably the last to die, had scratched out a shallow grave where she had half-buried her husband.[22] As Thomas Clarke put it:

> And (in the Countrey,) some were ty'd to poles,
> Dragg'd by the Neck with ropes, and pok'd in holes;
> Whilst other Carcasses were left in field,
> To see what Buriall Beasts and Fowls would yield.
> This like a second death here, did appear,
> Which did cost many a heart-peircing tear,
> Of such as did survive, fearing they
> Themselves, if seized, might go the same way.[23]

Public fairs had grown in popularity throughout the seventeenth century and featured public entertainment such as puppet shows, music and markets. All public fairs within a fifty-mile radius of London were banned, including Bartholomew Fair and Stourbridge Fair (where only a year earlier Newton had purchased several books). Houses were shut up in Dover, Canterbury and the key victualling town of Ipswich.[24] In Hadleigh, there was a scare when a number of Dutch prisoners died, but on inspecting the bodies it was found that plague was not the cause.[25] Plague arrived in the dockyard of Woolwich, and shipmaker Christopher Pett expressed 'fears it will prove very mortal'.[26] In Poole, anyone infected was removed to a pesthouse.[27] With no nurses to care for the sick, a young woman, sentenced to death in the town gaol, was persuaded to act as a nurse to the infected on the promise that she would be pardoned. She wasn't.

Most towns shut their gates to strangers. Ipswich admitted no one unless they had a certificate of health. In Bath, those with health certificates from infected places had to prove that they had been away for at least twenty days, and all vehicles and goods had to undergo a period of quarantine outside the city. Epsom, close to where members of the Royal Society had fled, shut its gates and banned the taking of lodgers. Yet despite precautions, plague entered. In Lichfield, an infected man entered an alehouse and a few days later the owner was dead. In Yarmouth, guards were stationed to prevent inhabitants leaving the town while butchers, bakers and others supplying food were forbidden from entering. The people began to starve so the Privy Council ordered the magistrates to find a way of feeding the inhabitants without weakening preventative measures; how this was achieved is unknown. Towns and cities linked to London by major highways like the Great North Road were particularly at risk, as were villages that lined the River Thames. The plague reached as far as Cheshire, where the Justices of the Peace closed inns to prevent it spreading. It also travelled to the Tyne in the North East via the coal ships from the Thames.[28]

One of the most notorious places to be hit by plague during this period was the small village of Eyam in Derbyshire. Legend has it that some patterns and fabric were received by the local tailor from a relative out of town; on opening the box of material the tailor noticed an odd damp smell and hung fabric near the fire to dry. The tailor, George Vicars, died soon afterwards of plague, and the disease quickly started to spread through the village. Church leaders such as William Mompesson saw that neighbouring villages would be at risk, so the 350-strong community of Eyam sealed itself off. Plague ravaged the village for months, and by the time it left only 83 people survived.

England's neighbours were fast to act. The Council of Scotland issued a proclamation prohibiting trade with London and any other infected English town, while all ships docking in Scottish ports from England had to perform quarantine. Merchants and travellers were stopped on the Scottish border and forced into quarantine, and anyone attempting to reach Scotland had to have a certificate of health. For the Scots, plague was not so distant: only in 1645, Edinburgh and Leith had suffered an outbreak during which tens of thousands had died. Across the Channel, France refused entry to any ship coming from England, on pain of death. The plague gave the Dutch cause to be happy, with the *Utrecht Couranter* reporting that

'The English nation is now brought down so low with Plague that a man may run them down with his finger.'[29]

Plague even assaulted the royal court, chipping away at several peripheral figures, and there were great fears that it had followed the king and queen to their retreat in Salisbury. A servant to the Spanish ambassador died of the disease in one of the town's streets; the wife of a groom to the queen's equerry, Mr Halsall, was struck down with it in the neighbouring village of Fisherton; and even the king's own farrier was shut up following suspicions of plague. Charles gave orders for the residents of the town to be taxed so that a pesthouse could be established, and while the court swelled the market town, no one was granted entry unless they had a certificate of health from the city's mayor. Naturally, the king was excluded from such strict rules. He came and went as he pleased, using his exile from the capital to make numerous trips by boat to ports to oversee and coordinate naval preparations, hoping to prove the *Utrecht Couranter* wrong.

Similarly, the Duke of York was in 'continual motion', travelling north with his wife, Anne, to meet loyal supporters and quash the threat of home-grown 'Fanaticks', nonconformists (this included Puritans) and Quakers: it was feared that these perceived Dutch sympathisers would aid the enemy if a land attack was launched.[30] Letters were sent to northern nobility to secure 'dangerous men' within their jurisdiction, and the king wrote to the Lord Lieutenants expressing his disappointment that plague had not suppressed seditious behaviour and asking for their help to subdue any potential risings. In Dover, a meeting of 300–400 nonconformists was ambushed and across the country dozens of 'Fanaticks' were apprehended. Among the nobility greeting the duke and pledging their support were the eccentric Duke and Duchess of Newcastle upon Tyne, William and Margaret Cavendish, whose estate of Welbeck Abbey was in Nottinghamshire.

Margaret defied almost every seventeenth-century stereotype of a noblewoman. A self-taught polymath, she was interested in science, natural philosophy, romance and, above all, herself. Her widely read 1656 autobiography *A True Relation of My Breeding, and Life* included the ravishing statement: 'All I desire in life is fame'. A Royalist to the core, she had been a maid of honour to Charles II's mother, Henrietta Maria, during the interregnum and had travelled with the royal court to Paris, Rotterdam and Antwerp, where she had fallen in love with and married the Royalist Civil War general William Cavendish. Unusually for the time, William, who was a patron of the playwrights John Dryden and Thomas Shadwell, encouraged his wife's learning, hosting meetings with leading thinkers. Margaret Cavendish is even depicted leading a group discussion in the frontispiece of one of her earlier books. They were a formidable couple.

By 1665, Margaret had published several works, the most recent being a series of letters addressed to an anonymous 'Madam', where she had laid out her views on the various philosophical topics of the day. One of her key arguments was that everything achieved by humans is material. Regarding the mind, she states that it is not 'composed of raggs and shreds, but it is the purest, simplest and subtillest matter in Nature'. Her works also touch upon the immaterial nature of God and faith, arguing that

> it seems as strange to me to prove the Immortality of the Soul, as to convert Atheists; for it is impossible, almost, that any Atheist should be found in the World: For what Man would be so senceless as to deny a God? Wherefore to prove either a God, or the Immortality of the Soul, is to make a man doubt of either.[31]

Yet the most important thread running through her writing is a clear desire to be accepted as an intellectual equal.

It was something she was yet to achieve. None of the thinkers alluded to in her texts had publicly engaged with her. John Evelyn, who had known the duchess for many years and regarded her warmly, referred to her in his diary as 'a might pretender to learning, poetry and philosophy'.[32] She was forward thinking, arguing that a woman's wit was equal to that of a man's, and that it was only learning that kept them apart.[33] She was also noted for her distinctive and 'very singular' style,[34] and her resistance to following modes of fashion. She rather marvellously adorned her footmen in velvet as she travelled around, and even Evelyn, who knew what to expect, was still struck by her 'extraordinary fanciful habit, garb, and discourse' when meeting her anew.[35] Her brash and confident demeanour provoked both fascination and repulsion from her contemporaries, and Pepys paints a glorious image of her a couple of years later when she and her husband visited London:

> The whole story of this lady is a romance, and all she do is romantick. Her footmen in velvet coats, and herself in an antique dress, as they say . . . so people may come to see her, as if it were the Queen of Sheba.[36]

At the time of meeting the Duke of York, she was preparing a new book for publication, an ambitious work of utopian science fiction entitled *The Description of a New World, Called The Blazing World*. It was an adventure story about a woman who travels to the North Pole and enters a new and fantastical land inhabited by hog-men, fox-men and sundry fantastical creatures.

The Cavendishes travelled for fifteen miles with the Duke of York and his entourage, attending them in Rufford before, presumably, returning to their estate. They promised the party a 'great entertainment' on their return.[37]

Just over a hundred miles south of Rufford, a Quaker named Thomas Ellwood was preparing for a humbler reunion. He had received word that his former master was soon to leave London, and had been tasked with finding a suitable retreat for the man and his family. Ellwood quickly found a 'pretty box' of a cottage in Chalfont St Giles, close to his own Buckinghamshire home. He intended to wait on their arrival, but unfortunately (although not for the first time) he was apprehended and sent to Aylesbury

Prison, probably because of his religious convictions. Nevertheless, his fifty-six-year-old master, accompanied by his flame-haired young wife, safely arrived in Chalfont in July. The master was John Milton and among his possessions was a ten-volume manuscript that he had been secretly working on for the past few years. It was not written in the author's own hand as he had been blind since 1652; instead, Milton had meticulously dictated thirty to forty lines at a time to various assistants and close relatives. Blindness had no more diminished Milton's intellectual ability than it had snuffed out his rather impressive ego.

Milton 'kept always a man to read for him', usually the son of an acquaintance or someone familiar.[38] One of his early assistants had been the poet Andrew Marvell (another alumnus of Trinity College, Cambridge) and in 1662 Ellwood had been recommended to Milton through mutual friends. Ellwood described going each afternoon to his master's house – which was then on Jewin Street in London – to read him books in Latin. Milton encouraged his pupil to improve his Latin by conversing 'with foreigners, either abroad or at home' in order to learn the correct pronunciation.[39] He was able to tell simply by the tone of Ellwood's voice whether his pupil had understood the words he was reading, and if he had not, Milton would stop his reader and explain what the words meant. Their time together was cut short when Ellwood became briefly ill, but the two remained on good terms so it was unsurprising that Milton turned to Ellwood when London became infected.

That Milton was not only alive, but a free man, is one of the great curiosities of the age. Charles II had been remarkably restrained when dealing with repentant Parliamentarians. The Act of Indemnity granted many of Cromwell's supporters clemency, with only fifty people specifically excluded. The full force of his retribution was reserved for those who had signed his father's death warrant. Milton, however, was a unique case and could well have been one of the fifty: while he had not been one of the signatories, he *had* been employed by the Cromwellian regime as Secretary of the Foreign Tongues, and had written a series of impassioned and widely read Puritan pamphlets staunchly defending the decision to execute Charles I. At Cromwell's death, the tide turned against Milton, and many of his tracts were publicly burned. Right up until the moment of the Restoration, when George Monck orchestrated the king's return, Milton had argued against the decision to reinstate Charles II, calling instead for a 'Free Commonwealth'. In his pamphlet published in the spring 1660, he argued:

> If we return to kingship, and soon repent (as undoubtedly we shall, we begin to find old encroachments coming on by little and little upon our consciences, which must necessarily proceed from king and bishop united inseparably in one interest), we may be forced perhaps to fight over again all that we have fought, and spend over again all that we have spent.[40]

Following the Restoration, Milton had been briefly imprisoned in the Tower of London, but the expert negotiations of his former protégé Andrew Marvell ensured his release. Afterwards, Milton went quiet, publishing nothing and regularly going into hiding. Perhaps it was this silence, combined with the king's pragmatism, which saved Milton's life.

As soon as Ellwood was released from his brief spell at Aylesbury Prison, he made the short journey south to visit his master at the cottage. After some polite discourse, Milton called for the manuscript he had brought with him from London. He gave it to Ellwood, asking him to read it at his leisure and, once finished, to come back and tell him what he thought. The text Ellwood carried away had started life as an outline for a play called *Adam Unparadized*, but had since been refashioned into an epic poem in the tradition of the *Iliad* and the *Odyssey*. It was called *Paradise Lost*.

Reading it for the first time, Ellwood found it to be 'a most excellent poem'. When he returned the manuscript to Milton he acknowledged the honour that his master had bestowed in asking for his opinion. At the cottage, the pair discussed the text, before

Ellwood said to Milton, 'Thou hast said much here of Paradise Lost, but what has thou to say about Paradise Found?' Milton did not answer, 'but sat some time in a muse' before breaking off their discourse.[41]

North Sea

Bergen was Norway's most important westerly port and its wooden town buildings formed a tight horseshoe around the narrow harbour. It was flanked on either side by the stone fortresses of Bergenhus and Sverresborg and beyond the town farmland fed into rocky hills. To reach the harbour, vessels had to navigate a series of narrow natural lanes formed by the scattered and rocky skerries. Rear Admiral Thomas Teddeman, who had been put in charge of the mission, lost several ships making the journey to Bergen – swept away by the high winds; the ships had drifted too far north – and even his own ship, the *Revenge*, had run aground and had to be worked free.

When his reduced fleet finally reached the mouth of the harbour, it was clear that the information they had received about Dutch merchant ships being in the harbour had been sound. They were in sight, already anchored. Strong winds meant that Teddeman's squadron immediately 'warp[ed] in close to the Dutch ships in the port and under the Castle' in order to anchor. It was then simply a matter of organising the attack, and it seems very likely that Teddeman expected assistance from Bergen. He soon received a message from the governor, Claus von Ahlefeldt, 'full of civility and offers of service', yet telling Teddeman that he must not 'bring above 5 men of war [warships] in his port'.[42] Teddeman explained that he 'must bring our ships into safety'. Messages went back and forth and Teddeman organised eight of his ships in line to bring 'our broadsides on the harbour'.[43] Montagu played messenger and explained their purpose to Ahlefeldt – namely, that they had arrived to seize the Dutch ships. Ahlefeldt's reply took them by surprise. He claimed that he had not received orders from Frederick III to cooperate with the English and said he 'would not violate the port, contrary to the Articles of peace'.[44] He asked the English to delay until he had received word from his king.

Days before and hundreds of miles away in Copenhagen, the English envoy Sir Gilbert Talbot, aware that Sandwich had decided to track the Dutch ships heading to Bergen, had sent a crucial letter to him explaining the developing diplomatic situation. The letter failed to reach Sandwich in time, let alone Teddeman's small squadron. In it he had warned:

> You are not to be surprised if he [the governor] seem to be highly displeased with your proceeding and that he make high complaint thereof against you, which nevertheless will be but in show to amuse the Hollanders and excuse himselfe outwardly to the world.[45]

At the same time, the Danes had dispatched a similar letter from Frederick III to the Governor of Bergen, explaining that a deal had been made. He told the governor to allow an English attack, but there was no mention of providing active support. From Frederick III's point of view, it would make much more sense to sustain the appearance of neutrality and take half of the prize should the English be victorious than to put himself at risk of war with the Dutch. But his letter, too, had failed to reach its recipient in time.

Teddeman's squadron was in an impossible situation. Supplies were dangerously low and a delay would seriously affect the health and morale of his men. There was also the suspicion that they were being played for fools. Clifford and Montagu continued to negotiate with Ahlefeldt, with Montagu even reportedly promising him great rewards,[46] including the Order of the Garter, but Ahlefeldt was not to be persuaded. Montagu changed tack, threatening the governor instead and warning him 'that he must defend himself as best he could'.[47]

For hours, messages went back and forth, but nothing happened. Led by captain Pieter de Bitter, the Dutch had been enjoying shore leave when the English arrived and appeared to have made themselves at home in Bergen. Were the Danes going back on their word? As night crept over the Norwegian harbour, Rochester was not alone in noticing how the Dutch seemed to be constructing temporary forts around the town under the cover of darkness and transporting cannons to the castle. Most tellingly, they also positioned their heaviest ships into a broadside line across the harbour. Teddeman smelled a rat and, as the sun rose on 2 August, he arranged his small fleet into a broadside half-moon, with the *Prudent Mary, Breda, Foresight, Bendish, Happy Return, Sapphire* and the *Pembroke* directly targeting the Dutch ships and the town, and the rest, including the *Revenge*, facing the coastal batteries.

Quietly, gunpowder had been transported by the youngest sailors from the safety of the storerooms in the lower decks of the English fleet, ready for battle. At 5 a.m., the English war drums began to beat, prayers were made, and Teddeman 'let fly' the fleet's 'fighting Coulours'. Fresh gunpowder was loaded into cannon barrels with cloth or old rope to keep it in place. The heavy gun carriages were rolled towards the bulwarks, enabling the barrels to protrude out of the gun ports. The cannons were immediately blasted at the enemy ships.

They were answered by a barrage of cannon fire from the Dutch ships. Teddeman would later say that he only fired on the town of Bergen after the castle and fortresses had fired on him. The Danes would say that it was only after an English cannonball hit their fortress, killing four people, that they began firing too. In the heat of battle, perhaps both sides thought their version was true. In any case, Bergen turned on the English.

Dutch artillery battered the ships, with the upper decks hit particularly hard. Each successful hit by a cannonball gave rise to a storm of dust and splinters from the ship, ripping through men's bodies and choking those nearby. Thomas Haward, captain of the *Prudent Mary*, was killed; Thomas Seale, captain of the *Breda*, was killed; John Utber, captain of the *Guernsey*, was killed, along with three other captains. The English were against the wind so the fire and smoke emanating from the battle billowed towards them. In such conditions, the use of the fireships, 'which' as Rochester overzealously noted later, would 'otherwise had infallibly done our business', would have been suicidal. As fast as they could, from the first and second decks of the English frigates, men stuffed gunpowder and cannonballs into the artillery and blasted more shots at the enemy. The tough work was made all the more difficult under fire; they were a mere 100 metres from the Dutch ships, but kept missing their targets. For three hours the battle continued.

On the *Revenge*, Rochester and his comrades were pounded with artillery from the Norwegian fortresses as well as from the Dutch ships. Despite their efforts, the 'Castles were not to bee [shot] down', not least because of the strong stone walls. Rochester's friend Windham began to tremble. It became so severe that Montagu rushed to his aid, holding the teenager upright, gunfire and cannons continuing all around them. Rochester heard a blast and saw a cannonball shoot into the pair, killing Windham instantly and ripping out Montagu's stomach. The English cut their anchor ropes and cast themselves adrift. In just three hours they had lost 500 men and six captains. Montagu's slow and horrifically painful death took six hours to conclude; he was reported to have been in good spirits to the end. Most of those whose lives ended that day sank into the water, their bodies offerings to the insatiable North Sea; but not Montagu and Windham. Their bloodstained cadavers were stored away in now-empty barrels, to be buried in English soil. Teddeman's squadron was shattered, and retreated, as Rochester described in a letter to his mother the next day, 'having beate the town all to pieces without losing one ship'.

After weeks at sea, it was a dreadful failure. Bad planning and slippery intelligence had led many ill-fed and ill-paid men to their deaths. Rochester waited all his life, but neither

Windham nor Montagu returned to tell him that there was a world beyond.

England

The fallout from the Bergen campaign was devastating for the Earl of Sandwich, but its effects were not immediate. The English were expecting to win the war; to their mind, they had better ships, better commanders and a strong recent history of beating the Dutch at sea, so when Clifford was sent to England with word of the defeat, there were profound psychological repercussions. The reality was that they were at an enormous disadvantage. For a start, there were no long-term funds for war – military costs were expected to be covered by Dutch prizes – and, unlike their enemy, the English had invested very little in the building of new warships. Losing the battle at Bergen was a real blow to morale: as the Duke of York's secretary William Coventry wrote in a letter to Arlington: to him, 'the consequences' of the ill-fated mission were 'not so great as the discouragement that it will give to the rest of the fleet, especially during the absence from them of so considerable a number of their body'.[48] In the Dutch Republic, coins were struck celebrating the victory. The action also worked to bind the Danes and the Dutch together.

Sandwich was shrewd enough to realise that his position was vulnerable, and spent the rest of the summer atoning for the disaster. In late August he took on 250 new recruits and replenished the fleet's provisions.[49] Early in September, he captured two Dutch East India vessels that had been driven away from the convoy during a storm. This was followed a few days later by the capture of eight Dutch merchant vessels and four warships. It was a tremendous turn of fortune and Rochester, who had remained with the fleet – conducting himself in a 'brave' and 'industrious'[50] manner – was sent to deliver news of the success to the king. At the start of the campaign it had been hoped that the capture of

Dutch merchant ships would be 'a booty that would pay for the powder and shot of a twelvemonths' war',[51] and it was anticipated that the gains would be worth £200,000 and help ease the financial pressure.[52] As Pepys wrote in his diary:

> The fleete come home with shame to require a great deale of money, which is not to be had, to discharge many men that must get the plague then or continue at greater charge on shipboard, nothing done by them to encourage the Parliament to give money, nor the Kingdom able to spare any money, if they would, at this time of the plague, so that, as things look at present, the whole state must come to ruine . . .[53]

Indeed, for the average seaman, the poor state of the navy purse had rendered his situation desperate. On shore, men were financially and physically broken, with their sporadically paid navy wages used to pay off debt. In the maritime city of Portsmouth, many unpaid men were 'turned out of doors by their landlords' where they perished 'more like dogs than men'. The navy had many men under its protection, but little with which to pay them. Thomas Middleton was in Portsmouth when he wrote an impassioned letter to Samuel Pepys, explaining: 'only pay these poor men board wages, and 200 will do as much work as 300 at the present time'.[54] For those given tickets in lieu of their wages, there was the option of exchanging them at extortionate discounts in alehouses or with moneylenders.[55] Sandwich's own force had returned from Bergen suffering from malnutrition.[56] In addition to this, the English were having to house and feed thousands of wounded seamen and make space for hundreds of Dutch prisoners, 'some of them very sick'. In the middle of September, Evelyn told George Monck that 'unless we had £10,000 immediately, the prisoners', who were under his control, 'would starve'.[57] A little later in the year, Pepys wrote of a terrifying incident involving a raid on the Navy Board in Greenwich: '100 seamen all the afternoon there, swearing below and cursing . . .

and breaking the glasse windows, and swear[ing] they will pull the house down on Tuesday next'.[58]

With plague affecting many parts of the country, casual jobs were scarce and normal trade was impossible. As the Earl of Peterborough put it, 'the plague is an infinite interruption to the whole trade of the nation'. Money was urgently needed.

In letters to Sandwich, both Coventry and Monck urged the admiral to keep safe from plunder and embezzlement the precious cargo he had won. Monck had already negotiated a deal for the East India Company to lend £5,000 to the Navy Treasury as part of the expected prize. What Monck and Coventry were soon to discover, however, was that many of Sandwich's officers had already taken a slice of the booty, before it had legally been declared a prize. Sandwich had turned a blind eye, principally to keep his flag officers onside: they would receive very little once the prizes were declared; it was viewed by many as just deserts; and keeping them onside would bolster Sandwich's chances of being given command of the 1666 campaign. It was a catastrophic error of judgement and, as the most senior and trusted member of the navy, Sandwich was fully culpable. He received a backdated authorisation from Charles, but it wasn't enough to plug the political volcano that erupted. Many officers who had been with him on the campaign refused to take a share and the Duke of York's secretary, William Coventry, smelling blood, orchestrated a fall.

He argued that the taking of prize goods before they had been properly declared should be made a felony, and pushed for Sandwich's impeachment. There was an extra layer to the hostility: Sandwich was the king's man and Coventry's grudge may well have been compounded by the resentment felt by his master, the Duke of York, at having been removed from active naval duty after Lowestoft. There were hints that Charles, who loved the sea, had been jealous of his brother's ability actively to lead the defence of the realm, and the reasons behind the duke's removal from active service were, to many, not satisfactory. To the king's most trusted advisor, the Lord Chancellor, the Earl of Clarendon, it was clear that courtiers were trying to encourage James to believe he had been treated unfairly.

While the royal brothers shared many experiences, their characters were vastly different. Charles was mentally agile, emotionally intelligent and a pragmatist to the core. He had an uncanny ability to read people and knew exactly how and when to please and impress. But his easy charm covered a naturally vulpine character. James, on the other hand, was not as intellectually sophisticated as his brother. He wore his heart, and his principles, on his sleeve, and often acted on impulse rather than design. He had inherited a stubbornness of character from his father; a trait that would have devastating consequences later in his life. That aside, what they did share was a resolute determination to continue the war against the Dutch, even if it was crippling the country's finances.

With the crown's purse empty, the calling of a parliament was of utmost importance. In early September, the court had moved from Salisbury to Oxford. A great Royalist city, Oxford had been a stronghold during the Civil Wars of the 1640s; it was also packed with buildings ostentatious enough to house royalty. Towards the end of September and beginning of October, MPs and nobility journeyed across the country to Oxford. James left his wife in York with her Master of Horse – 'the handsomest youth of his time'[59] Sir Henry Sidney – with instructions that she be treated as well as if he were still there (Sidney and the duchess were to take the duke's instructions a little too literally).

Shortly after the duke's arrival, the rivalry between the royal brothers intensified, but it had very little to do with matters of state. As soon as she had arrived at court in 1662 to be maid of honour to Catherine of Braganza, Charles had been infatuated with Frances Stewart. Beautiful, innocent but a flirt, Frances was described by Charles's sister as the 'prettiest girl in all the world and the most fitted to adorn a court', and Samuel Pepys found her to be 'the greatest beauty I ever saw, I think, in my life'.[60] But she was the rarest of things in the Restoration court: chaste.

When the queen became seriously ill in 1663, it was to this young ingénue that people looked when whispering about a possible new wife for the king. Perhaps she could see no benefit in following Lady Castlemaine's footsteps, perhaps she was too loyal to the queen, or perhaps she simply wasn't attracted to the king; whatever the reason, Frances would not submit to becoming the king's mistress and Charles felt the pain of unrequited love (or possibly unfulfilled lust). A poem he composed about her begins:

> I pass all my hours in a shady old grove,
> But I live not a day when I see not my love,
> I survey every walk now my Phyllis is gone,
> And sigh when I think we were there all alone.
> O then 'tis, O then, I think there's no Hell,
> Like loving, like loving too well.[61]

The lovesick king visited her chamber – along with the heavily pregnant Lady Castlemaine's – every morning before eating his breakfast. The duke was not blind to Frances's beauty, and he too became an admirer of the young woman. Confiding to Samuel Pepys 'as an infinite secret', William Coventry revealed that 'the factions are high between the King and the Duke, and all the Court are in an uproare with their loose amours; the Duke of Yorke being in love desperately with Mrs. Stewart'.[62] For her part, Frances seems to have been even less inclined to the duke's charms.

With affairs of the heart simmering in the background, Parliament was held on 9 October in the Great Hall of Christ Church, Oxford. It was presided over by Charles, with Clarendon delivering the details. In the session, the king pleaded with the house to grant the war effort more money, admitting that the war 'hath proved more chargeable than I could imagine it would have been', and assuring his subjects that he knew of 'no advantage they [the Dutch] have had but the continuance of the Contagion'. He also warned that he 'must not only desire Assistance to carry on this War, but such Assistance as may enable me to defend myself and you against a more powerful Neighbour [France], if he shall prefer the Friendship of the Dutch before mine'.[63]

Stoking anti-Dutch sentiment, Clarendon told the house that the Dutch have 'a Dialect of Rudeness so peculiar to their language, and their People, that it is high time for all Princes to oblige them to some Reformation', following that many 'infamous Prostituted persons of our Nation' had joined the Dutch 'wantonly put[ing] themselves on board the Enemy's fleet'.[64] Since the outbreak of war, a number of English subjects had indeed defected to the Dutch cause. A few had done so for ideological reasons, but many had been driven by their purse. Put simply: the Dutch paid. The house voted for a further £1,250,000 to be given to the war effort, with the Speaker of the House declaring: 'As Rivers do naturally empty into the Sea, so we hope the Veins of Gold and Silver in this Nation will plentifully run into this Ocean, for the Maintenance of your Majesty's just Sovereignty on the Seas.'

As the Member of Parliament for Dover and Weymouth and Melcombe Regis, the Earl of Sandwich was among the peers to vote in support of the war effort. Earlier that month, he had left the fleet and journeyed to Oxford in an attempt to neutralise the growing ill feeling towards him at court. Unfortunately for Sandwich, however, the political leader of the Dutch Republic, the Grand Pensionary Johan de Witt, had decided to put his fleet on the offensive and Dutch ships were spotted off the south-east coast. The Dutch found the English ships to be in such a sorry state that they retreated back to the Netherlands. With Sandwich absent, however, the incident gave George Monck an opportunity to assert his authority by mobilising the fleet as well as he could. Monck's case for leading the 1666 campaign got stronger.

While the furore continued, Montagu's body was transported to his family seat in Northamptonshire, where he was buried in the local church. News of his death had reached the court a couple of weeks after the disaster and had been announced in the *Intelligencer*, which noted: 'Among the slain was a valiant and worthy Gentleman Mr. Edward Mountague who together with Mr. Windham lost their lives honourably in the service of their Prince and Country.'[65] He was, however, little mourned; indeed, Lord Peterborough reflected that 'In my life I have not heard of any to whom death was soe usefull.'[66]

Across the Channel, the French threat grew. Over the course of the year, relations between England and France deteriorated dramatically. Technically, a 1662 treaty obliged France to aid the Dutch Republic if war were to break out with England, but it was a treaty that, up until the autumn of 1665, King Louis XIV had been reluctant to honour. While hatred of the French ran deep in the English psyche, many at Louis's court (not least his sister-in-law Henrietta) objected to a war with the English on grounds of principle. England was ruled by a seemingly pliable monarchy and the Dutch Republic was – just that – a republic. There was also the fact that the French navy was in its infancy and, despite a rapid building programme and expansion, it was still no match for the English in the Channel.

Oddly, it was the death of King Philip IV of Spain in September that drew France in. Philip IV's heir was four years old, frail and grotesquely inbred, so the question of who would inherit the Spanish territories was of utmost importance to Louis XIV. Louis wanted Dutch acquiescence to his planned expansion into the Spanish Netherlands, and he knew that he could get this by honouring the treaty. With the Spanish state weakened, English neutrality was no longer necessary. Moreover, it was becoming increasingly evident that the English posed a threat to the status quo in Europe. If Charles was successful in overthrowing the States General (the Dutch parliament), then the House of Orange – with its promising young Prince William – would hold the balance of power, effectively turning the Dutch Republic into an English protectorate. German princes were courted; Sweden was seduced by money; and pressure was put on the Danes.

The English had already captured several French merchant ships carrying Dutch goods, and in response to English insistence on being saluted by foreign vessels along the English Channel, Louis demanded that all vessels in the Mediterranean acknowledge French mastery of the sea by saluting French ships. This resulted in a number of skirmishes between the French and the English. Louis's admiral, the Duke of Beaufort, captured two English vessels and took them to Toulon. By December, most knew that a declaration of war by France was imminent.

The immediate threat of war did little to stem the court's lavish behaviour. Sir Robert Harley's French servant, Denis de Repas, was with the court in Oxford and described a place of jollity and extravagance, writing: 'There is no other plague here but the infection of love; no other discourse but of ballets, danse and fine clouse [clothes]; no other emulation but who shall look the handsomere . . . none other fight than for "I am yours" . . .' He even came across a rumour that a proclamation was to be ordered forcing everyone to be cheerful or they would suffer the pillory.[67] To long-time residents of Oxford, members of the court were seen to be 'rude, rough, whoremongers'.[68] The complex rivalries and romances; the backstabbing, drinking and politicking had worked to undermine any respect the inhabitants of Oxford may have afforded their social superiors. We know from Gilbert Burnet that following his return from sea, the Earl of Rochester '[fell] into company that loved . . . excesses' and released the natural 'intemperance' of his character. This 'company' probably included the burgeoning coterie of court wits such as the Duke of Buckingham and Lord Buckhurst. An interesting insight into the behaviour and dirty habits of the court in Oxford was offered by the contemporary academic Anthony Wood:

The greater sort of courtiers were high, proud, insolent and looked upon scholars no more than pedants or pedagogical persons . . . Though they were neat and gay in their apparel, yet they were very nasty and beastly, leaving at their departure their excrements in every corner, in chimneys, studies, coalhouses, cellars.[69]

Queen Catherine had remained in the university city with her ladies-in-waiting, one of whom, the king's mistress Lady Castlemaine, had become the focus of a vicious pamphlet campaign. Seemingly organised by university scholars, it climaxed in a note, written in both English and Latin, being pinned to the door of her chamber, declaring: 'The reason why she is not duck'd / Because by Caesar she is fuck'd'.[70] (It was not the first and certainly not the last time Lady Castlemaine would be likened to a prostitute.)

Even away from the main court, scandal followed the highest in the land. The royal brothers seemed to have a terrible knack of putting handsome young men in the paths of their wives. Following Edward Montagu's death, Queen Catherine took his brother Ralph, who 'doth both admire and Love himself', as her Master of the Horse. While it is highly unlikely that the pious queen strayed from her marriage, reports that, 'the Duchesse [of York] herself [had] . . . fallen in love with her new Master of the Horse, one Harry Sidney' were harder to shake. Sidney, who was also a Gentleman of the Bedchamber to the Duke of York, was purported to be 'so much in love with her' that the 'Duke for many days did not speak to the Duchesse at all'. It was a rift that only ended in the middle of January, when Sidney was banished from court.[71]

None of this was widely known, of course. While the court was in Oxford, official news was funnelled through a new mouthpiece, the *Oxford Gazette*. Organised by Henry Muddiman, the *Gazette* replaced the *Intelligencer* as the official English newspaper (although the word 'newspaper' was not actually used until 1670). News periodicals were relatively recent additions to society. They had actually originated in Strasbourg at the turn of the seventeenth century and over the course of the ensuing decades their popularity had spread across Europe, with publications established in Amsterdam, Basel, Paris and Antwerp. The earliest regular newspaper printed in England had been launched in 1621 and was a translation of a Dutch title. While this early paper offered readers information about foreign events, it contained no English news.

The breakthrough in the consumption of news in England had arisen during the Civil Wars when the need for information had taken on a new importance. The collapse of government had enabled a free press to emerge and the opposing sides founded publications to rally support and disseminate news at speed. Under Cromwell, controls were tightened once more, but the appetite for domestic news had been whetted and was not going to go away. The *Oxford Gazette* was printed on Mondays and Thursdays and based on intelligence gathered by Muddiman and his network of informers, most notably Joseph Williamson at the Secretary of State's office. It was delivered to readers through a mixture of subscription and on-the-day purchase. Appearing as one double-sided sheet of paper, the layout was recognisable as a newspaper, and it featured stories from the various regions of the British Isles as well as reports from ambassadors and correspondents abroad. The first edition was released on 7 November 1665 and Pepys thought it to be 'very pretty, full of newes, and no folly in it'.[72]

As 1666 drew ever closer, in other quarters there were signs of change. Ever since its inception, the Royal Society had drawn upon a network of knowledge from across the Continent, which was collated and disseminated by the society's secretary, Henry Oldenburg. Throughout the heat of the plague the society had kept busy: there had been experiments to improve ships and regular correspondence with scientists and thinkers. On 8 December 1665, Oldenburg wrote a curious letter to the Jewish philosopher Spinoza in Amsterdam, enquiring about a rumour that was circulating among his acquaintances in England:

Everyone here is talking of a report that the Jews, after remaining scattered for more than two thousand years, are about to return to their country. Few here believe in it, but many desire it. Please tell your friend what you hear and think on the matter. For my part, unless the news is confirmed from trustworthy sources at Constantinople, which is the place chiefly concerned, I shall not believe it. I should like to know, what the Jews of Amsterdam have heard about the matter, and how they are affected by such important tidings which, if true, would assuredly seem to harbinger the end of the world.

Believe me to be
Yours most zealously,
Henry Oldenburg[73]

PART II

1666

4

The Fateful Year

They that were drunken are drunken still; they that were
filthy, are filthy still; and they that were unjust and covetous,
do still persevere in their sinful course; cozening, and lying,
and swearing, and cursing, and Sabbath-breaking, and pride,
and envy, and flesh-pleasing, and the like God displeasing,
and God-provoking sins . . . do abound in London . . .

Thomas Vincent, *God's Terrible Voice in the City*[1]

LIKE A WORM that has been trampled on, London and its people
wriggled back to life. Plague had changed them, but they lived
and moved and talked and copulated and, by January 1666, a
semblance of normality began to return. Across the city, church
bells rang out for marriages and baptisms. Walter Smith and
Elizabeth More, Jonathan Perry and Mary Stanford, and John
Pagitt and Mary Johnson were wed at St Boltoph's Aldgate.[2] Sarah
Keepe, daughter of John and Margret; Anne Bomar, daughter of
Charles and Mara; and Joshua Defft, son of Anne, were baptised at
the church of St Bride's Fleet Street.[3] On 2 January, for the first
time since the previous June, the weekly Bill of Mortality revealed
the number of plague deaths to be under a hundred.

For the Drury Lane apothecary William Boghurst, who had
remained in one of the worst-hit areas for the duration of the
outbreak, this slowing down ratified his theory. Having spent
months with his finger on the pulse of the contagion, treating
many of those afflicted and recording their symptoms, he drew
upon his experience and observations to predict that the plague

would continue to decline in 1666. Writing in what would become a highly influential work on the Great Plague, *Loimographia*, he argued that 'the plague hath a long tail . . . going backwards and forwards in little increases and decreases till it be quite gone'. At its height the previous September, over 7,000 people in London were dying of plague each week, but by January this figure averaged around 90 deaths per week and there was every reason to think that the danger had passed.

For those that had fled, the signs were certainly encouraging. Throughout the month, merchants, priests, physicians and artisans streamed back into the capital. While Covent Garden and Westminster, where the richer portion of London lived, remained mostly deserted – with 'no Court nor gentry being there' – many shops in the centre of the city reopened, trading recommenced and 'the towne [was] full of people again'.[4] On 8 January, royal orders were issued to the Justices of the Peace in the City of London and Westminster to ensure that '. . . all the Bedding, and other Goods in the Several Infected Houses be well aired, the Rooms all new whited, and the Churchyards to be covered with Earth two foot high'.[5] Thomas Bludworth, the new Lord Mayor, who had been ushered in the previous October with minimal ceremony, sent out orders for the City of London to be fumigated.

With this programme of cleaning underway, the scattered bastions of English power prepared to return to the capital. By 20 January, the Exchequer had moved back to Whitehall from its exile at Nonsuch Palace; the Navy Board came back from Greenwich to Seething Lane; and, by the very end of the month, the king, the Duke of York, and a significant slice of the court left their base in Oxford and made their way to Hampton Court, with the intention of returning to Whitehall as soon as possible. Despite churches, such as St Olave Hart Street, still having 'so [many] graves' that lay 'so high upon the churchyards where people have been buried of plague',[6] the king was fixed on getting back to London. Writing to his sister Henrietta in France, he explained:

I have left my wife in Oxford, but hope in a fortnight or three weeks to send for her to London, where already the Plague is in effect nothing. But our women are afraid of the name of Plague, so that they must have a little time to fancy all clear.[7]

To Thomas Vincent, this all happened far too quickly and much too easily. The Puritan preacher, who had remained in the capital during the outbreak and had lost members of his own household to the disease, believed that many who had left had failed to use their time in wise contemplation. It was clear to Vincent that sinners were failing to heed God's warning and some, driven by greed, he complained, 'return to their Houses, and follow their worldly business, and work as hard as they can to fetch up the time they have lost'; with little effort made to 'improve [themselves] by the Judgment, and Gods wonderfull preservation of them'. Worse still were others, who Vincent saw 'sin as hard as they can, having been taken off for a while from those opportunities and free liberties for sin'.[8]

He was not alone in his concern. Comparing the outbreak of 1665 with previous plagues, John Bell, who was the clerk to the Company of Parish Clerks, asserted that 'all Plagues' were caused 'by the sins of the people'.[9] Unlike Vincent, however, Bell believed that the current plague was caused by the greatest sin of all: regicide. In his text *London's Remembrancer*, he asked: 'May not then this Nation justly expect Gods greatest judgements to fall on the people of it, for shedding the blood of their lawful sovereign?'[10] In early 1666, a printer called 'E. Cotes' compiled a collection of all the Bills of Mortality from the previous year to be sold as a memento mori at his printing house in Aldersgate Street. Cotes was the son, or perhaps nephew, of Thomas Cotes who had been responsible for printing many early seventeenth-century stage plays (including Shakespeare's Second Folio). Though just a 'Printer no Preacher', Cotes urged his readers to consider God's 'Mercy to Thee and Mee, that we are yet in the Land of the Living, to work out our

Salvation with Fear and Trembling', going on to write, 'O let us not imagine, that they were greater Sinners than we the Survivors!' before adding that a failure to repent would mean 'we shall all likewise perish'.[11] Cotes called his collection *London's Dreadful Visitation, Or, A Collection of all the Bills of Mortality for the Present Year* and within its pages urged his fellow man to:

> . . . search out the Plague of his own Heart and Brain and Purge our selves, by His gratious assistance, from all filthiness of Flesh and Spirit; that so He may in riches of His tender Compassion, return in favour to this sinful City, and restore Health to our Habitations.[12]

As a nonconformist minister, the plague had afforded Thomas Vincent the freedom to preach against sinful practices and encourage repentance, but this was stifled when official ministers began to return to their churches. Quaker meetings were regularly raided by militia dissident and anti-monarchical literature was suppressed; and nonconformists were actively sought out by officials. During this very year, perhaps the most famous nonconformist of the late seventeenth century, John Bunyan, was incarcerated at a prison in Bedford for attending unlawful religious meetings. He used his time to write and publish a memoir entitled *Grace Abounding to the Chief of Sinners* and to begin work on a colourful religious tract that he would later call *The Pilgrim's Progress*. Thomas Ellwood offers a taste of what religious dissidents had to endure when he describes one of his many arrests:

> . . . at a [Quaker] meeting at the Bull and Mouth, by Aldersgate, when on a sudden, a party of soldiers (of the trained bands of the city) rushed in with noise and clamour, being led by one who was called Major Rosewell, an apothecary, (if I remember not) and at that time under the ill name of a Papist. As soon as he was come within the room, having a file or two of musketeers at his heels, he commanded his

men to present their muskets to us, which they did; with intent, I suppose, to strike a terror into the people.

Then he made a proclamation, that all who were not Quakers, might depart if they would . . . The soldiers came so early, that the meeting was not fully gathered when they came; and when the mixed company were gone out, we were so few and sat so thin in that large room, that they might take a clear view of us all, and single us out as they pleased . . .[13]

From his residence in Hoxton, close to the now packed New Churchyard burial ground, Vincent watched agog as 'many spent their time . . . feeding and preserving their bodies . . . [with] no time in serious minding the salvation of their souls'. To him, 'when they apprehended the danger [of plague] to be over, they dropt asleep faster than before; still they are the same or worse than formerly'.[14] But his black and white view of humanity did little to illuminate the very real tragedy that scarred many of those who now returned or had remained in the capital: those whose reality had been decimated by the deaths of loved ones had no choice but to 'work as hard as they could' to scaffold something new out of the ruins.

At the beginning of the year, the Mitchell family of booksellers returned to their home in Wood Street and began to trade once more at Westminster Hall. They had lost their older son, on whom so much of their future had been pinned, to the contagion. Fortuitously, they soon discovered that his intended bride, Betty Howlett, 'did love' their younger son Michael 'more than the other brother' anyway.[15] The sought-after alliance with their trading neighbours, the Howletts, was sealed when twenty-two-year-old Michael and twenty-year-old Betty married in February. Their marriage licence, issued by the Archbishop of Canterbury, gave the couple permission to wed at either St Faith's (an independent parish church within the main body of St Paul's Cathedral) or St Mary Magdalen, in Old Fish Street, close to London Bridge.[16] The newly weds were set to move into premises in Thames Street, within an easy walking distance of both. Their new property, which had originally been promised to the older Mitchell brother and Betty, was where Michael would begin trading from the shop as a haberdasher.

Thames Street was one of the busiest places in all of London. Following the northern bank of the river and dotted with wharfs, it underlined the City of London. Stretching from Tower Hill past London Bridge and all the way to Baynard's Castle, it was home to an array of characters and businesses – from the widowed fishmonger Mary Bellamy and the tallow chandler Thomas Rosse, to Richard Spyre, the haberdasher and landlord of the Golden Hoope tavern, who paid his rent in 'canary sack' as well as pounds. There was also a substantial set of almshouses near to London Bridge, used to provide shelter to at least thirty poverty-stricken residents, and a cluster of printing houses to the far west, next to Baynard's Castle. It was a narrow place that was always busy with carts and people. On the rare occasion a foolhardy coachman attempted to navigate the street, he would risk getting stuck and being jeered at by 'street boys'. Though Michael and Betty's lives were tainted by the tragedy of Michael's brother's death, with their new home and business in this lively commercial hub, the future looked promising.

A soon-to-be neighbour of theirs, Anne Maxwell, also capitalised on the recent death of a loved one to define a new reality for herself. She lived in a substantial property of nine hearths, close to Baynard's Castle,[17] and had been married to the respected printer David Maxwell. In 1665, however, she became a widow after only seven or eight years of marriage. In the face of tragedy, like many widows of the time she continued the family trade. Printing was laborious work: texts needed to be typeset with individual characters then ink would be worked onto soft leather pads and patted onto the typeset texts, before going into the printing press where a stiff wooden lever would be pulled to ensure the ink marked the page. The process had changed very little since Johannes

Gutenberg first invented it in the 1430s. Although she didn't have any apprentices, Anne Maxwell did have two printing presses and does not appear to have struggled for work. In fact, at some point during this year, she received two manuscripts for publication from a very prestigious client – Margaret Cavendish, the Duchess of Newcastle. The first work, entitled *Observations upon Experimental Philosophy*, built upon many of her existing theories about the natural order of the world and explored the inner workings of (and relationship between) animate and inanimate matter. It questioned the ability of optics and micrography to reveal 'the truth' of an object and she opined that any experiment that rested upon the use of the senses was ultimately flawed due to variances in perception. The second work was her adventure story, *The Blazing World*, which would come to be regarded as one of the earliest examples of science fiction. In her address to the reader, Cavendish claimed to be as '. . . Ambitious as ever any of my Sex was' in the writing of it. She continued:

> . . . though I cannot be *Henry* the *Fifth*, or *Charles* the *Second*, yet I endeavour to be *Margaret* the *First*; and although I have neither power time nor occasion to conquer the world as *Alexander* and *Caesar* did; yet rather then not to be Mistress of one, since Fortunes and the Fates would give me none, I have made a World of my own: for which no body, I hope, will blame me, since it is in everyones power to do the like.[18]

A five-minute walk from the eastern end of Thames Street, slightly further into the city, was a busy street of fishmongers, butchers, coopers, vintners, and 'hooke and eye' makers. It was home to another family marked by the events of the previous year. They resided on a lane that had, according to the surveyor John Strype, originally been called Red Rose Lane, but over time its reputation as a place where butchers kept scalding houses and made 'their puddings with other filth [entrails] of Beastes', meant that it came to be known as Pudding Lane. If there was ever an archetypal seventeenth-century London street, this was it. Packed with trade signs – from the 'rose' and 'fish' to the 'Blue Anchor', 'Golden Bale' and 'Plasterers Arms' – and shadowed by overhanging timber-framed buildings, many of the shops doubled as homes. It was a place of pungent smells, thick smoke and hard work, and within an enclave along the lane, known as Fish Yard, a middle-aged, recently widowed man named Thomas Farriner lived with his daughter, Hanna, in a property with five hearths and one oven.[19]

Farriner was a baker. During 1665, he had lost his wife of twenty-eight years, Hanna,[20] though the cause of her death is unclear. A plague victim called 'Hana Farmer' is recorded as having been buried on 4 September 1665 at the church of St Mary, Whitechapel, one mile from Pudding Lane: Hanna's maiden name was Matthews so it is certainly curious that 'Hanna Farmer' was interred on the same day as a Judith and John Mathews,[21] but we cannot know with any certainty whether it was her. What we do know is that in the wake of losing his wife, Farriner seems to have had a stroke of luck: with victualling tenders returning once more to the capital, he was commissioned to supply the navy with 'ship's biscuit'.

The navy's victualling offices were based in East Smithfield, just north-east of the Tower of London and a fifteen-minute walk from Pudding Lane. The stocking of these offices was overseen by a multi-layered network of victualling officers, suppliers and clerks, all headed by the chief victualler, Denis Gauden. As surveyor general of victualling, Samuel Pepys had recently suggested reforming the system of 'Pursers', whereby a man on each navy vessel would be in charge of the ship's finances and the ordering of victuals. Under constant pressure, Pepys had remained in the city during the plague, only removing himself to Greenwich when the Navy Board was transferred for safety and even then making regular trips to the city. With the king, the Duke of York and many of his superiors at Hampton Court, he was keen to reintegrate himself into political life. On Sunday 28 January, he dressed in a velvet coat that he'd bought from Paternoster Row a few days earlier and prepared for a short trip to Hampton Court. Carrying all of his papers, he took a hackney coach through town to meet Lord Brouncker who would be travelling with him.

Brouncker was from a line of Irish nobility. While posterity would remember him, primarily, as the first president of the Royal Society, he was viewed by Pepys and his contemporaries as an esteemed mathematician and one half of a very public, and rather scandalous, romance with an actress called Abigail Williams. On this day, Brouncker waited for Pepys's arrival at his residence to the west of London, before the pair travelled in his coach with four horses. Earlier in the month, Pepys had described the thrill he felt travelling in such a manner through town: 'what staring to see a nobleman's coach come to town. And porters every where bow to us; and such begging of beggars!'[22] On this day, had the porters and beggars been around, they would certainly have had a spectacle to see when the coach suddenly halted at Brainford. Pepys described the reason for this as:

> Having need to shit . . . went into an Inne doore that stood open, found the house of office [the lavatory] and used it, but saw no people, only after I was in the house, heard a great dogg barke, and so was afeard how I should get safe back again, and therefore drew my sword and scabbard out of my belt to have ready in my hand, but did not need to use it, but got safe into the coach again, but lost my belt by the shift, not missing it till I come to Hampton Court.

At Hampton Court, Pepys waited for some time, before the king and the Duke of York emerged from council. Pepys kissed their hands and in turn, the king clutched the diarist 'very kindly by the hand'. A little later, Pepys found the king and the duke once more and the king came to him to say 'Mr. Pepys . . . I do give you thanks for your good service all this year, and I assure you I am very sensible of it.' The duke was also pleased with him, explaining how he had read over a note Pepys had written about Pursers and 'would order it that way'. Less than a year before, Pepys was not a man the king had known by face. Now, he was being invited to walk with the royals for private discussions 'quite out of the Court into the fields', before returning to the palace.[23]

The next day, John Evelyn arrived at the palace and the royal brothers followed the same pattern of gratitude. Describing his meeting with the king, Evelyn wrote:

> . . . his majesty ran toward me, and in a most gracious manner gave me his hand to kiss, with many thanks for my care and faithfulness in his service in a time of such great danger, when everybody fled their employments; he told me he was much obliged to me, and said he was several times concerned for me, and the peril I underwent, and did receive my service most acceptably.

This was followed by a private conversation regarding Evelyn's position and responsibilities. In a similar expression of gratitude, Evelyn recorded how: 'the Duke came toward me, and embraced me with much kindness, telling me if he had thought my danger would have been so great, he would not have suffered his Majesty to employ me in that station'.[24]

Like Evelyn, Pepys, Brouncker and two other gentlemen they had met along the way, many men flocked to Hampton Court to see the king and the duke. Sir William Penn, Sir William Coventry, Lord Mandeville, Sir George Carteret, Sir John Mennes, Sir William Batten and George Monck, Duke of Albemarle, were there, as was the troubled Earl of Sandwich, whom Pepys described as having 'a melancholy face, and . . . [suffering] his beard to grow on his upper lip more than usual'. Out of favour with most of the court following the disastrous end to the 1665 military campaign, Sandwich acknowledged that it would probably be best for Pepys not to be seen with him in public. The mentor/protégé bond that had served both men so well up until this point was frayed and close to breaking point. The following day, a council concerning navy matters, led by the Duke of York and the Duke of Albemarle, was held. During the meeting, Sandwich arrived late, 'very melancholy . . . and said little at all'. No room was made for him to sit down so Pepys gave up his own stool, before 'another was made' for him. Sandwich was soon to leave for Spain in a new role as ambassador and Pepys was all too aware that he would have to make new allies and befriend the very men who had castigated his former master, such as Sir William Coventry.

Following the meetings, the two great diarists of the age travelled in Lord Brouncker's coach back to London. There is no mention of the journey in Evelyn's diary – only that he left for home due to 'not being very well in health'. Pepys, however, recalled how they had 'excellent discourse' and how he found Evelyn to be 'a most worthy person'.[25] Upon Pepys's death, many years later, Evelyn would describe him as 'a very worthy, industrious and curious person' who was 'for near forty years so much my particular friend'.[26] It was during the period of the Second Anglo-Dutch War that their relationship was forged, and it is tempting to imagine the seeds of this enduring friendship being sown as they travelled home. They spent their journey voicing a shared disdain for 'the vanity and vices of the Court, which' as Pepys argued, 'makes it a most contemptable thing'.[27] There was plenty for the men to discuss; plague exile had done very little to constrain the increasingly loose morals of court, with indiscretions and extramarital affairs becoming public knowledge. More pressing matters, however, concerned the developing situation with the Dutch and the French.

As expected, Louis XIV officially declared war on the English in January. It was a decision that had not been without its problems – in France there had been real resistance from within the French king's own circle to declaring war on a monarchical state. The French navy was young but growing, with its main port at Toulon in the south of France. In England, preparations for the summer campaign were well underway. From as early as January, proclamations were made across the country which ordered all seamen to return to their ships by 20 February with the promise of pay even to those who had left without leave. Any who failed to return would be apprehended and face court martial. The aim was to have a fleet of '100 good ships'. With many vessels battered from the previous year, the dockyards were busy preparing and repairing. Money was tight, but the new funds granted by Parliament were put to use.

With the fall of Lord Sandwich, George Monck and Prince Rupert were asked to lead the 1666 campaign jointly. As one of the few peers of the realm to have remained in London throughout the contagion, Monck had initially refused, insisting that he would best serve his country by remaining in the capital to tackle the plague. His hesitation was brief, however, and in February, Rupert and Monck's elevation to chief commanders of the navy was officially confirmed. In a letter to both, the Duke of York declared:

> I do hereby constitute and appoint you my most dear and entirely beloved cousin Prince Rupert and George [Monck] Duke of Albemarle joint admirals and chief commanders of his Majts. Fleet, willing, authorising and requiring you to take upon you the charge and command of his Mast. Fleet accordingly, and to rule and govern in the same, and to execute all such orders and instructions as you have or shall from time to time receive from the King my Sovereign Lord and Brother, or from myself . . .[28]

They were to have the *Royal Charles* as their flagship. On 13 February, several sea commanders who had already served under Prince Rupert held a dinner in his honour where they pledged their loyalty and cheerful determination to go after the Dutch.[29] On 19 February, Pepys presented the state of navy accounts to Monck, Sir William Penn, the Lord Treasurer, and Sir John

Mennes. The navy had a 'debt of 2,300,000l' (excluding ordnance expense, the cost of caring for the sick and wounded or in fact wages from 1 August to 31 December 1665) and only '1,500,000l. to answer' it.

Concurrently, through a diplomatic back channel, the Secretary of State Lord Arlington (who had the unusual honour of having also fathered a child by the mother of Charles's first bastard child) had been brokering a peace deal with the Dutch through Sir Gabriel Sylvius, a nobleman in the court of Charles II with close connections to the House of Orange. In February, letters pertaining to the deal were carried to the Dutch Republic by a French messenger named Henri Buat. In return for peace, the English requested a sum of £200,000 from the Dutch as insurance as well as a position of power for the young Prince William of Orange (Charles's nephew through his sister). Buat carried the peace offer within a batch of letters that also contained a letter with instructions on action to take if the peace offer was refused. A coup d'état was suggested to overthrow Johan de Witt and his supporters and re-instal the House of Orange as stadtholders in prime positions of power. Whether de Witt would have agreed to the peace offer is not known because instead of delivering just the letter pertaining to peace, Buat accidently handed de Witt the whole batch. Realising his mistake, Buat asked for the letters back, but it was too late. The secret document regarding a possible Orange coup had been read. The mistake would later cost Buat his life, when he was executed by the Dutch as a traitor, and it worked to harden de Witt's resolve against a peace deal with the English.

At the beginning of February, as plague deaths dropped to fifty-six across London, the *Gazette* – now the only official paper – officially moved from Oxford to London. Towards the end of its tenure in Oxford, Muddiman's control of the *Gazette* appears to have been largely snatched away by Lord Arlington's secretary, Joseph Williamson, who began to act as editor. It was renamed the *London Gazette*, and printed directly by one Thomas Newcomb at his premises at the 'Porter's Lodge, part of King's College house',[30] in Thames Street. Newcomb was a canny fellow who had married into a large Thames Street printing business in 1648, when he took as his bride Ruth, the widow of the printer John Raworth. Ruth died following the birth of twins in 1653, but throughout the First Anglo-Dutch War Newcomb's business had not halted, printing official accounts of engagements as well as the government news periodicals: *Mercurius Politicus* and *Public Intelligencer.* Newcomb's role appears to have been much more than that of a simple printer, and closer to that of a publisher and manager. Records from the 1670s reveal that he was responsible for supervision of much of the newspaper's production: not only paying the salaries of the writer and the surveyor of the press, but also the French translator.[31]

While news was fed to Williamson from around the Continent and across the country by a series of informers, James Hickes at the General Letter Office routinely filleted private correspondence to gather material. This was no secret; in fact, in March 1666, an informer named Jo Carlisle wrote to Williamson, to say, 'I believe the last letter I sent you was intercepted for I find by Mr Muddimans Gazett the same words'. Then, in July, a disgruntled informer begged Hickes not to allow information from a previous letter to get into 'any paper of news'.[32] Not everyone was happy with what was included and excluded from the *Gazette.* Writing to Williamson on 2 February, John Evelyn argued that a report about the number of sick people being turned ashore should be included in the publication.[33] Williamson refrained.

One of the paper's first news stories as the *London Gazette* was an account of the king and court's return to Whitehall on 1 February. Published on 6 February, it described how: 'This day his Majesty, with his Royal Highness, arrived in perfect health from Hampton-Court, at His Palace at White-Hall, to the infinite Joy of this City.' The article continued by describing how the city had rung 'Bells and Bonfires, and such other expressions of publick rejoicing . . . for a return of a Blessing they had too long wished for'.[34] His return provoked people to 'bustle up and down' Whitehall in anticipation.[35]

As is often the case when conjuring images of life before now, the mind's eye tends to fix on the adult world of wars, politics, and affairs of the heart. Unless crucial to established narratives, children are forgotten. Yet the court of Charles II was brimming with young life. By 1666 Charles, as Pepys eloquently put it, 'hath many bastard children that are known and owned': besides his eldest child, the sixteen-year-old Duke of Monmouth, there was nine-year-old Charles Fitzcharles, whose mother was the actress Catherine Pegge, and from his long-term mistress Lady Castlemaine there was three-year-old Charles Fitzroy, two-year-old Henry Fitzroy, one-year-old Charlotte Fitzroy and a new baby, George Fitzroy, who was born just after Christmas at Merton College, Oxford.

The duke and duchess had a full and legitimate brood. Their eldest was a healthy three-year-old daughter named Mary, then there was two-year-old James, the Duke of Cambridge, followed by Anne, who was nearing her first birthday, and the duchess was pregnant with a fourth child throughout the beginning of 1666 (who had doubtless been conceived during their tour in the north of England). Away from the royal brothers, the Earl of Sandwich had a gaggle of children ranging from toddlers to teens, and Prince Rupert's mistress, Frances Bard, was pregnant with his first son.

There was one figure within this fertile court in need of a child more than anyone else: the queen herself. In early 1666, Catherine was indeed pregnant. Four days after Charles's triumphant return to London, on 5 February the royal physician Dr William Quatremaine wrote to Joseph Williamson at the office of the Secretary of State. Apologising for the delay in communication, he explained that: 'I had sooner written to you had I knowne what to say. I wish I had better newes now to send you than that her majestie has certainly miscarried.' Assuring Williamson that 'the evidence of fecundity must allay the trouble of this losse', and continuing, 'since the field appears fertile there is noe doubt butt if it bee carefully cultivated, it may yield ripe fruits here-after'.[36] It was hopeful thinking, for Catherine had suffered several miscarriages already. Present on the day of the miscarriage was Dr Clerke, who told Pepys a couple of weeks later that he 'had the membranes and other vessels in his hands which she voided, and were perfect as ever woman's was that bore a child'.[37]

By 16 February, Catherine had arrived at Whitehall with many of her ladies-in-waiting. Pepys saw her on 19 February looking 'prettily; and methinks hath more life than before'.[38] Whatever sadness she felt at the death of her Master of the Horse and now her unborn child she kept hidden. While this was no doubt a cause of personal sorrow for the queen, at this point her fertility issues were not a significant cause for national concern. Charles had many legitimate heirs: his brother James was of course his next-in-line, but as the two were only a couple of years apart, eyes naturally turned to the next generation, where there were healthy candidates in waiting – not least Charles's nephew, the two-year-old James, Duke of Cambridge.

As winter turned into spring, there was another matter causing a stir on the streets of London: rumours of a Jewish Messiah. If Henry Oldenburg, the secretary of the Royal Society, received a reply to his letter to the Dutch philosopher Spinoza, it has not survived. We do know, however, that shortly after its return to London following the contagion, the Royal Society – along with discussions about the merits of a new invention from Florence to destroy ships, creating a resolution to examine plague and giving the Earl of Sandwich a telescope to take to Spain – took an interest in the movement of Jewish people and a supposed Messiah figure in Judea. On 13 March Oldenburg wrote how 'the pre-tended king . . . is said not to assume ye dignity and office of ye Messiah, but to lead to him'.[39]

At St Paul's Churchyard, the bookseller Joshua Kirton began to sell copies of Francis Potter's *An Interpretation of the Number 666,* which was enjoying a resurgence in popularity. First published in 1642, the book was an examination of the biblical number of the beast, its relation to the End of Days and to the year 1666. Pepys had picked up a copy in February and returned to the book-sellers the next day where he heard a rumour, which he had heard twice already,

> of a Jew in town that in the name of the rest do offer to give any man 10l. to be paid 100l., if a certain person now at Smyrna be within these two years owned by all the Princes of the East, and particularly the grand Signor as the King of the world, in the same manner we do the King of England here, and that this man is the true Messiah.

He finished his diary entry that day musing: '. . . certainly this year of 1666 will be a year of great action; but what the conse-quences of it will be, God knows!'[40]

In Holland, similar stories emerged. There were reports that 'the Jewes hurry out of Amsterdam to their fraternity with great expectations for their new Massias . . . an ordinary silly fellow; the son of a baker'.[41] The English millenarian Nathaniel Holmes wrote how 'Mens Pockets are full of Letters; their Hands full of Gazetts; their Eares full of Reports and Tidings; and their Eyes sufficiently perceive the Jewes cease Trading, pack up, and are Marching.'[42] The appetite for news about the movement of Jewish people and the activities of Sabbathai Zevi in Persia was rooted in Christian doctrines about the Second Coming and the return of the Messiah. There was a sense of apprehension: Sir George Carteret shunned company for a number of days in February due to a great melancholy and a fear 'of a general catas-trophe to the whole kingdom', thinking that 'all things will come to nothing'.[43] Those with a keen eye for doom and gloom might have found extra cause for concern had they reread a 1651 pamphlet entitled *Monarchy or no Monarchy* by the popular astrolo-ger William Lilly. Within his heavily illustrated tract, Lilly had prophesied a period of reckoning in England where fire and disease would be rife.

At her printing house on Thames Street, Anne Maxwell published a short work entitled 'A New Letter Concerning the Jewes'. The tract was written by the Dutch millenarian (and the originator of many Jewish stories in European literature) Petrus Serrarius, and was one of at least half-a-dozen works, printed in early 1666, devoted to the activities of Jews. The works – with titles such as 'The Wonders of all Christendom' and 'Great Miracles, Wrought by The Famous Nathan, A Prophet of the Jews' and 'God's Love to his People Israel' – usually focused on the messiah figure and new 'King of Judea', Sabbathai Zevi, and addressed his plans to travel to Constantinople and take the Turkish crown. Serrarius's tract applied a Christian lens to the news, arguing:

> . . . as now they went to the sepulchre of Zachary the Prophet, to bemoan their sins against him; so the time shall come, that they shal go likewise to the Sepulchre of Jesus Christ, whom their Fathers once Crucified; and then will the King of Glory appear, and this King, Sabothi-Levi, and all other Kings, will submit unto Him.[44]

Questions over the authenticity of Sabbathai abounded: Was he the real Messiah? A prophet? A stooge of the Devil, or simply a fraud? Were they living at the End of Days? From the Royal Society and the Dean of St Paul's, to the transnational network of millenarians and the reading public, what was clear, and remained so, was an unceasing interest in events in Persia and Jerusalem.

On 21 March, a young man who was beginning to question his faith in the Christian religion was granted the position of Gentleman of the Bedchamber to the king. Although it would take another year for him to be sworn in, the prestigious role (that he shared with several others) would afford the Earl of Rochester time alone with the monarch. It is likely that it was during the spring of 1666 that the earl first fell into the company of the men who would come to be known as the 'Merry Gang' or the Court Wits. Though we cannot say with certainty, a man that would prove to be a huge influence on him, the playwright George Etherege, was likely to have been at court during this time too. He was still basking in the success of his 1664 play *Love in a Tub*, which had been performed at the Cockpit within Hampton Court that February.

It is also possible that Nell Gwynn formed part of this coterie. Her whereabouts during the plague year are unknown, but a hint that the king had started a relationship with an actress in 1666 can be found in John Evelyn's diary entry later that year. Disapproving of the trend among the nobility of taking actresses as mistresses, Evelyn wrote:

> . . . very seldom going to the public theatres for many reasons now . . . foul and indecent women now (and never till now) permitted to appear and act, who inflaming several young noblemen and gallants, became their misses, and to some, their wives.

He continued 'witness the Earl of Oxford, Sir R. Howard, Prince Rupert, the Earl of Dorset, and another greater person than any of them who fell into their snares, to the reproach of their noble families, and ruin of both body and soul'.[45] Even Pepys, while disproving of Brouncker's affair with Abigail Williams, had been enjoying the company of the actress Elizabeth Knepp in early 1666, at one point having her sing a song he had composed to accompany him on his flageolet.

Charles II, whether intentionally or not, took an informal approach to being the monarch; he walked every day through St James's Park, and allowed any personal criticism to go largely unpunished. Public awareness of his promiscuity ensured that the mystique of monarchy and the idea of the king being God's vessel on Earth were further dismantled. Looking back on Charles's reign in 1685, the Earl of Mulgrave (who was a teenage 'gentleman volunteer' in

1666), said that 'he could not on premeditation act the part of King for a moment, either at Parliament or Council, either in words or gesture; which carried him to the other extreme . . . of letting all distinction and ceremony fall to the ground as useless and foppish'.[46] Or, as George Etherege later wrote in his play *The Man of Mode*: 'Forms and ceremonies, the only things that uphold quality and greatness, are now shamefully laid aside and neglected.'[47]

It was becoming increasingly apparent that Charles was a monarch who appeared to endorse infidelity. Members of his court flaunted their mistresses, some from very lowly backgrounds indeed. Of course there had been vice at court before; the difference now was the public awareness of this vice, and the complete lack of effort to hide it behind formality. The honeymoon period of Charles's reign was coming to an end in 1666, and he was beginning to be seen as a man ruled by affairs of the heart and pleasure. The Earl of Rochester summed up the mood in a later satire, describing how 'His Sceptre and his prick are of a length; And she may sway the one who plays with th' other'.[48] In a culture where the Earl of Sandwich would refer to the Duchess of York as 'the veryest slut and drudge',[49] the Lady Castlemaine was repeatedly called a whore, and very few members of the court were free from censure.

The tangled liaisons within the court often resulted, unsurprisingly, in venereal disease. As early as 1664, there were rumours that the disease had penetrated the court via Prince Rupert. Pepys recorded in his diary how the Prince had undergone a process of trepanning to help alleviate the pains and sores on his head. In truth, Rupert's head wound was more likely to have been caused by an accident in the dockyard when a piece of apparatus had fallen on his head, but it was an easy story to believe. Sufferers of venereal disease underwent mercury treatment at establishments such as Madame Fourcords on Leather Lane, where they would be placed inside a fumigation mask to breathe mercury steam and sweat. Writing years later in July 1678, Henry Savile (later the Earl of Dorset) described his time at the well-known sweathouse:

When he sat for this portrait during the spring of 1666, Samuel Pepys complained, '[I] do almost break my neck looking over my shoulder to make the posture for him [the artist John Hayls].'

Willem van de Velde's illustration of the *London* warship as it appeared in 1656.

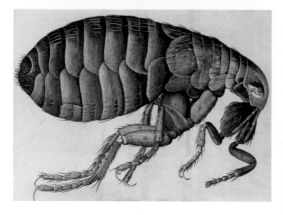

Robert Hooke's illustration of a flea, taken from *Micrographia*, published in 1665.

A contemporary engraving of physicians dissecting a plague-riddled human cadaver. The picture appeared in George Thomson's *Loimotomia, or, The pest anatomized*, 1666.

The plague in 1665 as depicted by John Dunstall. The illustration shows people leaving London and scenes of horror as mass burials pits are filled.

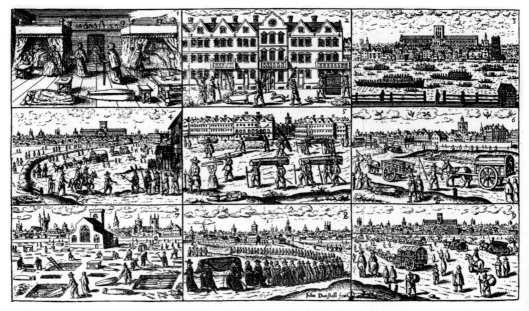

Eleanor 'Nell' Gwynn: orange-seller, actress and royal mistress.

Charles II, king of England, Scotland and Ireland. Famously described by the Earl of Rochester as 'a merry monarch, scandalous and poor'.

The Duke and Duchess of York by Peter Lely. The duchess's life was cut short by breast cancer within a few years of this portrait being painted.

'Man differs more from Man, than Man from Beast.' John Wilmot, 2nd Earl of Rochester, shown here holding a laurel wreath above the head of his pet monkey during the late 1660s.

Edward Montagu, 1st Earl of Sandwich, one of Lely's *Flagmen of Lowestoft*.

Action at the Battle of Bergen, 1665.

Sir Isaac Newton painted
by Godfrey Kneller some
years after 1666.

Seated to the right, Margaret
Cavendish leads a meeting of
men and women. This engraving
formed the frontispiece of her
book *Natures Pictures drawn by
Fancies pencil to the life*, 1656.

John Milton, as depicted
in the second edition of
Paradise Lost, 1675.

Aphra Behn by Peter Lely, *c.*1670. She declared, in 1686, 'I want fame as much as I had been born a hero', something she certainly achieved within her lifetime.

The Four Days' Fight, showing George Ayscue's *Royal Prince* run aground to the right and Michiel de Ruyter's ship *De Zeven Provincien* to the left. Painting by Abraham Storck.

The Great Fire of London seen from one of London's city gates, with St Paul's Cathedral ablaze in the background.

The fire observed from close to Tower Wharf, to the east of the city, with London Bridge visible ahead.

An engraving from William Lilly's *Monarchy or no Monarchy* (1651), depicting a city blazing with fire. It was one of several images within the text predicting the future state of England. Others included scenes of naval war, infestations of rodents, mass burials, drownings and rivers running red with blood.

The gravestone of Mary Godfree was unearthed during excavations in 2014 for the Crossrail project at Liverpool Street, London, upon the site of the New Churchyard. She was one of thousands to die of plague in 1665.

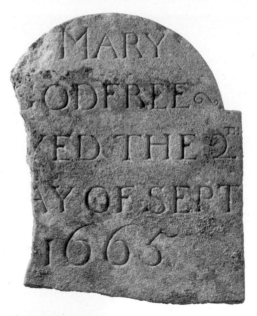

A skull unearthed at the Crossrail site, Liverpool Street.

A leather latchet shoe retrieved from the underwater wreck of the *London* by Historic England; excavations are ongoing.

I confesse I wonder at myself and that masse of mercury that has gone down my throate in seven monthes, but should wonder yet more were it not for Mrs Roberts [a minor mistress to several court figures] . . . what she has endured would make a damned soule fall a laughing at his lesser paines it is so far beyond description or beleefe.[50]

He then went on to describe how Mr Fanshawe – possibly the 'witty but rascally fellow, without a penny in his purse' mentioned in Pepys's *Diary*[51] – was also at the sweathouse and who:

will have his worse pox than ours pass for scurvy out of civility to his lady, though the rogue be a filthier leaper than ever was cured in Gospell . . . hee is the most incurable animall that now crawls upon earth[52]

The court was forced into sombre decorum at the end of March, when news arrived from Portugal that the queen's mother, Luisa de Guzmán, had died on 27 February. Luisa had been a driving force behind the marriage of her daughter to Charles of England, and the bond between mother and daughter was especially strong – in one of the many letters written by Luisa to Catherine shortly after she departed to marry Charles, she wrote: 'I have to tell you that I love you and that my worst torture is the loneliness that remained when you left.' Notices were pinned on the Queen's Chapel at St James's Palace inviting all 'good' Catholics to pray for the recently departed. When Catherine was told the news, she and her ladies-in-waiting went into official mourning. This involved wearing black 'with their hair plain and without any spots'. Stripped of her adornments, Pepys thought the Lady Castlemaine to be a 'much more ordinary woman than ever I durst have thought she was';[53] a far cry from the deified images of the court ladies being produced in Peter Lely's studio in Covent Garden.

Since at least March, the Dutch-trained artist had been in London working on two series of paintings, the first a romantic interpretation of the ladies at court that he had been working on for several years. Commissioned by the Duchess of York, it was to be called the *Windsor Beauties*, and featured the leading ladies of the day: the duchess herself, Lady Castlemaine, Frances Stewart, the Countess of Gramont, and eight others. Each lady was modelled on a figure from antiquity, with Frances Stewart taking on the part of the chaste Diana, and while certain characteristics made each image unique, they largely followed a uniform facial style: heavy lidded eyes, long noses and puckered lips.

The second series consisted of thirteen grand portraits of the commanders of the Battle of Lowestoft, which were commissioned by the Duke of York to hang in his chamber. Called *Flagmen of Lowestoft*, the series featured the Duke of York, Prince Rupert, George Monck, Sir Thomas Allin, Sir George Ayscue, Sir William Berkeley, Captain John Harman, Sir Joseph Jordan, Sir John Lawson, Sir Christopher Myngs, Sir William Penn, the Earl of Sandwich, Sir Jeremiah Smith and Sir Thomas Teddeman. Unlike his *Windsor Beauties*, Lely appears to have been honest with his subjects and each face was unique and full of character. Through Lely's brushwork, George Monck is revealed as a rounded man with an intimidating gaze and seemingly natural hair; the Duke of York is shown as a lean figure with long features and a full periwig; and Sir Christopher Myngs has a ruddy complexion and short light-brown hair. They were designed to celebrate England's maritime might after a glorious victory against the Dutch. Lely was an extremely busy man, however, and by April, as Prince Rupert and George Monck were making the final preparations to leave with the fleet, he had only got as far as the heads, 'some finished, and all begun'.[54]

At the Royal Mint, another Dutchman played his part in encouraging English patriotism by leaving a lasting mark on Britain as a whole. John Roettiers was the son of a Dutch goldsmith and had been invited to England, along with his brother, owing to a great skill 'in the arts of graveing and cutting in stone'.[55] In fact, the entire Roettiers family were so skilled and respected that its members held positions within the mints of

Spain, France and the Low Countries during the latter half of the century. Evelyn declared that John Roettiers's work 'emulates even the ancients in stone and metal' and on visiting his work-shop at the Mint, Pepys wrote how he saw 'some of the finest pieces of work, in embossed work, that ever I did see in my life, for fineness and smallness of the images thereon'.[56] Following Lowestoft, he was tasked with striking a commemorative medal of the battle. After a 1,500-year absence, the figure of Britannia, straddling the waves, was to adorn it – and who better to model her on than the most beautiful woman at court, Frances Stewart? On seeing the finished product months later, Pepys declared:

> At my goldsmith's did observe the King's new medal, where, in little, there is Mrs. Stewart's face as well done as ever I saw anything in my whole life, I think: and a pretty thing it is, that he should choose her face to represent Britannia by.[57]

Seated upon the waves, it is an image that still decorates British coinage today.

By April, preparations to defend Britain's seas were in full swing. On 5 April, a day of fasting was held, as the Essex vicar Ralph Josselin noted in his diary, 'for the good success in our naval forces'.[58] Evelyn, who also noted the fast day in his journal, speculated that the 'terrible war' was 'begun doubtless at secret instigation of the French to weaken the States and Protestant interest'.[59] Away from the court, Hannah Woolley, the forty-three-year-old author of books on female etiquette, got married for the second time on 16 April at the church of St Margaret, Westminster. Her new husband was a couple of years older than her and also a widower. There was a brief distraction when Thomas Chiffinch, the king's Keeper of the Private Closet – or royal pimp – suddenly died. Reports suggested he had been 'well last night as ever . . . and not very ill this morning at six o'clock, yet dead before seven'. With the contagion again on the rise, gossip spread that he might have had plague, but those close to him believed it to be 'an imposthume in his breast' – that is, a cyst or abscess.[60]

By 22 April, news arrived that the Bishop of Munster, previously a key English ally, had been persuaded by the French to defect to the Dutch cause.[61] With tickets still being issued in lieu of proper pay, it was difficult to recruit seamen voluntarily: bailiffs in Ipswich and Yarmouth were reprimanded for sending 'bad men or boys unfit for service'; each county was given a quota to fill, but many men went into hiding to avoid service, and on one occasion the horse militia was used to track down deserters in Essex Forest. Even when seamen reached the fleet, there was a risk that they would desert – Thomas Lane, recruited to serve under Sir William Berkeley on the *Swiftsure*, was accused of 'being a runaway', and there was a possible act of sabotage when one William Tiler set fire to the ship's Gunner's Cabin.[62]

Nevertheless, on 23 April, St George's Day, Prince Rupert and George Monck kissed the king's and duke's hands at Whitehall, bonfires were lit throughout the city, and they set off to command the fleet for the 1666 campaign. Joining them would be a solid block of experienced admirals, many of whom had fought at Lowestoft, though of course neither the Earl of Sandwich (who by then was thousands of miles away in Spain) nor Sir John Lawson (who was ten months dead) would be part of the action.

Throughout the month, navy matters dominated state correspondence, and new recruits flowed to the rendezvous point at the Nore. One such recruit was Balthasar St Michel – or 'Balty' as he was known to his brother-in-law Samuel Pepys. He was to join Captain John Harman's ship, the *Henry*, as muster-master. In his diary, Pepys (who had never really held Balty in high regard) expressed both anxiety and pride in having so near a relation set to conduct active naval duty. Requests streamed into the victualling office for extra supplies: beef, iron-clad casks for water and beer, ketches to carry the casks, and for 'flags and streamers' to distinguish the various squadrons.[63] Most unusually, a note was sent from the *Royal Charles* to Peter Pett at Chatham dockyard, which gave an order 'to send a bricklayer with 400 bricks and mortar suitable to them for accommodating the range of the cookhouse of his Majs. Ship the Royal Charles'.[64]

In London, as the fleet was being assembled, Nathaniel Hodges had other things on his mind. While the majority of the members of the College of Physicians had fled during the plague, Hodges had remained. He continued to work from his residence on Watling Street, Walbrook, as medical adviser to the City of London, overseeing the efforts of a lean group of physicians, many of whom perished. Although Parliament had recently been prorogued to prevent the 'hazardous consequences, and perils which may ensue' should large crowds gather in one place, it was accepted that plague 'by Gods mercy [was] almost totally abated' in London.[65] The contagion had now spread to the surrounding areas, with the towns of Ipswich, Colchester, Yarmouth, Norwich and Gravesend particularly affected. Against this backdrop, Hodges wrote a lengthy letter to an acquaintance, the contents of which provide a fascinating insight into the mind of a man of medicine during this time. Drawing on his experiences of treating plague, he addressed the 'first rise, progress, symptoms and cure of the plague' and detailed the intricacies of the disease as he saw it. Much of its contents would later be found in *Loimologia*, his seminal description of London's plague year, published six years later. He ended the letter with a touching reference to the peers he lost in the battle against the contagion:

> . . . so many Members of that most honourable Society have ventured their Lives in such hot Service; their Memory will doubtless survive Time, who died in the Discharge of their Duty, and their Reputation flourish, who (by God's Providence) escaped.[66]

He also used his time to write *Vindiciae medicinae et medicorum: an Apology for the Profession and Professors of Physic*, published in 1666.

It was both a rebuttal against the 'Pseudochymists . . . [and] ignorant Quacks',[67] who tricked the sick into using fake chemical
cures, and a warning to his peers who were strictly adhering to
many flawed Galenic remedies. He argued that the true physician
should sit between the two.

No amount of medicine could prevent the devastating consequences should a severe outbreak occur among the crew of the
fleet. When a small eruption of plague occurred on the *Princess*,
it was claimed to have been 'brought in by the women',[68] and it
became a solid basis for addressing one of the most pressing
concerns of the fleet in the early days of the summer campaign:
to rid the ships of women. Admiral John Mennes had written to
Pepys complaining how the ships are 'pestered with women' with
'as many petticoats as breeches', and one of the first letters sent by
Rupert and Monck after taking control of the fleet at the Nore
contained instructions for Thomas Allin to 'observe the ensuing
directions. Turn all the women to shore and suffer none to come
aboard.'[69]

On 8 May, Evelyn made his way to Queenborough on the Isle
of Sheppey and boarded the 'Richmond frigate' to sail to the
Nore to discuss business with Prince Rupert and General Monck.
There, he saw 'the most glorious Fleete in the World . . . now
preparing to meete the Hollander'.[70]

5

The Red Sea

Our fleet divides, and straight the Dutch appear,
In number, and a famed commander, bold:
The narrow seas can scarce their navy bear,
Or crowded vessels can their soldiers hold.

The Duke, less numerous, but in courage more,
On wings of all the winds to combat flies:
His murdering guns a loud defiance roar,
And bloody crosses on his flag-staffs rise.

John Dryden, Annus Mirabilis[1]

ON THURSDAY, 31 May, Ralph Fell took a boat from the Flemish port of Ostend. Originally from Newcastle, the sailor – who was most likely a merchant – was returning to England after a spell on the Continent. As he sailed across the Channel he sighted the Dutch fleet seven leagues out to sea. He continued his journey across the choppy waters and another fleet came into view around five leagues out from North Foreland, a stretch of land around the Kent coast: it was the English. Given the short distance between the opposing navies, Ralph Fell 'judged they might engage that day'.[2] He was a day out.

The next morning, on the English flagship *Royal Charles*, George Monck faced a difficult decision. A few days earlier he had received word from Lord Arlington at Whitehall that 'the Dutch Fleet would be out suddenly', and while he had been given 'no certain Time' of it happening, he had been instructed to prepare his own fleet for battle.[3] In doing so, he had sent a large fourth-rate frigate called *Bristol* to scout ahead of the main fleet and, at 6 a.m., from four leagues ahead, it 'made signall that shee discovered the enemies fleet'. Seamen, many of whom had only had a few hours' rest, scrambled up the ratlines of the *Royal Charles*'s rigging and from the top mast, with a strong south-westerly wind raging against them, sighted '8 or 10 sayle', that they recognised to be Dutch scouts.[4] After months of prepar-ation, the time for battle was drawing close. The English fleet – a mixture of first-, second-, third-, fourth-, and fifth-rate frigates, manned by seasoned captains, experienced sailors, fresh recruits, reluctant 'pressed' men, and army personnel, and packed with gunpowder and artillery – was as ready as it ever would be.

As co-commander of the navy, Monck had a distinguished and complicated military career: he had fought for the House of Orange during the Siege of Breda in 1637, supported Charles I during the Civil Wars and became commander-in-chief of Scotland under Cromwell, as well as a general at sea (the parlia-mentary equivalent of an admiral) during the First Anglo-Dutch War. He was now fifty-seven years old, but as confident as ever in his ability to lead a battle. The fleet had been carved into three robust squadrons – the red, the white and the blue – led by experienced naval leaders who commanded some of the best warships in the world. There was, however, a problem.

At just under 60 vessels strong, Monck's fleet was incomplete. Secret intelligence had arrived on 14 May explaining that French ships had been seen at Belle Ile, just south of Brittany, and that more were expected, led by the French Duke of Beaufort.[5] A decision was made to split the navy in two in order to protect both sides of the Channel; while Monck had charge of the major-ity of the fleet to the east, his co-commander, Prince Rupert, led a taskforce of 20 'good' ships and 5 fireships and had set off to 'joyne with a squadron of 30 sayle' to the west, at Plymouth. Travelling in the first-rate frigate, the *Royal James*, Rupert was joined by Sir Thomas Allin, Sir Edward Spragge, and Sir

Christopher Myngs – who commanded an especially loyal crew on the *Fairfax*. Allen, Spragge and Myngs had all received their knighthoods following their conduct during the Battle of Lowestoft the previous year. They were capable naval commanders. Myngs, in particular, was renowned for his ability to inspire 'courage and spirit' in his men, a skill he had doubtless honed during years of pirating: having led a series of barely legal and extremely violent buccaneering raids in the Caribbean, in the eyes of the Spanish he had become as notorious for his piracy as Sir Francis Drake earlier in the century. By 1 June, Rupert's squadron was close to the Isle of Wight, which was at least a day and a half away from Monck.

Unfortunately for the English, their bold precaution was unnecessary. As Monck and Rupert deepened the distance between their respective flotillas, the French fleet was thousands of miles away, anchored near Lisbon. Even if the French had wanted to aid the Dutch (which at this point, they clearly did not), it would have taken well over a week, if not more, for the Duke of Beaufort's ships to reach the English Channel. Writing from Paris at the beginning of June, the Venetian ambassador, Alvise Sagredo, illuminated the calculated game the French were playing: 'It was agreed between France and Holland these last weeks that the most sure and certain way to bring the English to reason was that of time and not of arms and that the best way to conquer was to tire them out.'[6] It was with this logic, the ambassador reasoned, that the French fleet under the Duke of Beaufort had tarried. It may well have been that Louis XIV also wanted to sit out the first great clash of 1666 so that he could assess the relative strengths of the two nations and, perhaps most importantly, preserve his own fleet. There was also the possibility that while the Dutch and English battled, the French could take advantage of the open seas to usurp English and Dutch maritime trade and commerce networks, particularly in the Americas.[7] Just like the disaster at Bergen, bad intelligence had given the English an unnecessary handicap.

At 7 a.m., Monck summoned the flag officers from their various ships and called a council of war on board the *Royal Charles*. The size of the Dutch fleet was uncertain, but there were reasonable fears that the English would be outnumbered. Only a few days earlier, Monck had calculated that he would need a fleet of 79 or, at a push, 70 ships to engage the enemy successfully.[8] Frustratingly, many warships, including the *Loyal London*, which had been built to replace the *London*, still remained in various dockyards, incomplete and unready for battle. It meant that Monck had a total of 54 ships – a handful of which were captured and refashioned Dutch vessels of little value – plus 4 fireships. Monck also felt that Prince Rupert had cherry-picked the best of the fleet's ships to take on his covert mission against the French, leaving behind 'very heavy Ships, and many of them Merchantmen, and Dutch Prizes'.[9]

Sitting in the richly decorated stateroom of the *Royal Charles*, Monck's flag officers publicly and privately weighed the risks against the gains. It would later be reported that 'two-thirds of the commanders' at the council meeting were secretly against engaging the Dutch that day, but 'durst not oppose . . . for fear of being called cowards'.[10] Indeed, Captain John Harman of the *Henry* thought it to be 'against his reason to begin the fight then' because 'the wind being such, and we to windward', the choppy waters would render the lower gun decks useless.[11] Yet Monck was a formidable figure: he was the man responsible for the Restoration; the man whose arrival into London immediately before Charles II's return had been celebrated with bonfires and bells; the man who had remained in the plague-ridden capital when everyone else had left; and, most importantly, the man to have beaten the Dutch at sea before 'at as great disadvantage'.[12] Buoyed with confidence, Monck saw no question of retreating and, despite any private reservations, his flag officers unanimously agreed with their commander. They would engage the enemy.

On the *Royal Charles*, Sir William Clarke, the Secretary of War, penned a letter to Whitehall to relay the developing situation. He explained that they thought there were '20, or 30 sail, some say 40' just off the coast of Flanders, near to Dunkirk. At 11 a.m., Clarke added a postscript: '75 sail are now in sight'.[13] As the letter was wax-stamped and sent on a packet boat back to London, the signal was given for the fleet 'to drum into a line of battle'.[14] Monck had decided to ambush the Dutch as they lay at anchor. With key commanders seconded to Rupert's mission, the flag officers had been reordered, with a couple of notable promotions, including Robert Holmes who had returned to the fleet following a short resignation to become rear admiral of the Red Squadron under George Monck.[15] For Holmes, the promotion to flag officer on board the *Defiance* was long overdue; despite his notable successes conquering Dutch fortifications along the West African coast, he had been overlooked at Lowestoft in favour of Captain John Harman.

With the wind behind their sails, the fleet cruised across the Channel. Voyaging under a pale blue sky, gulls swooped, squawked and snapped at the waters as they trailed the ships.[16] From the flagstaffs of each and every vessel, white flags stained with the blood-red cross of the English flapped in the gusty sea air, along with the union flag of England and Scotland; on board, thousands of men readied themselves for battle. Gunpowder was transported from the powder rooms, gunners primed the artillery, and surgeons and parsons prepared to heal bodies and souls. In less than an hour, Monck's fleet was just a league and a half from the Dutch, who were anchored seven leagues from Ostend. From the quarterdeck of the *Henry*, Samuel Pepys's brother-in-law Balty would have been well placed to see the Dutch ships as they came into view. The combined fleets of Holland, Zeeland, Friesland, Groningen and the other major maritime provinces of the Dutch Republic numbered 84 in total, all under the control of Admiral Michiel de Ruyter.[17]

On sighting the English, the Dutch ships cut their anchors and began to position themselves ready for battle. Significantly outnumbered, Monck's plan was to concentrate initial fire on the Dutch rear squadron, which was under Lieutenant Admiral Cornelis Tromp, before the rest of the enemy fleet had time to intervene. At half past one in the afternoon, war drums beat and across the English fleet captains stirred their crews ready for combat. According to enemy reports, the English were naturally disposed to 'insolence and customary arrogance' and fired several blank shots at the Dutch 'as a sign of contempt and contumely' and then began to sing hymns and joyful songs, including the *Te Deum*, 'with a loud voice'.[18] The Dutch, 'burning with wrath to see themselves disdained in this strange fashion', were the first to fire, according to the English, when one of their guns blasted the third-rate English frigate the *Clovetree*. The English responded with an intense assault on Tromp's rear squadron. Gunfire followed gunfire as shots of death and destruction exploded in both directions. The lowest gun decks of the largest English ships were only a matter of feet from the waterline, and with the fierce winds whipping up the waves, the gun ports had to remain closed and useless.[19] They were also on shallow water, estimated at only fifteen fathoms deep, which required them to change tack.[20] But the English had taken Tromp by surprise and his fleet was forced to retreat across the shoals.

Breaking away from the main body of the English fleet, who had turned north-west to face the rest of the Dutch, Vice Admiral Sir William Berkeley noticed that Tromp's flagship had collided with another Dutch vessel. In his 66-gun ship, the *Swiftsure*, Berkeley swooped towards the enemy to capitalise on its vulnerable position. Unfortunately, the captains of two other Dutch vessels saw what Berkeley was trying to do and moved to rescue Tromp. A fierce bombardment ensued, with the *Seven Oaks* and the *Loyal George* gearing towards the fight to aid Berkeley. A Dutch chainshot blasted the *Swiftsure*, completely destroying the rigging. Crew from the Dutch ship *Hern*, commanded by Henry Adrianson, exploited the damage and boarded the *Swiftsure*.[21] Berkeley refused to surrender, shouting 'You dogs!' just before a musket ball blasted into his throat, killing him. Deep in the ship's powder room, the constable of Berkeley's ship attempted to blow it up to prevent the Dutch taking it as a prize, but his own crew cut his throat before he was able to. The *Swiftsure*, the *Loyal George* and the *Seven Oaks* were all captured by Tromp's men.

Meanwhile, further down the channel, Prince Rupert's fleet faced a harsh south-westerly wind and came to anchor at St Helens on the Isle of Wight at 10 a.m. Here, they were met by two ketches, one of which had 'a packet from his Royal Highness' for their 'return for the Downs to join with his Grace the Duke of Albemarle, for the Dutch fleet was put out to sea'.[22] These orders had actually been signed off two days earlier, long before the battle had commenced, and had been delivered to Rupert much later than intended. Although he denied wrongdoing, the fault lay firmly with the Duke of York's secretary, William Coventry, who after the decision had been made to recall Rupert had rushed to wake 'the Duke [of York], who was then in bed, to sign them',[23] but instead of sending a messenger on horse had sent this 'packet' of such importance and urgency 'by the ordinary post'.[24] His failing might have been overlooked if Rupert had directed his fleet to join Monck straightaway. Perplexingly, however, rather than act on the instructions hastily, Rupert and his fleet waited at St Helens until 4 p.m. that day before setting off to join the action.[25] By this time, the battle between the English and the Dutch navies was well underway.

Under Admirals Michiel de Ruyter and Cornelis Evertsen, the Dutch had formed a broadside line, ready for battle. As Monck arranged his own fleet into a broadside line against the enemy, he had no clue that Berkeley had already been killed and the *Swiftsure* captured. Despite pleas for more ships, he had also not been privy to the decision to recall Rupert. For now, this was it. Once face to face with the full might of the enemy, the English can't have failed to notice just how busy their counterparts had been. Since Lowestoft, de Witt had ordered a thorough programme of rebuilding. Unlike the English, whose new ships were still being built, the Dutch fleet was bolstered by a raft of new fighting vessels. The English had, quite literally, written the book on broadside naval fighting: the process of concentrating artillery fire from one side of the ship, stretching the fleet into a long line, had transformed the pattern of battle, resulting in ships often being battered on just one side. It was a strategy at which the Dutch were now equally adept, and the wind was on their side.

The two sides pounded each other for hours in a brutal and relentless close-range bombardment. Several Dutch ships were set alight,[26] and one of the Dutch admiral's ships was 'made a hull' while 'six or seven [Dutch ships were] maimed'.[27] Captain John Hart's ship, the *Rainbow*, which held 310 men, was attacked by 12 Dutch vessels and 25 of its crew were killed or wounded; it was 'so disabled in masts and rigging that she could not keep up' with the rest of the fleet and tailed away to refuge at Ostend for the night.[28] The flagstaffs of the *Royal Charles* and the *Defiance* were fired at, bringing them crashing down. A natural target for the Dutch, the sails of Monck's flagship became 'so shot that they had to anchor to get fresh ones'. But the *Royal Charles* was afforded very little respite; a gunshot hurtled towards it, tearing into Sir William Clarke's leg, and Monck was battered and bruised from the same shot; it 'tore his breeches and coate in many pieces'.[29] Many good English ships retreated 'immediately after the first passe without any notice of their condition given'.[30] Damaged, they had taken themselves back to the English coast for repairs, without asking permission or giving warning. As the English position weakened, the Dutch curved their broadside line into a half-moon partially to cocoon their enemy. As the ambassador in France vividly reported:

> Inspired by fury, drunk with hate and the smoke, both sides blinded by passion, no longer men but wild beasts, they left it to inhumanity and desperation to do their worst in that conflict, which lasted, day and night . . . with the perpetual discharge of guns, the flames of burning ships, masses of black smoke, which encumbered and confounded the air, the noise of masts and spars falling and breaking, the shouts and groans of poor wretches who were in pain.[31]

Deep in the belly of each ship, surgeons were kept busy conducting emergency amputations to remove damaged arms and legs, with many seamen having 'themselves bound up' before returning to their stations above deck.[32] Among the number of wounded treated by the surgeon was Sir William Clarke, whose partially severed leg was amputated with a sharp knife, a strong saw and a steady hand. In his diary, John Evelyn gives a vivid account of what it was like to witness, let alone experience, an amputation:

> that morning my Chirurgeon cut off a poore creaturs Leg, a little under the knee, first cutting the living and untainted flesh above the Gangreene with a sharp knife, and then sawing off the bone in an instant; then with searing and stoopes stanching the blood, which issued aboundantly; the stout and gallant man, enduring it with incredible patience, and that without being bound to his chaire, as is usual in such painefull operations, or hardly making a face or crying oh: I had hardly such courage enough to be present, nor could I endure to see any more such cruel operations.[33]

The terrifying procedure must have been excruciating, but Clarke 'bore it bravely'.[34]

As the day drew to a close, the English fleet numbered around 40 vessels. At 10 p.m., battered and in desperate need of repairs, the opposing fleets began to retreat for the night. Unfortunately, Captain John Harman's 72-gunned flagship *Henry* drifted into enemy lines. Having fallen into 'the body of the Dutch fleete', Harman attempted to navigate his way out, but was swiftly set upon by fireships. With him throughout was Pepys's brother-in-law Balty, who remained on the quarterdeck as the *Henry* desperately tried to escape the chase. One after another, 3 fireships ploughed into them, and Harman's panicked crew fell into a frenzy. In fear, the parson jumped ship and drowned, followed by nearly a hundred men 'and a good many women':[35] despite the drive to rid the fleet of women earlier in the year, many had remained on board Harman's ship. Who they were and why they were there can only be guessed at.

At this point, Harman drew his sword and threatened anyone that wanted to abandon ship with death, which succeeded in calming the panic. Coordinating the assault on the *Henry* was the fifty-six-year-old veteran Dutch commander, Cornelis Evertsen. The son of one of the most famous Dutch commanders in history, Evertsen had been temporarily imprisoned by the English during the First Anglo-Dutch War. Sensing that the *Henry* was almost at its end, he asked Harman if he wanted to surrender, but after restoring some order to his ship Harman was in no mood to give up. Evertsen continued his attack. The fiery mast of the third fireship smashed down onto the *Henry*, breaking Harman's ankle as it fell. The crew managed to put out the fire and made one last attempt to escape, with a final shot at Evertsen's ship. Whoever fired the shot either had a perfect aim or uncanny luck. It pounded into Evertsen himself, cutting the Dutch admiral in two. Against all odds, the *Henry* miraculously escaped.[36]

John Evelyn's garden was beautiful. A neatly sculpted melody of courtyards, orchards and groves, it was home to a variety of elm, beech, ash and oak trees. Inspired by 'Solomon's Garden' in Sir Francis Bacon's *New Atlantis* and the botanical gardens of European universities, it was also a kind of outdoor laboratory, where Evelyn cultivated and experimented with exotic plants, rare seeds and spices from far-flung places. Only a couple of years earlier, he had published a work called *Sylva or A Discourse on Forest Trees*, in which he had stressed the importance of using garden space for the production of key materials for the navy, in particular timber. Evelyn had visited some of the finest gardens in France and Italy, and the splendour of his garden at Sayes Court represented a little slice of Renaissance landscaping in England.

At 6 p.m. on 1 June, he was in his garden when the air suddenly cracked with the sound of cannon fire – or, as Evelyn put it, 'the great guns go thick off'. Taking a horse, he rode that very night to Rochester, twenty-six miles away, to see if he could gather any news. The next day, from Rochester, he galloped to the coast where he met the lieutenant of the 42-gunned fourth-rate frigate *Hampshire* who told him what had passed, 'or rather what had not passed', at sea the previous day. Evelyn also discovered that although he had heard the guns from his garden on the outskirts of London, there had been no sound of battle on the south-east coast near Deal and Dover. Fuelled with fresh intelligence, he took to his horse once again and thundered back to London.

On the morning of Saturday 2 June, the king received Sir William Clarke's letter, sent the previous day from the *Royal Charles*. While Clarke's report confirmed that the fleet was preparing to engage with the Dutch, it had been sent just after 11 a.m. and offered no information about the ensuing clash. There had also been word from Rupert's squadron at the Isle of Wight, confirming that he had received the king's orders and was making his way to join the rest of the English fleet. No doubt aware that the orders to Rupert had been late in their delivery, and perhaps to distract himself, the king took a walk through St James's Park.

Following the Restoration, the park had undergone a significant redesign. A long canal was under construction, the open areas were now decked with avenues of trees, and a grand decoy had been created to encourage and house wildlife. The park was also home to an array of interesting creatures – from antelopes, elk, deer and roebucks, to pelicans (a gift from the Russian ambassador), swans and ducks. One particularly curious inhabitant was a Balearic crane that:

> having had one of his legs broken and cut off above the knee, had a wooden or boxen leg and thigh, with a joint so accurately made that the creature could walk and use it as well as if it had been natural; it was made by a soldier.[37]

Charles had opened the royal park to the public (though horses and carriages were forbidden) and, seven years later, it would become the focus of one of the most infamously lewd poems in English literature. In 'A Ramble in St James's Park', Charles's new Gentleman of the Bedchamber, the Earl of Rochester, presented a place where natural beauty disguises the carnal activities of its visitors:

> Whence rows of mandrakes tall did rise
> Whose lewd tops fucked the very skies.
> Each imitative branch does twine
> In some loved fold of Aretine,
> And nightly now beneath their shade
> Are buggeries, rapes, and incests made.[38]

It was in St James's Park that Evelyn found the king 'impatiently expecting' news. Speaking directly to Charles, Evelyn revealed that he had spoken to a lieutenant of the fleet that very morning about the previous day's action.[39] The king was 'greatly rejoiced' by the news, but surprised to learn that the guns had not been heard on the south coast. Orders were given for 200 soldiers to be sent immediately to join the fleet, and Charles and the Duke of York boarded the royal barge for Greenwich.

At the Navy Board, news of Clarke's letter had put everyone 'into a tosse'. Pepys rushed to the victualling office at Smithfield and then to Greenwich to dispatch the soldiers, who were instructed to march to Blackwall. After securing some yachts to carry the army recruits to the fleet, he walked to Greenwich Park with Captain George Erwin, where they heard the distant sound of cannon fire. Unlike St James's Park, Greenwich Park was closed to the public. Bordered by a twelve-foot brick wall that had been built during the reign of James I, it contained a substantial hill in the centre that provided a high vantage point from which to view London. In ten years' time, this hill would be the foundation to an ambitious new scientific laboratory, known as the

Royal Observatory, but for now only the remains of a medieval watchtower marked the park's highest point. At around 4 p.m., Pepys met the king and Duke of York as they arrived and walked with them to the park, where they also heard the gunfire. Travelling to Blackwall, Pepys found the soldiers, 'who were by this time gotten most of them drunk', and recounted how they 'kissed their wives and sweethearts' goodbye, and then 'shouted, and let off their guns' before setting off. Their fate and the hopes of naval success seemed to depend on how fast Prince Rupert could reach the main body of the fleet, as Pepys wrote:

> All our hopes now are that Prince Rupert with his fleete is coming back and will be with the fleete this even . . . great hopes, the wind being very fair, that he is with them this even, and the fresh going off of the guns makes us believe the same.[40]

But Rupert had not reached the fleet, nor would he that evening. At 5 a.m. on 2 June, his squadron had been parallel to Beachy Head and had spent the day, 'it being very clear weather', sailing along the south coast; from Fairlight to Dungeness and finally Dover, the whole time hearing nothing of the battle. At Dover, word did arrive from a 'Capt. Jacob' (possibly Jacob Reynolds, captain of the fifth-rate frigate *Great Gift*[41]) that one Ralph Fell had seen the Dutch and English fleets abroad two days before. Rupert intended to make sail to travel further, but the weather was too calm so his squadron anchored all night near to Dover, so close but so far from the action.

Meanwhile, thirteen to fifteen leagues away, the English fleet was 'engaged very hotly' in the second day of the battle with the Dutch.[42] At 3 a.m. Monck sighted the enemy fleet to the leeward side of his own. Then, at 5 a.m., he also spotted a small group of enemy ships to his windward side. The English supposed this small detachment to be enemy supplies or 'part of their fleet which wee had severed the night before'.[43] Early in the morning, Monck had sent his disabled ships and wounded men (except Sir William Clarke) back to shore. At 7 a.m., the reduced fleet of around 40 vessels set off from their position south-west to hack its way through the Dutch line.[44] Unfortunately for the English, de Ruyter had plans of his own and smashed into them first, guns blazing. A 'very . . . sharp encounter' ensued which saw several captains lose their lives and limbs (on the *Antelope*, Captain Holles's arm was shot off),[45] and many English ships were disabled.[46] After this first confrontation Monck noticed that more of his ships had left the scene of the battle, including the 58-gun frigate *Anne*, helmed by Captain Robert Moulton; the 52-gun *Bristol*, whose captain Philip Bacon was killed; the *Baltimore*, which had taken a serious battering resulting in extensive body damage and dangerous leaks;[47] and at least two others.

The English had a stroke of luck when it became clear that the small detachment of Dutch ships that had separated from the main Dutch fleet was in fact Tromp's vulnerable rear squadron. As the focus of the English attack the previous day, his squadron was now extremely thin. Some of his ships had returned home for repairs, while others had taken captured English ships back under escort (Monck still had no idea that Sir William Berkeley had been killed and the *Swiftsure* taken). The English attacked the remainder of Tromp's rear squadron, sinking one of his ships, killing a vice admiral and setting another vessel on fire. The assault on Tromp was so intense that the Dutch admiral, de Ruyter, had to lead a rescue mission, breaking the English line and forcing through to his comrade's exiled ships.

Gaining the weather gage, George Ayscue, the admiral of the White Squadron, saw that Tromp and de Ruyter were isolated and attempted an assault, but de Ruyter again managed to break through the English line and return to the main Dutch fleet. At one point, de Ruyter was reportedly urged to board an English ship, possibly the *Royal Charles*, but having been forbidden from placing himself in personal danger, he refused. Monck was attacked by a Dutch vice admiral's ship, that got so close 'the Yard-Arms touched' and attempted to board, but Monck 'received him with so full a broadside, besides a volley of small shot, that the enemy immediately fell to the Stern, and appeared no more . . .'.[48] The Dutch knew that if the English feared their ships might be captured, they would blow them up,[49] and the Dutch believed their failure at Lowestoft to have occurred because the high command had been wiped out. De Ruyter was under strict orders to stay alive, and with his ship damaged, he left the battle and returned to the Dutch coast for repairs.

Amidst the action, a small six-gunned ketch made its way from Harwich to the English fleet and, at 2 p.m., its passengers Sir Thomas Clifford and Lord Ossory boarded the flagship. On hearing news of the impending battle, they had ridden the eighty or so miles from Hampstead to Harwich the previous day to join the fray. Clifford's report to his patron Lord Arlington was to become one of the key testimonies of the battle, and one of his first observations was that 'there was nothing to be heard amonge the comen [common] Seaman but complaints against dividing our fleet and sending away Prince Rupert'.[50]

Shortly after Clifford's arrival, a (seemingly) fresh squadron of 12 Dutch vessels was seen on the horizon. In truth, they were the ships that had given chase to the *Rainbow* the day before and were now on their return. With 5 more English ships shattered, many others 'disabled in their masts, Sayles, & Rigging' and the fleet overpowered & . . . much wearyed',[51] Monck began a retreat so that his fleet could attend to crucial repairs.[52] He used 16 of his best ships, including his own, as a bulwark to shepherd the remaining fleet back to the English coast, under attack the whole time by 'the Dutch fleet of 66' ships.[53] A greatly damaged fourth-rate frigate called the *St Paul* straggled behind. To prevent the Dutch taking advantage of it, Monck ordered the seamen on board to abandon ship and join other vessels. The ship was then set alight in an act of deliberate sabotage: as the report back to

Whitehall stated, 'wee burned the St Paul for fear she could not keep company'.[54]

Sunday 3 June began pleasantly enough in London. At Whitehall, there had been word from a Captain Thomas Elliot of the *Portland*, a ship that had been disabled on the first day of action. He reported that he had seen 'one of the Dutch great ships blown up, and three on fire' and that aside from one other ship that he had seen coming into port at the same time as him, he knew 'of no other hurt to our ships'. William Coventry passed the information on to Pepys who, in turn, whispered the news 'with great joy' to his fellow parishioners from the pews of his local church, St Olave Hart Street.[55] This joy, however, was short-lived.

By late morning, news filtered into the capital of a letter from Prince Rupert that had arrived in Whitehall that morning, in which he confirmed he had remained at Dover all night. It was the smoking gun in a blame game that swept through the politicos and chatterers of the city. The Exchange was full and busy with conversation about the fight; Pepys declared that many talked 'highly of the failure of the Prince in not making more haste after his instructions did come', and of the bad management in not getting word to him sooner and 'with more care'.[56] There were whispers among the city victuallers that both Monck and Holmes had had their ships' flags shot down, and there was also news that the ship Captain Elliot had seen coming into port was in fact the *Henry*, not the *Portland*. Not only was the *Henry* a key vessel of the White Squadron, containing a rear admiral, it was also the very ship on which Pepys had secured a position for his brother-in-law Balty. There were reports that it had suffered terrible casualties from being attacked by Dutch fireships.

As many in London began to consider the possibility that an English victory might not be guaranteed, under a fresh easterly wind Monck's greatly diminished fleet of 34 fighting ships finished repairs and prepared for a third day of battle. For most of the morning the Dutch had remained about two leagues from the

English, but as midday approached the enemy fleet under the Dutch commander, Van Nes, began to advance. When they were within range, cannon fire was exchanged and the battle was resumed. Then, at 3 p.m., the English spied from their topmasts a large group of warships in the distance to the south-west. As the ships drew closer, with flags and hulls coming into view, the English realised with a wave of ecstasy and relief that Prince Rupert had finally arrived with 20 fresh warships. So great were the 'acclamations of joy . . . from ship to ship'[57] and so unanimous was the shouting of the whole English fleet,[58] that the Dutch momentarily ceased firing, some even shortening their sails to drop back to the 'Body of their Fleete'.[59] It was a moment that was glossed with poetry and captured for posterity by John Dryden in *Annus Mirabilis*:

> For now brave Rupert from afar appears,
> Whose waving streamers the glad general knows:
> With full spread sails his eager navy steers,
> And every ship in swift proportion grows.[60]

From his flagship the *Royal James*, Prince Rupert – who had travelled with the tide that morning and packed all of his squadron's storage chests onto a small ketch for safety – watched as the English fleet retreated under a Dutch assault. Having met 'no Intelligence in the Downes' of the ensuing fight, he had continued to travel north-east before sighting Monck's fleet.[61] On noticing Rupert's approach, the enemy split into two parts: the first, of 40 ships, continued the attack on Monck's fleet, while the second, of 30 ships, geared towards Rupert. There was still some distance between Rupert's ships and the Dutch threat and it was imperative that he join together with the main body of the English fleet before they were forcibly kept apart. The path to union, however, was obstructed by a danger below the waters: with the tide now low, the perilous stretch of shallow sea known as Galloper Sands lay between Rupert's squadron and Monck's fleet.

Monck risked the hazardous shoal and sailed to meet his co-commander, but it didn't take long for his ship to become grounded in the raised sand, quickly followed by the 76-gun *Royal Katherine* and the 92-gunned *Royal Prince*. Monck's ship and the *Royal Katherine* managed to work themselves free, but the *Royal Prince*, helmed by Admiral George Ayscue, 'drawing more water than either stuck fast'.[62] Smelling an opportunity, Lieutenant Admiral Cornelis Tromp quickly moved in with some of his smaller ships; taunting their prey, the Dutch nudged the *Royal Prince* with fireships, and threatened to board. The rest of the fleet could only watch in horror as one of their most prestigious warships lay helpless. Launched in 1610 at Woolwich, the *Royal Prince* was a first-rate ship of the line, one of the largest vessels of the English navy and, along with the *Sovereign*, carried the most guns. Designed to hold 630 men, it had participated in the First Anglo-Dutch War and the Battle of Lowestoft, but it was now isolated from the rest of its fleet and in danger.

Monck sent a handful of small frigates across the shoal in an attempt to fend off the attack, but it was to no avail. As Thomas Clifford reported from the *Royal Charles*, 'to the wounder of the whole fleet' the *Royal Prince* unexpectedly raised its flags to surrender to the Dutch 'when she had not her selfe either shot ten guns in her defence or received ten shot from the enemy'.[63] The Dutch boarded the ship and took Vice Admiral George Ayscue as a prisoner, along with some of his officers. Unable to budge the gargantuan vessel, de Ruyter ordered that the ship be destroyed and the rest of its crew be taken as prisoners. Somewhere within the Dutch fleet, an artist called Willem van de Velde watched the drama unfold with a keen eye. From rough sketches made during the battle, he would later transform this most humiliating moment in English naval history into a striking and realistic work of art. Watching the vessel blaze from afar, Clifford was dumbfounded, believing that 'a little resistance would have [saved] her'; like 'a castle in the sea', he argued that the *Royal Prince* was 'the best ship that ever was built in the world to endure battering'.[64] But she was gone, and so was Ayscue, sent to The Hague as a prisoner on a galliot the next morning;[65] the last admiral of the Royal Navy to be captured by an enemy at sea.

A council of war was held on the *Royal James* with the remaining flag officers, where it was decided that Rupert's fresh squadron would lead an attack the next day.[66]

Navigating the streets of London, the two men made their way to the Navy Board in Seething Lane. What a sight they must have been. One had a face 'as black as the chimney . . . covered with dirt, pitch, and tarr', with his right eye concealed by a makeshift eye patch; the other had 'endangered another eye' and was, presumably, of a similar condition.[67] Along with twenty or so wounded men, they had left the *Royal Charles* at 5 p.m. the previous day, travelling on a ketch and reaching Harwich at 2 a.m. Able to ride, the pair had taken to horses and galloped all the way to the capital, arriving in London just before midday. Pepys met them at the Navy Board offices and escorted them across town to the king. All the while, eager eyes stared at the battle-wearied men, expecting news of the fight. At Whitehall, their escort left them at the lodgings of William Coventry while he went to find the king. Returning a little while later, Pepys asked the men to follow him to another room of the palace, where they gave their account of the battle to the monarch in person, explaining the sequence of events and that Monck and Rupert had finally joined forces the previous day. The king 'was mightily pleased' with the news and gave the no doubt exhausted men twenty pieces of silver for their troubles, before they were sent to see the surgeon. The news soon spread throughout London.

Privately, Pepys was not as pleased with the news as the king appeared to be. Following a brief meeting with the scientist Robert Hooke, who was compiling a list of naval terms and words for a new book about the 'Universal Language' by his friend Dr Wilkins, Pepys reflected on the state of the navy. To him, Monck 'hath failed of what he was so presumptuous of' and had acted far too rashly in going to war against the Dutch when the numbers were so unequal. He felt that more consideration should be made before conducting battles with 'people that can fight, it seems now, as well as we'.[68]

At 5 a.m. on Monday 4 June, the fourth day of fighting, the English fleet of 60–65 ships advanced towards the Dutch fleet of 68–70 ships. The irascible maritime figure Sir Christopher Myngs was placed in charge of the front squadron, Prince Rupert held the centre and Monck took the rear.[69] With Sir William Berkeley missing, Captain John Harman disabled and Sir George Ayscue recently captured, Sir Thomas Allin and Sir Edward Spragge (who had been travelling with Rupert) were welcome additions to the fleet, which was also bolstered by 5 fresh ships that had recently arrived from the English coast. Numerically, it was the first occasion throughout the entire battle when the English and the Dutch were on an equal footing, but as the day progressed, the odds, once again, stacked in favour of the Dutch.

Once level, the opposing fleets attacked one another in a broadside line. De Ruyter was back leading the Dutch and had won the weather gage, but the English made significant inroads, with Sir Christopher Myngs and Sir Robert Holmes breaking up the Dutch line. Despite doing them 'much mischeife', the enemy soon came together again.[70] During this first pass, English fire-ships managed to burn 2 or 3 of the Dutch ships and disable many others. However, there were complaints that the 'nimble frigots [that] should have destroy'd those of theirs that were disable[d] . . . omitted their duties'.[71] The *Convertine*, the *Clovetree*, the *Essex* and the *Black Bull* were all either lost to the Dutch or destroyed.

From the front, Sir Christopher Myngs on the *Victory* locked into a close-range duel with Vice Admiral Johan de Liefde on the *Ridderschap*. Surrounded by the Dutch and targeted by a marksman, Myngs was fired at by a musket. The first hit cracked into his cheek. The second smashed into his shoulder. He lingered on for a few days, but the wounds were a death sentence. Another towering maritime figure gone. The English flagships were disabled, with the *Royal James* losing its main topmast and the sails of the *Royal Charles* (specifically targeted by de Ruyter) being fired at so much that they were torn to shreds. After several hours, a mist rose from the waters, casting a fog over the battlesite, and Rupert coordinated an English withdrawal having, as the Dutch claimed, 'never committed himself so far as to allow himself to be cut off and destroyed'.[72] It would later be claimed that the withdrawal was intended to repair the tattered fleet, but the Dutch saw it for what it really was: a full retreat. Victory lay with de Ruyter, but (as was the case with the Duke of York at Lowestoft the previous summer) he could, and probably should, have given chase to the English. Instead, he regrouped his ships and returned home, leaving it open for English command to claim that the Dutch had in fact fled.

Despite claims that Monck had 'absolutely ruin'd the Dutch Fleete', the English were in no position to carry the battle into a fifth day. The night was spent mending sails and rigging, but it was found that there was no more ammunition. Even the *Royal Charles* only had two more rounds left. In four days, the total number of English and Dutch killed numbered 3,000. The Royal Navy had lost half of them, as well as 23 ships. There were 1,450 Englishmen wounded and 1,800 captured. On their side, along with their dead, the Dutch had lost just 4 ships and had 1,300 wounded. It was one of the largest and longest battles in the age of sail. As one report back to England stated: 'by the inspection already made, this appeard to be the sharpest conflict that ever was fought on the ocean'.[73]

Reports of the Dutch victory trickled back to the Dutch Republic and France, with Ambassador Sagredo opining that the English:

had the everlasting shame of their unbridled arrogance, their lunatic haughtiness and their overweening pride, shown in the hymns which they sang before the battle which made it appear that they had first made war on Heaven . . . and thereby undoubtedly provoking its wrath and their losses.[74]

Sleep deprived and battle weary, Sir Thomas Clifford composed an eleven-page, day-by-day account of the action as he had experienced it. It wasn't perfect – as he confessed himself, writing: 'I doe almost forget what I am to say next' – but it covered everything he had witnessed on the *Royal Charles* since his arrival on the second day of the fight. Throughout that time he claimed to have 'not slept two houres of every fower and twenty'. In the letter, without being explicit, he admitted the defeat: 'be for the present some honour to them [the Dutch] and may abroad somewhat lesser our reputation'. As a counterweight to the bad news, he also stressed the importance of rearming and repairing the fleet as soon as possible so that it could re-engage with the Dutch. To his mind, three things were crucial: first, that the fleet was resupplied with men, stores, victuals and ammunition; second, that funds for the payment of arrears were made available; and third, that the fleet set out again 'before the Hollanders'. Signing off his letter he added:

I would not have lost seeing [the fight] for halfe I am worth there were so many occasions not only to observe great conduct and much experience in it but the whole was so interwoven with such various accidents that the like perchance will never happen.[75]

6

Fantastic Fortune

Fantastic fortune thou deceitful light,
That cheats the weary traveler by night,
Though on a precipice each step you tread,
I am resolved to follow where you lead.
                                    Aphra Behn, *The Rover*[1]

THOMAS CLIFFORD'S LETTER was sent to Lord Arlington in
Saxham and then forwarded to Whitehall, with strict instructions that it be preserved after the king had read it.[2] But before the
court could read Clifford's account, they received another testimony. On 6 June, the Duke of York was walking in St James's Park,
where 'every body [was] listening for guns', when he was handed
a letter that had been sent by express from Harwich dockyard.
Written by Captain John Hayward from the *Dunkirk*, it painted an
English success, explaining that the commanders were well and
inaccurately reporting that the Dutch fleet had been halved by the
English attack. The duke ran straight to the king – who was
worshipping in the chapel at Whitehall – to pass on the good news.
The king and the congregation were thrown into 'a hubbub, being
rejoiced over head and ears in . . . [the] good newes'.[3] The battle
was taken to be an English victory, and the king ordered a public
thanks to be given in celebration with notices sent to St Paul's
Cathedral and Westminster Abbey. When word reached the City
of London, the Lord Mayor, Thomas Bludworth, and the city
magistrates travelled to Whitehall to praise the king. Celebratory
bonfires and bells were ordered throughout the city.

Yet no sooner had the good news been absorbed than fresh details emerged. Clifford's account arrived, describing great English losses, the capture of Admiral Ayscue, the destruction of the *Royal Prince* and the number of missing ships. Evelyn, who had been in the chapel with the king, witnessed the change of mood at court. The news hinted at a much less certain conclusion to the battle, which Evelyn recognised to have been 'rather a deliverance than a triumph'. Like Pepys, he was fast to place full blame on Monck:

it pleased God to humble our late overconfidence that noth-ing could withstand the Duke of Albemarle, who, in good truth, made too forward a reckoning of his own success now, because he had once beaten the Dutch in another quarrel; and being ambitious to outdo the Earl of Sandwich, whom he had prejudicated as deficient in courage.[4]

For his part, Monck complained that he had 'never fought with worse officers in his life, not above twenty of them behaving themselves like men'.[5] There was certainly a sense that many of the younger gentlemen captains had left the action unduly or as a consequence of very minor damage to their ships. Sir Edward Spragge and Sir Christopher Myngs were singled out for particu-lar bravery, as was Sir Robert Holmes – who was praised for 'keeping himself in good order and within bounds' (but, as William Coventry warned, 'a cat will be a cat still, and some time or other out his humour must break again').[6] The heroics of Captain John Harman (who had escaped with a broken ankle) provided much fodder for discussion, while Pepys was greatly relieved to discover that his brother-in-law Balty had survived the action. For a short while, several false rumours circulated; that Sir William Berkeley and the *Swiftsure* had returned safely to the Nore,[7] that de Ruyter had been killed in the action and that de Witt (who hadn't even been present) had had his leg shot off. Most of these stories were put to bed when a letter arrived from an English informer in The Hague. It was discovered that Berkeley had in fact been killed and his ship taken and that while Dutch losses had been substantial ('the sails of those that are come in, look like so many Nets, so sharp was the service on our side'), they were celebrating a fantastic victory and de Ruyter was not only alive,[8] but 'exalted with the greatest praises'.[9]

News of the Dutch triumph was quick to reach England's enemies. In Paris, Sagredo noted how the 'delight which the Dutch feel over it is inexpressible'.[10] The question of how the English would react to the humiliation remained open, with the ambassador musing:

> What effect this serious and ill-fated disaster will have upon the presumptuous and proud spirit of the English, is not yet known, but it is easy to see that it may bring about some disturbance in the government and involve peril to the king personally.[11]

But there was a simple way to deal with the defeat that the ambassador had not considered: to deny it had happened in the first place. Privately, many knew that the English fleet had suffered terribly, but the official account declared an English victory and celebrated the valour of Monck and Rupert, while downplaying the level of loss. At his printing house near to Baynard's Castle, Thomas Newcomb was fed the official state-vetted reports for typesetting and when he printed the 7 June–11 June edition of the *London Gazette* it reported 'a Happy Victory obtained against the Dutch'.[12] Conceding that there had been some English losses, most notably the destruction of the *Royal Prince* and the capture of Sir George Ayscue, the newspaper suggested that it was only due to a lack of ammunition and bad winds that the English fleet had not continued the fight to an even greater 'victory'.

When the Venetian ambassador received copies of the *London Gazette* in Paris, he was astonished to discover how: 'they have studied to deceive the people by making them believe that the fleets separated with little disparity of advantage, and that if anything it lay on their side'.[13] It was perhaps because of this perceived deception that a pamphlet entitled 'A Relation of the Passages in the Battel at Sea, Between the Fleet of England and the United Neitherlands: Collected according to the charge & order of the Lords States General' made its way onto British shores. Translated from the official Dutch account of the battle, the anonymous publisher claimed to have printed the pamphlet for the 'undeceiving of the English nation' and celebrated a clear Dutch win. Expanding on particulars of the fight, it ended: 'the inhabitants of the Confederate Neitherlands are bound to give the highest thankes unto God thee Lord, who hath given them so eminent a Victory'.[14]

For those directly affected, the reality was clear. Echoing similar protests earlier that year in Rotterdam, around three hundred women flocked to the navy offices at Seething Lane to demand money in lieu of captured loved ones. Pepys was there and recalled 'the yarde being very full of women . . . coming to get money for their husbands and friends that are prisoners in Holland'. So rowdy was the crowd that Pepys was almost too frightened to send a venison pasty he had planned to have for supper to his bakers for cooking in case the women seized it. All day the protesters 'lay clamouring and swearing and cursing' at Pepys and his colleagues, at one point even reaching the diarist's window where they 'tormented' him. He confessed:

> their cries were so sad for money, and laying down the condition of their families and their husbands, and what they have done and suffered for the King, and how ill they are used by us, and how well the Dutch are used here by the allowance of their masters, and what their husbands are offered to serve the Dutch abroad, that I do most heartily pity them . . .[15]

As the crowd dispersed, Pepys called one of the women over to him and gave her some money; she blessed him and went on her way. But it wasn't just families that were broken. Visiting the fleet near to Chatham on 18 June, Evelyn saw first-hand what the *London Gazette* called the 'honourable marks of this Glorious Action' and was deeply troubled, writing:

> I beheld the sad spectacle, more than half that gallant bulwark of the kingdom miserably shattered, hardly a vessel entire, but appearing rather so many wrecks and hulls, so cruelly had the Dutch mangled us. The loss of the Prince, that gallant vessel, had been a loss to be universally deplored, none knowing for what reason we first engaged in this ungrateful war.[16]

To Monck and Rupert, there was only one way to atone for the calamity that was now being called the Four Days Fight and that was to win a clear victory against the Dutch – and fast. To do so, the tattered fleet had to be mended at breakneck speed. Despite Evelyn's private horror, much of the damage to the navy was in fact reparable, and the dockyards were sufficiently supplied to handle the repairs. There was ready timber, with more being felled in the New Forest, and there were skilled carpenters and new supplies of artillery.[17] Rupert also pushed for every flagship to have its own fireship and a fifth-rate frigate to carry messages back and forth, arguing that the lack of support vessels had affected the outcome of the previous engagement.[18] The dockyards, however, had long been hotbeds of corruption and double-dealing, which had resulted in bad management, the slow delivery of ships, unhurried repairs and incomplete supplies. Monck and Rupert were quick to highlight the deficiencies at the dockyards and the 'great Negligence of the Commissioners of the Navy', especially the slow delivery of key warships such as the *Loyal London*, the *Warspite* and the *Greenwich*. With time of utmost importance, they took matters into their own hands and sent some of their own officers and seamen to oversee the work – which was completed, they said, 'in a very few Days'.[19]

With so many men taken prisoner by the Dutch and killed or wounded during the battle, fresh recruits were desperately needed. Monck and Prince Rupert called for an extra 3,000 men to replace the crews that had been lost; Sir Thomas Allin needed '1,000 able seamen' for his squadron alone. Writing from Aldeburgh on the Suffolk coast to the Secretary of State's chief assistant, Joseph Williamson, 'J. Knight' reasoned that 'experience makes devils wise, much more week mortals'. He reported that such a spirit had got into the seamen that it would be difficult to get them to return to their ships. Contrary to Clifford's advice, he argued that pay 'only helps them run away' and named 6 that had recently escaped, 20 to 30 more that were 'ready to do so' and many more that had fled to King's Lynn and Wells in Norfolk, with some even reaching as far as Bilborough in Nottinghamshire, where 40 were apprehended.[20] He also reported that a troubling reminder of the deadly battle had flowed 'for miles' around the Suffolk coast, with the sea appearing to turn red. It was probably the result of fish spawn, but many swore it to be the blood of those slain during battle.[21] In London, around 300 men were pressed and sent to Bridewell Prison where they remained for several days without proper food or pay; an act that Pepys declared was 'contrary to all course of law'. They were sent to join the fleet but there was a mutiny while travelling along the Thames; and the ringleader was apprehended and sent to the Tower of London, with the rest 'quietly' continuing the journey to the fleet.[22] In London, the Frenchman Denis de Repas witnessed a priest begging a press officer to set free a recently pressed father of five, only for the priest to be taken instead and told 'then you must come with us, you are so much fitter, you shall pray while the others fight'.[23] Three hundred more were pressed and sent from Plymouth. Around the country many of the pressed men were reportedly 'pitiful fellows' with 'no shirts and scarce rags to cover them, and fall sick in three or four days; some come sick, not without suspicion of plague'. Knight suggested that to lighten the burden on the naval purse, the sick men should be discharged rather than sent to navy hospitals.[24]

Running parallel to the navy preparations was a drive to mobilise the militia. The fear of a coordinated Dutch and French land attack was very real and towards the end of June intelligence arrived from The Hague confirming that the Dutch fleet was carrying 5,000 soldiers. Written in orange juice to keep the subterfuge hidden from Dutch surveillance, the letter stressed that while there was talk of landing in England, the government should not 'prepare for it that the fleet be less manned'.[25] Likewise, Prince Rupert and George Monck played down the risk, arguing that 'there is no ground for the great apprehensions of the enemy's landing, as they have no horse'.[26] Nevertheless, on 27 June orders were sent to the lieutenants of the counties to assemble their respective militias and 'unite the gentry'. Anyone with a ready horse was invited to join the regiments. The coastal beacons were to be watched and fired if necessary, and a £70,000 militia tax was to be raised.

The Dutch, it seems, believed the level of unrest within England to be much greater than it actually was. There were certainly individual instances of severe grievance, as one anonymous appeal written in late June attests:

> The people are in a desperate condition, housekeepers so oppressed with taxes that they dare not open their doors, or the tax gatherer will carry away a bed or a dish; the people curse the King, wish for Cromwell, and say come Dutch come devil, they cannot be worse, so that where one would fight for His Majesty, 10 would fight against him; there are not 10 amongst the gentry whom they would follow.[27]

However, England was a country where civil war was still within living memory, plague was rife and anti-Dutch and French feeling potent; a substantial and widespread uprising in favour of a foreign ruler was unlikely. The Dutch reportedly had an informer near to the Thames Estuary who would give the signal if he detected widespread support for an invasion. No signal came. Failing to find any straggling vessels or land support, the Dutch abandoned their plans for a land attack and left the troops across the water. By the middle of July they could be seen on a stretch of the Thames Estuary known as the Gunfleet 'drinking healths, vapouring, and firing guns'.[28] All the while, a two-way exchange of covert intelligence continued. Despite firm restrictions on travel, details of England's internal affairs were smuggled across the Channel by French and Dutch agents and leaked to spies 'on the other side'.[29] Likewise, the English drew on their network of informers to keep tabs on their enemy. On 9 July, a letter was sent to Whitehall from an informer in Bristol confirming that the French fleet, under Beaufort, was still at Lisbon. The Channel was open for another Anglo-Dutch battle.

As the situation developed the Earl of Rochester, now nineteen, took a keen interest. His exploits at sea the previous autumn had seen him bestowed with several honours, including a £750 'free gift'. Until very recently he had been in close proximity at court to Elizabeth Malet, the young heiress he had attempted to kidnap the previous summer. In early July, however, she formed part of the coterie of ladies who left Whitehall to take the waters at Tunbridge Wells with the queen.[30] Their departure was probably a welcome relief to the king. In the middle of June, he had had a disagreement with his principal mistress, Lady Castlemaine, over his where-abouts after he left her chamber at 'one, two, or three in the morn-ing'; Castlemaine had declared, in front of the queen, that he must have found somewhere else to stay. Unlike the king, Rochester did not have a marriage and a long-term mistress to sustain. Perhaps it was because of the sadness at Elizabeth Malet's departure, perhaps it was the languid state of the court in general following the Four Days Fight, perhaps it was stories of warfare from his peers, or perhaps it was simply his restless spirit – but in the middle of July, the earl left Whitehall abruptly 'without communicating his design to his nearest relations' to re-join the navy.[31]

At noon on Friday 20 July, the fleet approached a stretch of sea in line with Ipswich known as the Middle Grounds. On board the *Royal Charles*, Thomas Clifford wrote to Lord Arlington and reported that 'my Ld Rochester came to us this morning he says he will stay on board Sr Ed Spragg[e's ship]'. The historian and future bishop of Salisbury, Gilbert Burnet, would later describe Rochester as having 'a strange vivacity of thought and vigour of expression: his wit had a subtlety and sublimity both, that were scarce imitable' so it was perhaps no surprise that he would opt to join Spragge's flagship.[32] Spragge was cut from the same cloth as many of Rochester's future companions, with an equally ready wit and cheerful demeanour – he had a secret wife who, that very month, had been making claims on his fortune.[33] Clifford also revealed that another volunteer had arrived, called Sir Robert Leach, to join Sir Robert Holmes's ship. Leach, he explained, had 'a full persuasion grounded upon many dreams' that he would personally kill de Ruyter 'with his fuser'. He added that 'I know not what he will doe but I'll undertake Sr Rob Holmes will bring him neer enough to shew his skill and fancy.'[34] Reflecting on the fleet, Clifford wrote:

> I wish his majestie had but seen us yesterday under saile I am sure he would have been infinitely pleased we took up in length 9 or 10 mile and almost as much now at anchor . . . I confess I was never more pleased with any sight in my life and there is a new air and vigor in every mans countenance than when we ley at the boy of the nore.[35]

Now fully manned, victualled and repaired, the navy had replenished itself at surprising speed. The co-commanders George Monck and Prince Rupert resolved that this time the entire navy would stick together. They also knew that, to be successful, they would need to have the weather on their side, so they waited for exactly the right conditions to get out to sea from the Thames Estuary, ready to face the Dutch. On 23 July, the

89-strong English fleet was assembled near to the Gunfleet; with the Dutch fleet of 88 ships in sight, all believed that the action would commence the following day. From the *Royal Charles*, Prince Rupert wrote directly to the king to confirm that they would stick to their instructions. He also mentioned that a shallop he'd had specifically made at Harwich the previous week had arrived; he christened the small boat *FanFan*.

The fleet would have to wait a little longer for action, though, because that night there was a terrific thunderstorm. The wind and rain forced many ships apart, scattering some of the smaller vessels and damaging others. The 50-gunned fourth-rate frigate *The Jersey* was struck by lightning, with a jagged white knife of electricity splitting its mainmast in two; the vessel was sent to shore for repairs and its 185 men were distributed across the fleet. Rupert and Monck spent the day of 24 July reordering the weatherworn navy, which they organised into three squadrons: as the co-commanders of the navy, they were to lead the Red Squadron on the *Royal Charles*, with Sir Joseph Jordan as vice admiral on the *Royal Oak* and Sir Robert Holmes as rear admiral on the *Henry*; the White Squadron was to be led by Sir Thomas Allin as admiral on the *Royal James*, Sir Thomas Teddeman as vice admiral on the *Royal Katherine* and Captain Utber as rear admiral on the *Rupert*; the Blue Squadron was to be led by Sir Jeremy Smith as admiral on the *Loyal London*, with Sir Edward Spragge as vice admiral on the *Victory* and Captain Kempthorne newly promoted to rear admiral on the *Defiance*.

On 25 July, St James's Day, the English moved north with the Dutch fleet pursuing from a leeward position. Monck was convinced that this time he knew how to beat the Dutch – and he must have been aware that his reputation as a military leader would either be cemented or destroyed as a result of the day's action. The English had a stroke of luck when the winds changed in their favour. Turning the fleet to face the enemy, Monck and Rupert won the weather gage and forced the Dutch into a precarious area of water known for its high pressure. Leading the

Dutch front squadron was Lieutenant Admiral Johan Evertsen, whose brother had been killed during the Four Days Fight by Captain John Harman's ship. He was sixty-six years old and a very experienced commander but, handicapped by the weather, had difficulty keeping his ships in line.

A fresh breeze gave wind to the English sails and, at 10 a.m., Sir Thomas Allin's White Squadron ploughed into Evertsen's splintered fleet. From his flagship, the *Royal James*, Allin coordinated a particularly sharp and bloody attack, battering Evertsen's ships. Intense cannon-fire saw many Dutch vessels disabled and, like his brother less than two months earlier, Evertsen was killed – as was a vice admiral, while a rear admiral lost his leg and arm to a cannon shot. The wails of the wounded could reportedly be heard above the gunfire. By 11 a.m., the Red Squadron, under Prince Rupert and George Monck, had joined the White Squadron to form a solid broadside line against the Dutch fleet. The English still held the weather gage and the Dutch line fractured even further during the bombardment. The *Royal Charles* twice engaged in a duel with de Ruyter's flagship, the second time joined by the 92-gunned *Sovereign of the Seas*. Rupert and Monck's flagship became so damaged that the commanders had to change ships, moving to Allin's *Royal James* to continue the fight. The English lost the *Resolution* to a fireship, but most of the men were saved. In the heat of the action, some of the most badly damaged vessels from the Dutch front squadron managed to escape.

Meanwhile, a battle on altogether different terms had been waged by Lieutenant Admiral Tromp on Admiral Jeremiah Smith's Blue Squadron. Watching on as the centre and the front of his fleet was decimated, Tromp made the decision to break away from the main body of the Dutch fleet to target Smith's squadron at the rear of the English fleet. Swooping behind the English line, he carved a watery path between the Blue Squadron and the rest of the English fleet. Unlike the rest of the Dutch ships, Tromp's squadron managed to win the weather gage and pushed Smith's ships ever further from the rest of the English navy – putting them under heavy attack as he chased them west.

Supporting Smith in the Blue Squadron was Sir Edward Spragge's flagship, the *Victory*. Among the 450 men on board the 76-gunned second-rate ship was the Earl of Rochester, who experienced some of the worst of the fight under Tromp's relentless onslaught. A fellow gentleman volunteer on his ship, Mr Middleton, had his arm shot through, and many of Rochester's shipmates were seriously injured. So confused did the fighting get that at one point there were reports that some of Smith's great warships were in danger of being set upon by his own fireships.[36] With the conduct of one of the captains being called into question, Spragge sought a messenger to make the perilous journey from the *Victory* to another frigate to carry a letter of reproof. But he 'could not easily find a person that would cheerfully venture through so much danger to carry his commands'. Rochester volunteered and under heavy gunfire 'went in a little boat, through all the shot, and delivered the message, and returned back'. It was a daring display of courage that 'was much commended by all that saw it',[37] but it wasn't enough to change the outcome of the fight between the opposing rear squadrons. Tromp defeated Smith, whose flagship, the *Loyal London*, was so badly damaged that it had to be towed away.

After five hours of fighting, the White and Red Squadrons under Monck and Rupert forced de Ruyter into a retreat. They gave chase, following the Dutch all night and through to the morning. Two Dutch ships were captured, and although the vice admiral managed to escape, Rupert and Monck took the crews on board as prisoners and set fire to the ships, not having enough manpower to secure them. Then they sank a further two ships.[38] On inspecting the Dutch prisoners it was clear that many of them were 'landmen', and the English officers were informed that there had been trouble recruiting able seamen for the Dutch fleet. With de Ruyter injured and humiliated, Rupert took one last swipe, sending his little boat the *FanFan* to row up to de Ruyter's flagship and 'with her two little guns, ply him for an hour with broadsides, to the amusement of the English, and indignation of the Dutch to see their admiral so chased'.[39]

Even with the defeat of Smith's rear squadron, the English had secured an overwhelming victory. In less than twenty-four hours, Monck and Rupert had won back their reputations, and English pride. Early estimates put the number of Dutch dead and wounded at 5,000, with only 300 English dying or being seriously injured during the battle. It was an astonishing turn of fortune and Londoners, bruised by a recent defeat and eager for news after hearing gunfire all through St James's Day, celebrated a welcome victory. It was proof – if ever it were needed – that in a sea battle of equals, the weather is always the winner.

In times of war, it was dangerous to cross the Channel. Merchant ships were regularly raided by the enemy, putting passengers at risk of imprisonment, death, assault – and losing their goods. When a ship was captured by the Dutch the previous year, it was reported that the seamen had been 'stripped to their shirts and beaten, some breaking limbs'.[40] However, in the middle of July, an Anglo-Dutch prisoner exchange took place, which afforded a rare opportunity for individuals with business on the Continent to travel in relative safety. The English prisoners arrived first: ninety-six seamen who, Sir Thomas Clifford complained, were 'weak, old, or children, 20 being under 12 years of age'.[41] In return, a ship full of carefully selected Dutch prisoners waited for transportation (Clifford expressed 'hopes that able seamen will not be released in exchange'[42]). The remaining space on the ship was allotted to a handful of private individuals with business across the Channel. The list included several women travelling independently: Mary Vandermarsh, a woman recorded simply as 'Jacomyna' and also one 'Mrs D Escluse'.[43]

Another young woman poised to voyage across the sea in July was Mrs Aphra Behn. Without the security of a prisoner exchange ship, her journey held far greater dangers. Poor intelligence had been at the root of the failures of both the Battle of Bergen and the Four Days Fight. As such, a tighter grip on foreign activities and a better-informed ring of spies was desperately needed. One way to gather intelligence was to target known dissidents and republican exiles with promises of pardons and money. Once seduced, they were often kept on side with threats of exposure. One such figure was William Scot, the son of the regicide Thomas Scot. He had run up considerable debts in England before fleeing to Surinam in the early 1660s and then making his way to the Dutch Republic. Unlike his father, who had steadfastly stuck to his commonwealth ideals even during his trial, Scot was a creature of dubious morals and suspect loyalty. For a brief time in 1665 he had floated around de Witt's circle, and he had already toyed with and then exposed one English informer. In the summer of 1666, he was living in The Hague with Oliver Cromwell's former spymaster, Joseph Bampfield. Lord Arlington, the Secretary of State, had Scot earmarked as someone who might be bought. The person to do the buying would be Aphra Behn.

For the woman who would go on to become the most prolific female playwright of the seventeenth century, and a good while after, it is a curious entrance into the history books. The records relating to Aphra Behn begin not with a baptism or a marriage, but with a memorandum of espionage instructions when she was a fully formed adult in her mid-twenties.[44] It is likely that she was one 'Eaffrey Johnson' who was born in December 1640, but most of her youth is shrouded in mystery. It is not even known with any certainty how she came to be a 'Mrs', but she was certainly a free agent when she travelled to Gravesend with, as she wrote, 'her brother one Mr Cherry and her Mayd' to board a merchant ship called *The Castel Rodrigo* for Ostend.[45]

Her later letters hint at a familiarity with the theatre manager and court wit Thomas Killigrew, suggesting a prior connection, and it may have been Killigrew who put Aphra forward for the mission.[46] Armed with clear instructions, a false name ('Astraea'), a cypher and £50, she was joined on *The Castel Rodrigo* by Sir Anthony Desmarches as well as Viscount Stafford and his son, John Howard. Aphra hadn't met Desmarches before but, judging him to be a reliable confidant, revealed the details of her mission to him. He offered her guidance and the promise of help in transporting her letters back to Whitehall, assuring her that his route was the safest. When their ship reached Ostend they found that the plague was too 'hot' there, so they took a different route, chartering a smaller boat to take them further along the coast so that they could make their way to Bruges, a few miles inland. By early August, the group was in Antwerp, in Flanders, and settled in a residence called the Rosa Noble.

Aphra set to work and within two weeks of landing she had made contact with William Scot – whom she referred to in code as 'Celadon'. She persuaded him to leave Holland and meet her in Antwerp where, at his suggestion and Aphra's expense, they took a coach out of town so that they could discuss matters in greater privacy. Aphra found that 'at first he was very shy', but wrote to her Whitehall contact that: 'I had use all my arguments to him that weare fit for me he be came so extreamly willing to undertake yr services'.[47] He was in the service of an English regiment of the Dutch army and told her:

> . . . that at present his being in the troops has hinderd him from being so wise as he would have bin but now upon a dislike of his imployment it being troublesome he is quitting it which will be wthin three or fouer days & he goes to the Hague & designes a life more close & less troublesome to him . . . [48]

In many ways, Aphra appears to have been out of her depth and she initially took much of what Scot told her at face value. In some parts of her first letter back to England she forgot to use the code that she so diligently used in other parts – explicitly naming Lord Arlington and Sir Anthony Desmarches. She appears to have been excited at making contact with Scot, but also full of apologies for not sending any substantial intelligence. She stressed that she had run out of money and needed more to get to Holland, where she had agreed to meet Scot once more. There was another problem, too: she wasn't the only spy in town, and her actions were being monitored and critiqued by one Thomas Corney, the very man Scot had revealed to Dutch authorities the previous year. Corney wrote to Whitehall that since Scot 'cannot speake 3 words of Dutch' he would not have anything of value to report and that his ties with leading Dutch figures had disappeared: 'De Witt will as soone entrust the Divell as him'.[49] What is more, Aphra was not being as discreet as she perhaps imagined: Corney revealed that her choice of residence, Rosa Noble, was a 'place where all the Hollanders come every day; and believe knoweth her business as well as her selfe'.[50]

In years to come, when she looked back at her time as a spy, Aphra seems to have retrospectively excused her naivety by declaring her mission to have been 'unusual with my sex, or to my years'. However, while it might have been unusual, female spies were not unheard of. By their very nature, spies are hard to identify – indeed, some of the 'merchant' passengers on the prisoner ship may not have been as innocent as they appear – but some names do emerge from the records. In the 1650s, the Leveller Mary Sexby travelled across the Channel with pistols and 1,000 coins hidden underneath her bodice, to provide money to the opponents of the Cromwellian regime, while Diana Gennings had used an alias to infiltrate a group of Royalists, including the 1st Earl of Rochester, in a tavern in Brussels.[51] And, just over a year before Aphra's trip, Katherine Haswell had petitioned the king for an office for her husband, citing her loyalty in 'many services in carrying letters'.[52]

As their correspondence continued, Scot urged Aphra to travel to The Hague where he would be able to speak to her with greater ease: he told her that Bampfield watched his every move and would be suspicious if he were to leave Holland again. Aphra, seemingly persuaded, at first resolved to travel to him but, on the advice of Desmarches, for safety suggested Dort on the border of Flanders and Holland as a rendezvous instead. She hoped that another meeting with Scot would bring him onside, but her mission was about to get more problematic: a couple of days after dispatching her first letter back to London, a man who had been uncharacteristically restrained during the last two naval battles orchestrated a vicious attack against the Dutch.

On 9 August, Sir Robert Holmes approached the Dutch island of Vlieland on the 40-gunned fourth-rate frigate *Tiger*. Without adequate supplies to sustain a long-term naval blockade of the Netherlands, the navy commanders Monck and Rupert had decided to follow their recent victory with an intense attack on a Dutch port. The largest, Amsterdam and Rotterdam, were either too heavily fortified or too difficult to reach, so instead, on the advice of a Dutch traitor named Captain Lowris Van Heemskerk who claimed to have been ill-used by de Ruyter, the English decided to target the islands of Vlieland and Terschelling. Heemskerk, who had a wife and children waiting for him in Dover, had told the English commanders that the waters behind the islands were used to anchor rich merchant vessels and the islands were home to 'Store-houses both for the States, and the East-India Fleet, and riches to a good value'.[53] Despite the challenging shoals that provided a natural defence, he convinced Rupert and Monck that the area was not well guarded and that an attack would be possible.[54]

During a council of war on the *Royal James* a couple of days earlier, it had been decided that Sir Robert Holmes would navigate the shoals to coordinate the attack with a taskforce of 7 medium-sized vessels, several fireships and 900 men (300 from each navy squadron) to raid the town and naval storehouses. Accompanying him would be Sir Philip Howard, who would command a troop of

120 gentlemen volunteers for the land attack. The rest of the fleet would remain safely outside the shoals, anchored a little out to sea so as to intercept any escaping Dutch vessels. Given his successes and experience on the West African coast, Holmes was exactly the right man for this kind of job. His orders were to sack the stores and premises believed to be on the island of Vlieland first before setting fire to the Dutch vessels. Prince Rupert's small pleasure boat, *FanFan*, was sent to scout ahead and discovered 'a considerable Fleet of ships near [Vlieland]', close to 170 merchant ships and two warships that had convoyed the merchant vessels during the final stretch of their journeys from the Guinea Coast, Russia and 'the East Countries'. The rest of the vessels, of all different sizes, were described as being 'equally laden'.

Holmes held a short council on the *FanFan* where he decided to disregard his orders. The promised storehouses on Vlieland were of very limited size and estimated worth – the island being, as Holmes described, not 'so considerable as it had been represented'.[55] Instead, he resolved that the *Pembroke* and the 5 fireships would make a speedy attack of the enemy's merchant fleet. The attack began on the morning of 9 August and the Dutch were both surprised and unprepared when one of the English fireships, helmed by Captain Brown, ploughed immediately into the biggest warship and, as the official account reported, 'burnt him down-right'.[56] The other Dutch warship managed to escape the initial attack from the fireship only to be set upon and fired at by longboats. The remaining English fireships hit 3 great merchant ships, carrying flags in their topmasts, and burned them. 'Spreading an indescribable confusion and terror among the crews', as it was later reported to the Venetian ambassador,[57] Holmes ordered Sir William Jennings to make full use of their advantage by burning and destroying all that they could but, as he declared, 'with strict instructions not to Plunder'.[58] The various English captains set to work burning the Dutch ships 'some 12, some 15 apiece', with a south-westerly wind driving the Dutch vessels towards their attackers. In the end, the English set fire to around 150 Dutch ships, with only 8 or 9 managing to escape. In their confusion, according to the Venetian ambassador in Paris, the Dutch captains had 'thought more of saving their own skins than of defending their ships'.[59] The first stage of Holmes's attack had proven to be a tremendous success.

The next day, Holmes drove his taskforce closer to the island of Terschelling, where the land forces disembarked. At Terschelling they were met with little resistance, and encountered only 'some few scattered fellows', but the island seemed to be of little consequence, consisting only of a handful of warehouses of little worth. Leaving 1 of his 11 companies (each containing 100 men) behind to keep watch of their boats, Holmes marched his men three miles inland to what they later described as the 'very fair Town' of West Terschelling, which contained 'above 1000 Houses'. Holmes held back 5 companies of men on the outskirts of the town so as not to be surprised by an enemy counter-attack, and sent the other 5 companies into West Terschelling to 'fire and burn the Town'. He knew that success depended on not only attacking the Dutch, but making a speedy getaway. To his annoyance, the men he had sent took too long executing his orders, so he suspected they had started to loot the town.[60]

Taking matters into his own hands, Holmes set fire to some of the buildings in the eastern part of the town. The consequences were so savage and sudden that it was claimed that Holmes did it only to 'perfect the Work, and hasten his Men away'.[61] It had been a very dry summer, however, so the town burned with such a violence that in half an hour most of it was consumed by flames, and within a matter of hours the entire town had been almost wholly burnt. Only thirty houses survived along with the town hall, an important church and the lighthouse. According to the English accounts, there were 'very few people [in the town] . . . having had time to run away from the danger, except some old Men and Women, who were used with all gentleness and humanity'.

With the wind on their side and a high tide, Holmes's taskforce was able to make a relatively easy escape; many of the soldiers were laden with booty they had picked up along the way. Seamen on the 40-gunned fourth-rate frigate *Dragon* encountered some difficulty in the shoals, becoming so lodged that the only way to shift their vessel was to throw bulky victuals overboard: they lost '8 guns, 12 tons of beer and 3 casks of flesh'.[62] Aside from this, English losses were minimal, with only half-a-dozen men killed and the same number injured. In less than forty-eight hours the Dutch had lost 150 merchant ships, an estimated 'million sterling', an entire town and the States' pleasure boat, which the English captured on their retreat.

The rising smoke and fire could be seen by the rest of the English fleet. Monck and Rupert sent a messenger to tell Holmes to retreat immediately. Rupert's secretary, James Hayes, who had remained on the *Royal James*, wrote that Holmes had made 'bonfires for his good success at sea' and declared that the incident would 'make great confusion when the people see themselves in the power of the English at their very doors'. But the incident didn't just confuse, it also appalled: many condemned the attack on a Dutch town as being outside the rules of war. When news reached Amsterdam, the city was devastated, and the tensions between the Orangist Tromp and de Witt intensified. Rioting took place and, in her second letter to Whitehall, Aphra Behn reported that following the burning of the ships and the town of West Terschelling she 'saw a letter from a marchants wife that desires her husband to com to Amsterdam home for that theare never was so great a desolation & mourning'. Anti-English feeling was so intense in Holland that Behn felt she 'dare as well be hangd as go'.[63] The Venetian ambassador reported how 'The tears and lamentations of those poor wretches are indescribable, and from what to-day's letters from those parts report the universal desperation of the people is something to be feared'.[64] The event would come to be known as Holmes's Bonfire.

In marked contrast, when news reached London it was universally celebrated. The Duke of York took time during a Navy Board meeting to get out his books to show 'the very place and manner' with which the navy had done it, explaining that it had not been the fleet's design to achieve so much, but only to have landed at Vlieland and burned their stores.[65] Once more, bonfires and bells were seen and heard throughout the capital. As one triumphant poem described,

> Our streets were thick with bonfires large and tall
> But Holmes one bonfire made, was worth'em all
> Well done Sir Robert, bravely done I swear,
> Whilst we made bonfires here, you made'em there.[66]

Coupled with the St James's Day Fight, the success at Vlieland and Terschelling served fully to restore Monck and Rupert's reputations, though Pepys doubted whether Monck had had much to do with the success, asserting: 'But, Lord! to see what successe do, whether with or without reason, and making a man seem wise, notwithstanding never so late demonstration of the profoundest folly in the world.' The official account, which ran to five pages, was sent to the printer Thomas Newcomb to publish and distribute as a newsbook. Even with English bias it is hard to ignore Holmes's surgically precise talent for devastation.

With only six Englishmen injured, the attack on Vlieland and Terschelling must have been a welcome relief to John Evelyn, whose role as one of the commissioners responsible for the care of wounded seamen and prisoners of war had been severely inhibited by a lack of funds. Nevertheless, on 25 August, he visited the Savoy Hospital on the banks of the Thames to the west of the city, to 'give some necessary orders'. Its current master Henry Killigrew, younger brother of the theatre manager Thomas, had been in charge since 1663, but the hospital had been a military one since 1642, and it now contained many of the war wounded. During his visit, Evelyn witnessed 'the miserable dismembered and wounded men dressed', a reminder that many survivors of the various naval battles faced a lifetime of disability.

By now, London had almost completely returned to normal following the outbreak of plague – rehearsals had begun for the new theatre season, and churches were busy with worship rather than mourning. Yet while plague seemed to have vacated the capital city, it continued to devastate the peripheral towns and other major cities around the country. Portsmouth, Deal, Dover and Cambridge had all been badly hit by the contagion, with death bills reporting increasing losses. The cloth trade in Colchester was ravaged by the deaths of 3,500 people in 1666, Norwich experienced a peak of 203 plague deaths in August 1666 and the quarter sessions courts had to be moved out of Winchester due to growing concerns about plague. Closer to London, Greenwich was suffering from an occurrence, and Evelyn's local town of Deptford was experiencing an ever-worsening outbreak. The churches, as Evelyn noted, were no longer safe places to be, and it seemed as though people were now travelling to London for refuge. It was a stark contrast to the previous summer.

Following his visit to the Savoy Hospital, Evelyn visited the Lord Chancellor, Clarendon, in Whitehall, where it was confirmed that he had been selected as one of three surveyors of the repairs to St Paul's Cathedral. They were to be tasked, as Evelyn wrote in his diary, with considering models for 'the new building, or, if it might be, repairing of the steeple, which was most decayed'.[67] Originally built in the eleventh and twelfth centuries, St Paul's Cathedral was a huge Gothic box of a building that had been deteriorating ever since the Dissolution of the Monasteries, when its wealth and Catholic iconography were plundered and destroyed. In 1561, the gigantic spire – thought to be one of the largest in Europe – had been struck by lightning during an electrical storm, causing it to crash into the nave of the church. The spire had never been rebuilt and the structure was insecure. There had been attempts to improve the building, most notably under Charles II's grandfather James I who, in the 1620s, had commissioned the architect Inigo Jones to conduct work. He rebuilt some of the structure and added a grand, although rather incongruous, portico to the west of the building, but the Civil Wars put a halt on further improvements, and by August 1666 it had become a glorious medieval relic in semi-terminal structural decline.

On 27 August, Evelyn joined workmen and gentlemen, including the Bishop of London, the Dean of St Paul's and Evelyn's long-time acquaintance Dr Christopher Wren to survey the cathedral's decaying structure and decide on what would, as Evelyn wrote, be 'fit to be done'. The building was already covered in wooden scaffolding, to support the dilapidated structure and in anticipation of the impending work. Touring the space, the men discussed whether to repair the steeple using its original foundations or to create a new foundation: both Evelyn and Wren preferred the latter, arguing that it was not only necessary but would also improve the aesthetic of the design. In the seventeenth century, there was no such thing as an architect in a modern sense. Like many intelligent and well-educated men of their age, however, Wren and Evelyn took a polymathic approach to the world around them: feasting on the curiosities of nature, marvelling at new technology, absorbing the wisdom of classical thinkers, examining the built environments in which they lived and pursuing a deep understanding of mathematics.

Wren had already put his skills in mathematics and knowledge of building design into practical use. In 1663 his uncle, Matthew Wren, had given him the commission of designing a small chapel for Pembroke College, Cambridge. Alongside this, he had also been given the job of constructing the Sheldonian Theatre in Oxford, a place that Wren designed to host academic ceremonies, anatomical demonstrations and the staging of plays. He had recently returned from France after spending nine months studying Continental architecture and soaking up the expertise of acclaimed sculptors and designers such as Gian Lorenzo Bernini and François Mansart; this was to be his only spell outside Britain. St Paul's Cathedral, however, had long been part of Wren's life. Since the early 1660s, he had been consulting with the dean of the cathedral on how best to restore the failing structure and, shortly after his return to England in March 1666, he suggested creating a huge cupola on the top of the cathedral as 'an Ornament to His Majestie's most excellent Reign, to the Church of England, and to the great Citie'. By the end of August, his designs were complete.[68]

Wren wasn't the only figure during the summer to galvanise the power of mathematics in order to push forward a vision of the world. Thomas Hobbes was now seventy-eight years old and living under the patronage of the Duke of Devonshire. Despite being in the twilight years of his life, Hobbe's academic curiosity had not waned. Peculiarly for a man of his intellect, connections and interests, Hobbes had never, and would never, become a member of the Royal Society: frosty relations with several of the society's founding members, especially the scientist Robert Boyle and the mathematician John Wallis, might possibly have been the reason behind this.

It is perhaps unsurprising, therefore, that in August 1666, shortly after the publication of Hobbes's work on mathematics entitled *De principiis et ratiocinatione geometrarum*, a savage review of it appeared in the Royal Society's affiliate journal *Philosophical Transactions*. The review went:

> It seems that this Author is angry with all Geometricians, but himself; yea he plainly saith in the dedication of his Book, that he invades the whole Nation of them . . . he will acknowledge no judge of this Age, but is full of hopes that posterity will pronounce for him.[69]

Another letter to the journal complained that Hobbes's latest work was 'A New Book of Old matter: Containing but a

Repetition of what he had before told us, more than once; and which hathe been Answered long ago'.[70]

The truth was that for a long time Hobbes had been very limited in what he could write and publish publicly, and mathematics was a crowded genre. *Leviathan or the Matter, Forme and Power of a Common Wealth Ecclesiasticall and Civil*, arguably his greatest work and certainly the tract he was most renowned for, had been published fifteen years earlier, and met with widespread censure for its seemingly heretical views. With its subversive message regarding the Church and provocative views on religion, the text firmly marked its author out as a dissident, and possibly even an atheist. Fortunately, the Act of Oblivion, a law whereby the large majority of 'crimes' committed during the Civil Wars were indemnified, covered the publication of *Leviathan*. Hobbes was doubly protected by his link to Charles II himself, having been the king's childhood tutor. That said, from as early as 1661 there were whispers of heresy, and Hobbes had become fearful that the church bishops were baying for his blood.

For all the indignation *Leviathan* engendered, the work was undeniably groundbreaking. Taking the eponymous biblical sea beast linked to Satan as its key metaphor, the text argued that because humans were inherently selfish, pursuing desires and ensuring self-preservation above all else, an absolutist state under the authority of a monarch was the only way to prevent disorder. Most controversially, at the time at least, were Hobbes's theories on religion; he doubted the authenticity of other peoples' religious 'visions' and reasoned that because all things in the universe, including humans, were simply matter in motion, this must also apply to God. Despite its ban, the book's influence, most notably in the assessment of human nature, can been found in the letters, poems and diaries of many of the period's most notable figures – from Rochester and Dryden to Pepys and Margaret Cavendish.

★

Out at sea, war continued. With Monck and Rupert keen to seal one last victory before the end of the summer campaign, ships were re-victualled and the fleet was prepared for another engagement. As of yet, there had been no sign of the long-expected French fleet, but, by the end of August, the Duke of Beaufort had at least reached the Bay of Biscay. Despite being much further away than even the Dutch expected, the aim was to conjoin the two allied fleets and assault the English by stealth and numbers. It was a foolhardy plan and, given that the allied fleets were based on opposite sides of the European continent and needed to pass through enemy territory just to meet each other, a sizable dose of optimism was required on both parts. The Dutch, however, had issues that ran deeper than an unreliable ally. Following his actions during the St James's Day Battle and the public mood after the English raid on Vlieland and Terschelling, an Orange-shaped wedge had been driven between Tromp and the States regime of Johan de Witt.

The terms of peace following the First Anglo-Dutch War, fought when England was a republic, specified that members of the House of Orange were to be excluded from the position of Stadtholder. Despite being an elected role, the position had traditionally gone to members of the House of Orange. With the fall of Richard Cromwell and the Restoration, this rule was overturned. But the Orange heir was still only a child in 1660 so, despite the change, the position of Stadtholder in most of the provinces of the Dutch Republic lapsed. In 1666, William was to turn sixteen and many Orange supporters, including the formidable Tromp family, rallied around the boy prince and promoted his cause. The likes of de Witt and de Ruyter feared that, as nephew to the King of England, William's allegiance might sit with the English crown above all else; so concerned was de Witt that he decided to take over the young man's education.

On Friday 31 August, the English spied the Dutch fleet, under de Ruyter, but a brisk gale scuppered any plans they might have had for tackling the enemy. Some English ships became tangled in the Galloper Sands and one of the English fireships ran into Vice Admiral Sir Thomas Teddeman's flagship, damaging the vessel and knocking down the mast. The fleet separated, with the Blue Squadron moving further away from the others. During the early hours of the following day, Sir Thomas Allin recorded 'several flashes of fire which we judged to be guns between the Dutch and the Blue [squadron]'. As daylight dawned, there was no sign of the enemy. Just after midday, they finally caught sight of the Dutch along the French coast, near Calais. There followed a minor skirmish, with cannon fire exchanged between de Ruyter's ship and the *Guinea* and the *Assurance*. De Ruyter retreated and, as daylight failed, the English fleet also returned to the coast, sustaining several injuries on the way from ships crashing into one another. At 2 a.m. on 2 September, the fleet spied the Dungeness Lighthouse, a cylindrical brick building on the southern Kent coast, with flaming coals on top.

With the widespread expectation of a final battle against both the Dutch and the French, the English fleet stayed close to Portsmouth for the next couple of days, with several ships returning for repairs. Then, late in the afternoon on 5 September, an urgent letter arrived for Monck from the Secretary of State, Sir William Morrice, in Whitehall. In tandem, another letter was also sent to Thomas Clifford from Lord Arlington, which read:

God has visited the city with a heavy calamity; a fire began on Sunday at one a.m. in Pudding Lane, and has burned since both ways, towards the Tower and Westminster, and as far into the body of the city as Paul's, with such violence that no art can meddle with it. All hopes now rest in cutting off a part of the town by Holborn bridge down to Bridewell. The consequences are terrible by the disorders likely to follow. The King, with the unanimous concurrence of the Council, wishes the Lord General were here, and Sec.

Morice is sounding him to know whether he would be willing to be ordered home.[71]

Monck surrendered his control of the fleet and began the seventy-
five-mile journey to London the very next day; he had tears in
his eyes.

7

Fire! Fire! Fire!

War, fire and plague against us all conspire;
We the war, God the plague, who raised the fire?
Andrew Marvell, 'The Third
Advice to a Painter' (1667)[1]

London, a few days earlier . . .

As THE SUN set on another hot day, an easterly wind danced
through the capital, weaving its way westward. From Islington,
Samuel Pepys and his wife journeyed home after watching a new
puppet show on Moorfields before sharing food and wine with
their friends, Mary Mercer and Sir William Penn. The Pepyses
could have travelled any number of ways home, but the quickest
route was to head south in their coach towards the scaffolding-
heavy St Paul's Cathedral, before turning east along the historic
throughway and marketplace of Cheapside, following the road
through to Lombard Street and then Eastcheap, before finally
reaching their home in Seething Lane.

If they had taken this particular route, Thomas Farriner might
just have heard the 'mighty merry' pair singing cheerfully as their
coach skimmed past Pudding Lane. Farriner's working day was
drawing to a close and at 10 p.m. he raked through the coals in
the oven of his bake-house to subdue the tired fire. Tomorrow
was the Sabbath, so several pots of meat were dotted around
the room, ready for dinner the next day. As one of the navy's

suppliers, the end of the working week was doubtless a welcome respite and would probably be spent worshipping at the local parish church of St Magnus the Martyr, where Farriner had held the position of churchwarden just before the outbreak of plague. This evening Farriner kept company with his daughter Hanna, his apprentice son Thomas, and their maid. At around midnight, his daughter went downstairs to the bake-house to get a light for a candle. There may or may not have been timber for the following week drying close to, or perhaps inside, the oven. In any case, it was later claimed that there hadn't been enough fire in the oven to light the candle so a flame was found elsewhere. Soon afterwards, the family, like the rest of London, was asleep.

Between 1 a.m. and 2 a.m., at roughly the same time the fleet had sighted the Dungeness Lighthouse, the Farriner family awoke choking; smoke was filling their living quarters. It seemed that a fire had started in their bake-house and the blaze had become so well established that thick fumes and orange heat roared up the stairs of their ramshackle house. With their main exit blocked, the only means of escape was through a window and over the roof. Thomas and his adult son and teenage daughter climbed out to save themselves; his daughter scorched her skin a little during their escape. Too fearful to follow, their maid remained behind and perished in the flames. As they scrambled to safety, the bundles of faggots stored in Farriner's yard quickly caught alight and the blaze began to spread to the adjacent houses.[2]

'Fire! Fire! Fire!' was shouted out in the surrounding streets as neighbouring citizens woke from their sleep, looked out of their windows, dressed and ran to see what the commotion was all about. With the alarm raised, the city watchmen alerted the mayor, Thomas Bludworth, who quickly arrived on the scene. London knew fires; they happened frequently with varying severity. As such, there were procedures in place to deal with blazes which, when coupled with human instinct (i.e. it not being wise to stay in a burning building), were usually successful. First, water pipes, which ran under the pavement, were severed to fill and refill leather fire-buckets – some brave souls even attempted to use ladders to tackle the flames from above. Fire engines, which worked by pumping water through a squirt, were sent for but found to be too cumbersome to navigate the maze of narrow alleys in and around Pudding Lane.[3] One of the most effective procedures was the rather rudimentary practice of pulling down surrounding buildings to create a firebreak.

Seeing how rapidly the fire was spreading down Pudding Lane, this was suggested to Bludworth by some seamen who were helping to fight the fire.[4] They pressed upon him the need to act fast, but the Lord Mayor was acutely aware of the financial demands that would be levelled at him should properties be unlawfully demolished. He reportedly told the seamen that 'he durst not do it without the consent of the owners'.[5] However, the majority of Farriner's neighbours were tenants rather than owners and could not offer the permission Bludworth required. Confused by the speed of the destruction, they looked to save themselves and their goods instead of, what the official report would later claim, 'preventing the further diffusion of it, by pulling down houses as ought to have been'.[6] With, as the puritan preacher Thomas Vincent put it, 'neither brains nor hands to prevent its ruin', in a very short time, the furious fire became too big to control.[7]

By 3 a.m., Pepys was awoken by his maids. They told him of a 'great fire they saw in the City'. Putting on his nightgown, he looked out of the window and saw a fire several streets away. Judging it to be some distance from his house, he went back to sleep. While he slumbered, the fire travelled south down Fish Hill towards the River Thames – like lava, it claimed everything in its path. By the time dawn arrived, the ancient church of St Magnus the Martyr, a place that should have been being preparing for the day's sermons, had become the fire's first ecclesiastical victim; its windows cracked and its stones disintegrated. The adjoining churchyard served as a throughway to London Bridge and as the fire continued its march south, it was only prevented from travelling across to Southwark by a gap about a third of the way across the bridge, caused by another fire thirty years earlier. Instead, the furious river wind nudged the flames towards the commodity-rich Thames Street.

It was a street almost custom-built for burning. Wooden storehouses chock-full of combustible matter such as oil, wine, pitch and tar, decked either side of the road, while businesses and homes clogged up every inch of available space. One of the street's first casualties was the grand Tudor-built Fishmongers' Hall, just to the west of London Bridge. Its occupants managed to salvage many of the guild's most important assets, including company silver and valuable documents, before the building became the first livery hall to be taken by the blaze. From there, the insatiable fire took hold of building after building, wreaking havoc along the waterfront. Thomas Vincent was in the city and likened the fire to an awakened beast running westward: 'where having such combustible matter in its teeth, and such a fierce Winde upon its back, it prevails with little resistance, unto the astonishment of the beholders'.[8]

With their residence either within, or very close to, the Old Swan tavern at the London Bridge end of Thames Street, Michael and Betty Mitchell's new home and haberdashery business was directly in the line of fire. Betty was around two months pregnant with the couple's first child (a fact that she may have still been unaware of) and for the past few weeks her relationship with her husband had been under noticeable strain. They had been arguing and both of their respective fathers had complained that Michael had been unkind to his wife. Even Pepys, a persistent admirer of Betty, had found the usually polite and submissive young woman to be much more detached than usual when he visited in August. Any existing marital problems vanished into the hot air as they awoke to find themselves in mortal danger, and frantically packed away their possessions before their home and livelihood went up in smoke and fire. Their neighbours fared no better. Tavern-keeper Richard Spyre,[9] married couple Mr and Mrs Dunstan,[10] ageing merchant Walter Boothby, fishmonger Mary Bellamy,[11] tallow chandler Thomas Rosse,[12] and the many poverty-stricken inhabitants of the riverside almshouses, all lost their Thames Street premises to the flames.

By 7 a.m., Pepys had woken once more. This time his maids informed him that the fire had taken 300 houses and was 'burning down all Fish-street, by London Bridge'. He quickly got himself ready and walked east, to get a better grasp of the scale from the vantage point of the Tower of London, which was a five-minute walk from his home on Seething Lane. Joined by the Lieutenant of the Tower's son, he saw what he described as 'an infinite great fire' taking hold of the southern part of the city surrounding London Bridge. The diarist took to the water and as his boat emerged from the shadow of London Bridge, he was hit by the scale of the devastation. The blaze had overwhelmed the waterfront and reached as far as the Steelyard. Along the riverside, hordes of people threw their worldly possessions into waiting boats while others remained in their houses – some still in bed – until the very last moment before dashing towards the river, clambering from one set of steps to another in an effort to secure safe passage.[13] Pepys could see pigeons hovering near to windows and balconies, only to have their wings burnt and fall down.[14] Most concerning of all, however, was that nobody appeared to be attempting to quench the fire. He feared that if robust action wasn't taken soon, it might spread still further. He directed his boat to Whitehall.

Whether he was the first to deliver the news to the king is unknown; Charles was skilled at letting people believe what they wanted to believe. Nevertheless, when Pepys relayed what he had seen to the king and the Duke of York, it certainly *seemed* as though the news was fresh. Although he had very little experience of such fires, he felt confident enough to tell the king that unless a command was made for houses to be pulled down, nothing would stop the inferno. London was under the control of the Lord Mayor and the aldermen, and city fires did not fall under the direct jurisdiction of the monarch. Charles, however, told the diarist to find Bludworth at once and order 'him to spare no houses, but to pull down before the fire every way'. The Earl of Craven was to be charged with aiding the Lord Mayor and the magistrates in their efforts to stem the blaze. The duke and Lord Arlington, secretly and rather astutely, also instructed Pepys to offer the Lord Mayor military assistance in the form of armed bands of soldiers.

Pepys and a companion took a coach back to the City of London to find Bludworth. Alighting at St Paul's Cathedral, they walked all the way down Watling Street against a tide of people, horses and carts fleeing the affected area, and found Bludworth in Canning Street, where the fire was fast encroaching. With a handkerchief around his neck, the fifty-six-year-old Lord Mayor seemed to be drained with fatigue and worry. After delivering the king's message, Pepys observed how the Lord Mayor cried 'like a fainting woman, "Lord! what can I do? I am spent: people will not obey me."' He told Pepys that he had no need of soldiers and admitted that he had already been pulling down houses, but confessed that 'the fire overtakes us faster than we can do it'. Then, astonishingly, he declared that 'he must go and refresh himself, having been up all night' and left.

The city was less mobile on a Sunday so many of those living in the suburbs did not receive news of the fire until late morning. At 11 a.m., at Westminster Abbey, the schoolboy William Taswell stood on the steps leading to the pulpit. He was attending Sunday's service when people at the back of the church started to run to and fro in confusion. As a pupil of Westminster School, Taswell had only four months previously resumed his studies, following a ten-month hiatus during the plague epidemic. Now whispers reached the congregation of another calamity, a great fire in the city. Hearing reports that 'London was in a conflagration', Taswell took leave of the minister and walked down to the riverbank where he saw four crowded boats, whose passengers were covered in blankets.[15] They were some of the first wave of many to escape the burning metropolis.

By midday, it was clear that a major disaster was unfolding, but rather than put a collective effort into suppressing the fire, it seems Londoners – confirming a Hobbesian view of human nature – prioritised their own individual needs by carrying personal goods away from the danger zone. Moving their possessions from one burning house to another, many called on family and friends for help. Near to Dowgate, just west of the Steelyard, for example, a handsome merchant named Isaac Houblon stood at his door, dressed in finery but covered in dirt as he received his brothers' goods; within hours they would need to move still further. Believing stone would offer protection, belongings were stored in the city's many churches. St Paul's Cathedral, some distance from the outbreak, was thought to be one of the securest places in the city and was commandeered by the Stationers' Company and the city's many booksellers as a storehouse for their stock. Underneath the cathedral, care was taken to ensure that every last gap of the arched ceiling of the Church of St Faith's – positioned to the east end of the cathedral's west crypt – was blocked before it was packed with hundreds of books, papers and manuscripts.[16] Given the thickness of the cathedral's walls and its positioning a fair distance from any other buildings, it was assumed that St Paul's would offer security.

When news of the calamity reached the diarist John Evelyn at his home in Deptford, he took a coach with his wife and eleven-year-old son to Southwark. Viewing the fire from across the river, they were astonished to behold the terrible spectacle of London aflame and Evelyn worried for the maimed seamen under his charge at the Savoy Hospital. From his viewpoint across the water, Evelyn estimated that the fire was creeping towards Cheapside to the north-west of the epicentre, but saw no efforts to stop it.[17] With horror, he mused that: 'The conflagration was so universal, and the people so astonished, that, from the beginning, I know not by what despondency, or fate, they hardly stirred to quench it.'[18] His fears were echoed by Clarendon, the Lord Chancellor, who claimed that 'all men stood amazed as spectators only' with no one knowing how to halt the fire.[19]

By the afternoon, the situation had deteriorated to such a

degree that the king and the Duke of York took the royal barge from Whitehall to the parish of Queenhithe, in the centre of the city. With the fire glistening on the river around them and boats filling the Thames, the royal brothers arrived at St Paul's Wharf. Pepys had joined them and was instructed, once more, to give the king's orders for houses to be pulled down quickly. There was hope that swift action would stop the fire progressing at the Three Cranes (literally, three manual cranes positioned close to the river to lift and load goods onto cargo boats) to the west, and St Botolph's Wharf to the east side of London Bridge. The greatest fear was that the fire might reach the Tower of London which was just east of St Boltoph's Wharf.

But the flames were nigh on impossible to contain. Feasting on an endless supply of timber and rubbish, and buoyed by the whispered encouragement of the same easterly wind that had kept the English and Dutch fleets apart, the infernal heat continued to push west and devour the city's buildings. It was a fire of such power that when Pepys took to the river a few hours later he found that when his face was to the wind it was 'almost burned with a shower of firedrops'. The usual Sunday soundscape of church bells, chatter and song was replaced by the sharp cracking noise of buildings collapsing into ruins. Evelyn could hear nothing but the 'thunder of the impetuous flames, the shrieking of women and children, the hurry of people, the fall of towers, houses, and churches'.[20] 'Rattle, rattle, rattle', Thomas Vincent claimed, 'was the noise which the fire struck upon the ear.' To him, it was like 'a thousand Iron Chariots beating upon the stones [pavement]'.[21]

As night arrived, the wind changed and the flames began to push north as well as west. It climbed up church steeples, rolling from house to house, and even appearing to leap through open spaces. In the darkness of Sunday night, an arch of fire developed from one side of London Bridge to the other, trailing uphill for a mile. In their individual accounts, both Pepys and Thomas Vincent likened its shape to that of a bow: 'a Bow which had

Gods Arrow in it with a flaming point' reported Vincent.[22] To Pepys, the blaze had morphed into a 'most horrid malicious bloody flame, not like the fine flame of an ordinary fire'. He joined the multitude of Londoners stunned by its ferocity and confounded by its scale. That evening, he wept for his city.

Meanwhile, at the General Letter Office at Post House Yard, near Threadneedle Street, the deputy postmaster general, Sir Philip Frowde, and James Hickes were on tenterhooks. Their office was about a third of a mile north-west of Pudding Lane, sitting just north of the Royal Exchange. While the threat of fire was real, it was not quite imminent. It was in nobody's interest to cut off the main method of communication so they continued to receive dispatches well into the night. At midnight, as the fire crept ever closer, Frowde and his wife made the decision to leave with their possessions. James Hickes, who had weathered the plague the previous year, kept his wife and children in the General Letter Office for another hour until the situation became too dangerous. He wrote to Joseph Williamson at the Secretary of State's office, to explain that, trying his 'wife and childrens' patience [he] could stay no longer' and left Threadneedle Street, carrying the Chester and Irish mail with him. Hickes sent his family to Barnet for safety and established a de facto Letter Office at the Golden Lyon in Red Cross Street outside the walls. Communication with the wider world had suffered its first major blow.

Fifteen minutes away, at the western end of Thames Street, Thomas Newcomb was one of a cluster of printers close to Baynard's Castle whose livelihood was under threat. Published on Mondays and Thursdays, Newcomb's most lucrative publication, the *London Gazette*, had become a crucial source of news relied upon not only in London, but across the country too. The latest issue, which featured foreign reports regarding Anglo-Dutch tensions, was due the next day. Luckily, its contents must have been typeset earlier that day, because as the fire crept closer the issue was almost ready for disseminating. Before evacuating his premises, Newcomb added a final paragraph to the newspaper, offering readers the briefest of reports on the disaster. It began:

> About two a clock this morning a sudden and lamentable Fire brake out in this City, beginning not far from Thames-Street, near London Bridge, which continues still with great violence, and hath already burnt down to the ground many houses thereabouts[23] . . .

The *London Gazette* went out, but there would be no issue that Thursday.

By the end of the first day, roughly a quarter of the historic walled City of London was engulfed in flames. The fire raged either side of the throughway to London Bridge, pushed west along Thames Street, almost as far as Baynard's Castle, and reached as far north as Cannon Street. One thousand homes and shops had been destroyed, nine churches had been taken, six of the livery halls were gone, and most of the waterfront warehouses were ashes. What had started as a simple house fire was now stalking ever closer to some of London's most important buildings: the Guildhall, the Royal Exchange, the Tower of London, the Inns of Court and even St Paul's Cathedral. Something had to be done.

Overriding the Lord Mayor's authority over the City of London, that evening, Charles put his brother in charge of the effort to halt the fire. The Duke of York's first instruction was for the deputy lieutenants and Justices of the Peace to summon enough workmen and tools for the next day. He sent letters advising that there were large metal hooks stored within the city's churches that could be used to pull down houses in times of fire and requested that they were made ready that night for use first thing the next day. Command stations were assigned around the city, to be manned by small teams of the noblemen who were not out at sea: Lord Belasyse would be stationed at St Dunstan's Church in the east, Sir Charles Wheeler at Clifford's

Inn, John Berkeley at Fetter Lane to Shoe Lane, Colonel Whittley at Holborn Bridge, and Sir John Fayers at Cow Lane and Cock Lane.[24] All would be supported by the local constables and men who could help. At the Tower of London, Lord Berkeley requested a warrant for all the water engines at Deptford and Woolwich shipyards to be prepared and sent to London along with, as he wrote, 'all persons, capable by hand or judgment to assist in the preservation of the Tower'.[25] Tomorrow would be the first day of a concerted effort to tackle the fire.

Before dawn broke on Monday 3 September, Pepys's household was awake and on the move. The blaze had continued throughout the night and had grown so large that it could be seen from ten miles away.[26] Pepys's much loved home on Seething Lane was just streets to the east of the inferno and protected only by the direction of the wind. Over the past few years, he and his wife had extensively refurbished the premises, renovating the space, adding new flooring and upholstering the various rooms with decorative hangings and paintings. Now they were in danger of losing it all so Pepys decided to take precautions. At 4 a.m., he packed his belongings onto a cart supplied by Lady Elizabeth Batten. Along with her husband, Sir William Batten, Sir William Penn and several others, she had negotiated space for their possessions at Sir William Rider's residence in Bethnal Green. In his nightgown, Pepys travelled on the cart a mile and a half out of the city to Rider's home, which he found to be packed full of goods, and spent the rest of the morning transporting his household things to and fro, by boat and cart. At one point, he found the wharfs so crowded with people trying to escape danger that he was unable to help an acquaintance that he spotted nearby with her goods.

With so many Londoners abandoning their homes, the fire also brought opportunism. To facilitate the evacuation, some of the capital's poorer inhabitants played the role of porter, transporting the goods of the wealthy to safety. Boatmen and coachmen increased their rates, with Sir Edward Atkyns report-ing that prices went up to £10 a cart,[27] and Thomas Vincent claiming that some carts, drays and coaches charged as much as £30. As news trickled out to the countryside and peripheral towns and villages, anyone and everyone with a cart or a coach made their way to London to make money, resulting in the city gates becoming gridlocked with traffic going into and out of the city. There were also reports of theft and cases of porters making off with household goods. The nobleman Windham Sandys declared: 'For the first rank, they minded only for their preserva-tion; the middle sort so distracted and amazed that they did not know what they did; the poorer, they minded nothing but pilfer-ing . . .'[28] This description was perhaps a little unfair, but lawless-ness did abound. The master of a Watling Street tobacco house found a man in his attic behaving suspiciously and, forcing him out of his house, could be heard shouting in the streets 'you rogue, do you come to rob me?'[29] William Taswell's father also experienced theft first hand when someone claiming to be a porter stole £40 worth of his possessions.[30]

Of course, most people had to carry their own belongings. Observing the scenes of despair all around him, the preacher Thomas Vincent asserted that it 'would have grieved the heart of an unconcerned person, to see the rueful looks, the pale cheeks, the tears trickling down from the eyes'. Offering a glimpse into the desperate plight of London's evacuating citizens, his testi-mony reveals distressed men and women lamenting their ill-fortune as they asked for help or shouted at anyone who would listen; pregnant women, new mothers and the dangerously sick being carried out of their houses to the surrounding fields; and scores of men and women hunched under the weight of their possessions. The heaviest load of all, Vincent wrote, was 'the weighty grief and sorrow of heart'. He wondered that they did not sink with the anguish of it all.[31] Across the River Thames, Evelyn – who had returned this day on foot to Southwark – described the 'miserable and calamitous spectacle' of what he

estimated to be 10,000 houses aflame. By his rudimentary calcu-
lations, the smoke had reached a length of nearly fifty miles.
Evelyn watched streams of homeless people flow towards
Moorfields and other green spaces surrounding the city. By the
afternoon, he could no longer bear to watch so returned home,
leaving behind a city that he pronounced 'a resemblance of
Sodom, or the last day'.[32]

Even in the midst of this despair, efforts to contain the fire
were well underway. At the various command stations across the
city, the Duke of York's teams of gentlemen, supported by constables, 100 men and 30 foot soldiers, managed the firefighting
efforts. Each station had been provided with £5 worth of bread,
cheese and beer for sustenance, and shillings would be distributed
to hard-working volunteers. Stationed at the church of St Dunstan
in the east (where the naval commander Sir John Lawrence had
been buried just over twelve months earlier), Lord Belasyse was
not only supported by Cambridgeshire MP Sir Thomas Chicheley
and architect and scientist Hugh May, but a group of adolescent
boys. These were pupils at Westminster School who had been
marched from one side of London to the other by the Dean of
Westminster to aid the firefighting efforts. William Taswell was
among their number and recorded how he and his peers fetched
water back and forth to assist the gentlemen, adult volunteers and
foot soldiers.[33] By halting the fire's progress towards St Dunstan in
the east, the firefighters hoped to prevent it creeping towards the
Tower of London. Unlike the stations to the west and north of
the city, the wind was in their favour and Belasyse's taskforce had
initial success. By the end of the day, the church, although badly
damaged, remained standing; their combined efforts seemed to
have blocked the fire's path.

Concurrently, two companies of armed guards, including the
Lord General's Regiment of Foot Guards (trained guards responsible for the protection of the City of London) patrolled the city
and Moorfields for looting and violence. In normal circum-
stances, these trained soldiers would have fallen under the control

of the Lord General, George Monck, but he was yet to be summoned back from the fleet and was thus oblivious to the scale of the devastation. Instead, their actions were coordinated by the Duke of York. For all his faults (and there were a great many), the duke possessed the type of dogged confidence that people could easily follow during times of great strife. Leading by example, he rode through the city offering encouragement and active help to those attempting to extinguish the fire. His presence appears to have allayed the panic and disorder that was on the brink of breaking out.

Despite their best efforts, the fire had become almost too great to combat. It pushed ever further north and along the final stretch of Thames Street, taking hold of Thomas Newcomb's recently evacuated printing house. The place that had fixed so many of the year's greatest catastrophes and victories for posterity was soon destroyed.[34] Miraculously, Anne Maxwell's printing house, managed to escape the fire. By the afternoon, the financial heartland of the city was under threat as the blaze raged down Lombard Street and the surrounding throughways, but much of the city's wealth was saved by the swift action of the district's goldsmith-bankers: Aldermen Robert Vyner and Edward Backwell, men who had a muscular hold on the finances of the city, evacuated their premises in Lombard Street and sought refuge at Gresham College.

The Lombard Street bankers and the Thames Street printers should not have been surprised that their houses were at risk. They were in the line of fire and the wind pushed in their direction. Many of those who had gone to bed the previous night, however, judging their homes to be a safe distance from the inferno, had been awoken before dawn to find their houses burning. The wind had fanned the fire with such fury that flakes of burning material flew through the air and scattered around untouched areas of the city, setting houses ablaze almost independently. As Pepys described: 'houses were burned by these drops and flakes of fire, three or four, nay, five or six

houses, one from another'.[35] William Taswell saw the phenom-
enon too, writing that he 'saw great flakes carried up into the
air at least three furlongs; these at last pitching upon and uniting
themselves to various dry substances, set on fire houses very
remote from each other in point of situation'.[36] Thomas Vincent
described them as 'horrible flakes of fire' that mounted up the
sky.[37] With many places seemingly catching alight spontan-
eously, the Lord Chancellor recalled: '[it] kindled another fire
in the breasts of men, almost as dangerous as that within their
houses'.[38]

People couldn't understand how houses that were far from
the epicentre of the fire could suddenly start burning. In the
midst of the confusion, a rumour began that the fire was a work
of arson, conspired by the Dutch and the French. Breaking into
hysteria, 'the ignorant and deluded mob', as Taswell described
it, became consumed with a 'kind of phrenzy' and directed
anger towards the many foreigners living in the city.[39] The
previous day, from the top of a church steeple near to the Three
Cranes, one Thomas Middleton thought he saw the fire 'break
forth out of several houses . . . a good distance from [the main
fire]' and was convinced that the whole thing was not an accident, but in fact 'maintained by design'.[40] When Sir Edward
Atkyns wrote from London to his associate in Bath, he claimed
that from the very beginning 'there was a cry in the streets, the
Dutch and French were in arms, and had fired the City'.[41] Denis
de Repas declared that gangs of 'English women . . . did knock
down severall strangers for not speaking good English. Some of
them were armed with spits, some with bread staffs, and the
captain with a broad sword'.[42] Taswell witnessed a blacksmith
using an iron bar to fell a Frenchman – the schoolboy watching
as the victim's blood flowed down to his ankles. He also saw a
French painter's house burnt to the ground after he was robbed
by a group of angry Londoners. Taswell's brother reported
seeing another Frenchman 'almost dismembered' in Moorfields,
because the tennis balls he had been carrying with him were

mistaken for fireballs.[43] Perhaps an embellished version of the same incident, a similar story told of a Frenchwoman having her breasts cut off in Moorfields after chickens she had carried under her apron were, once again, mistaken for fireballs.[44] Lady Isham heard rumours 'that there is daily taking of men, and some in woman clothes with fire balls'.

Lord Hollis, who had been tasked with patrolling the area near to Newgate Market stumbled upon a mass maiming of a man that he recognised to be the Portuguese ambassador's servant. He found him being 'pulled and hauled and very ill used' without his hat or his cloak and having his sword taken off him. Those in the crowd swore that they had seen the Portuguese man throw a fireball into a house that was now on fire. When Hollis relayed the accusations to the suspect, he denied the charge and claimed that what had actually happened was that he had seen 'a piece of bread upon the ground' which he took up, and laid upon shelf in the next house'.[45] A cursory search of the area turned up the piece of bread, but Lord Hollis sent the man to the constable anyway, for his own safety. Aware of the threat to anyone suspected of being French or Dutch, the Spanish ambassador turned his house into a sanctuary for all foreigners needing to escape the multitude of angry Londoners. Others remained in their homes and shut the doors.

With tempers flared, the armed guards focused their attentions on rounding up and rescuing many foreigners from the clutches of the angry mob. It was thought that in prison they would be 'in much more security than they could have been at full liberty'.[46] Most, it was claimed, had been committed for their own safety, but some weren't happy about it. A Dutch baker by the name of Cornelius Reitvelt was incarcerated at the Gatehouse in Westminster, along with others, on what Reitvelt claimed were 'false rumour[s] that they set their own house on fire'. News of his arrest travelled fast, with one Anne Hobart writing a letter to her cousin from Chancery Lane on Monday morning about a Dutchman being 'taken in Westminster [after] setting his outhouse on fire'.[47] When petitioning Lord Arlington for release, Reitvelt claimed that his goods had been taken by the 'violence of the multitude' leaving him with no money to survive.

Spurious rumours were easily believed. There were claims that the fire was being aggravated by French arsonists who had thrown fireballs into houses at random, that Dutch merchants had started the fire in retaliation for Holmes's Bonfire, and even that a force of 4,000 French papists was on its way, hell-bent on death and destruction. Even level-headed Pepys, who from the very start had been told that the fire had started at a baker's house in Pudding Lane, was concerned about the 'discourse now begun, that there is plot in it, and that the French had done it'.[48] In Westminster, Elizabeth Green from Chequer Alley, Richard Doe from Covent Garden, Anne Cave and Alice Richards presumably from nearby also, claimed that they had overheard one Anne English declaring that five or six Frenchmen had arrived at her master's house a few weeks before, saying that all of his street would be burned down to the ground. Perhaps fearing repercussions, Anne English at first refused to reveal her master's name, but then admitted that she lived with William Peck on James Street in Covent Garden, and denied saying anything.

Johan Vandermarsh, a recently naturalised middle-aged Dutch merchant who lived with his family in Lime Street, would have been a prime target for plundering, or worse. He had already organised to have most of his valuable goods transported to safety, but the threat of fire had become an ever-pressing concern. Pushed by the easterly wind, the inferno had so far scorched its way west across the city, leaving many streets to the east of Pudding Lane relatively secure. Now, however, the fire crept along Fenchurch Street and worked its way towards his street. Vandermarsh's brother-in-law's home was burnt and his neighbours Robert Gefferey and Peter Hoet saw their premises crumble — the latter was left with only his warehouse after his entire house and garden were destroyed.

When the fire began to torch part of Vandermarsh's home, he raided what remained of his coffers and paid £50 to encourage men to help pull down the affected parts of his premises. His intention was not only to save the rest of his house, but to block the fire's path along the rest of Lime Street. Despite his best efforts, the walls on one side of his home became so badly burned that they fell down, exposing the building from top to bottom and the ceilings and floors were drenched in water, which had presumably been used to quench the flames. He might have failed completely to salvage his own home, but his neighbours would later testify that Vandermarsh had been instrumental in saving many of the adjacent houses. Those who witnessed his efforts would comment on his 'great industry' in preventing the fire spreading further along Lime Street.

There was no such luck for the nearby Royal Exchange. The fire swept through the galleries, filling the air with flames and smoke and consuming the whole structure. Built during the reign of Elizabeth I, the building's wrought-iron framing and giant metal bell melted as the statues of kings and queens lining the piazza fell face first to the ground. The only figure to remain intact was that of Sir Thomas Gresham himself.[49] Thomas Vincent lamented that in the demise of the Exchange 'the glory of the merchants' was irreparably broken.[50] One of the final buildings to succumb on Monday was the magnificent medieval palace of Baynard's Castle. The robust stone structure was steeped in history, having been the stronghold of the House of York and the place where Edward VI and then Mary I were crowned king and queen, respectively, over a century earlier. Its current occupants were the Earl of Shrewsbury and his promiscuous wife, Anna Maria Talbot. When the fire hit, the castle's sturdy facade crashed into the Thames and the building burned all night until only a central tower remained. It served as a terrible warning – if Baynard's Castle could fall, anything could.

By the end of the second day, the fire could be seen from forty miles away and had taken out the entire middle chunk of the walled City of London, spreading across the waterfront – from Billingsgate towards Baynard's Castle – and peaking at Gracechurch Street, the main throughway northwards.

Early on Tuesday, the king gave orders for the most valuable commodities within Whitehall Palace to be transported to Hampton Court. Following the lead of the wealthy inhabitants of the great houses along the Strand, the monarch's servants filled royal boats on the Thames and headed west with great chunks of Whitehall's wealth. He also ordered many houses, some of them newly built, surrounding Whitehall to be pulled down as a precaution. There was a pressing reason for this. Early that morning, hopes that the River Fleet might serve as a crucial natural firebreak to the west of the city were dashed when the fire leapt over the River Fleet.

The Fleet fed into the Thames and was a physical barrier between the walled City of London and the suburbs leading to Whitehall and Westminster. In crossing the river, the fire cut through the Duke of York's fire post at Temple Bar and, for the first time, posed a genuine threat to the palaces of governance and the western suburbs. Immediately at risk, however, were the Inns of Court and what had originally been known as Bridewell Palace. Residents evacuated their premises at the Inns of Court, but refused to preserve the possessions belonging to absent lodgers. Their argument, unsurprisingly, rested on the legality of 'break[ing] up any man's chamber' without their knowledge.[51] Built as a royal residence for Henry VIII, Bridewell had served as a jail since 1553 and it was a place that the baker Thomas Farriner knew well.

In 1627, a boy of ten or eleven named 'Thomas Farriner' was discovered alone by a city constable in the area of Walbrook, within the walls. He had run away from his unnamed master and had caused enough of a nuisance to be detained and sent to Bridewell Prison. As well as being a jail, Bridewell was also a house of correction – it housed dozens of waifs and strays found around London who were educated and, in many cases, taken on as apprentices by the prison's patrons. Despite its status as a prison, the building was a grand place. John Milton's friend, the Quaker Thomas Ellwood, had spent time in there in 1662, describing one of the rooms he was held in as:

> one of the fairest rooms that, so far as I remember, I was ever in, and no wonder, for though it was now put to this mean use, it had, for many ages past, been the royal seat or palace of the kings of England, until Cardinal Woolsey built Whitehall.

The boy found in 1627 was given a hearing where it transpired he had attempted to run away from his master three or four times previously. His details were recorded in the book of minutes and he was released. Then, in 1628, the same boy appeared at Bridewell Prison once more, accused of exactly the same thing.[52] A year later, in 1629, Thomas Farriner was taken on as an apprentice to one Thomas Dodson and his career as a baker began.

Thirty-seven years later, as the fire pushed into new territories outside the city walls, it didn't take long for Bridewell Prison to fall, taking with it the city's crucial store of corn, £40,000 worth. King Charles II cannot have been ignorant of what the loss of London might do to his hold on authority. His pragmatic approach to kingship was born out of the bloodshed of the Civil Wars and the boredom of exile. Perhaps more than any monarch before or after him, Charles was acutely aware of the fragility of power. He knew that holding London was the key to controlling England. His own father had lost his head shortly after London had declared its allegiance to Parliament; and it was only when George Monck had secured the capital that the Restoration had been possible in 1660.

All day the king rode with the Duke of York across town with very few attendants. Joining those attempting to extinguish the fire, he laboured in person, rewarded and encouraged the firefighters and permitted the use of gunpowder had been used to blow up buildings near to the fire and create large firebreaks. The royal brothers were a visible presence and seen by many. Sir Edward Atkyns reported that 'the King and Duke of York were exceeding active';[53] Evelyn wrote in his private diary about the 'extraordinary . . . vigilance and activity of the King and the Duke'; and the official report would later declare that 'even those persons whose losses rendred their conditions most desperate' were glad of the sight of the king and the duke helping extinguish burning buildings and offering advice.[54] Yet, with thousands upon thousands of Londoners lying destitute in the fields surrounding the city, the pressing need to restore order drove Charles to write to the fleet and recall George Monck. It is a stark insight into the mind of the king, hinting that he believed that Monck was the most capable leader in the realm, a greater commander than himself and even his brother. Monck certainly had the respect of the masses and could wield martial control with greater ease than the king or duke. It was hoped that Monck would bind the miserable citizens of London together again and prevent widespread disorder.

By now, the city was becoming tired. Those tackling the fire and transporting their goods had been surviving on very limited sleep. Even the king and the duke suffered from 'as much fatigue as the meanest'.[55] At his residence in Seething Lane, Pepys was so tired that he began to wonder what day it was. With all of his stuff in Bethnal Green, he had been living off Sunday's leftover food for the past couple of days, and had no dishes. During Tuesday afternoon, he sat in a state of melancholy in his garden with Sir William Penn. They were certain that the navy offices would not survive the inferno, and wanted permission to pull down the surrounding houses as a last precaution – if the navy offices were destroyed, Pepys thought it would 'much hinder, the King's business'. He wrote to William Coventry to seek the duke's permission, while Penn rode to Deptford to gather extra men for the task of fighting the fire. Resigning himself to the probable loss of his home, Pepys followed the example of Sir William Batten and made a couple of pits in his garden: one to bury his remaining navy papers and the other for his wine and Parmesan cheese.

To the north of the city, efforts to contain the fire were having success. Under the charge of Lord Craven, the flames were held at bay for most of the morning. In the afternoon, however, the many branches of the fire conjoined to conquer Cheapside, burning as Thomas Vincent proclaimed 'the very bowels of London' in a matter of hours; most notably, the Mercers' Company at the east end and the Goldsmiths' Hall towards the west end. Packed with combustible materials, the street raged with fire and the hurried wind rushed the flames further west and north. This was the worst day, with dozens of livery halls and countless churches destroyed, and the fire breaking through Ludgate and reaching as far as the Inner Temple with, as Evelyn described, all 'Fleet Street, the Old Bailey, Ludgate hill, Warwick lane, Newgate, Paul's Chain, Watling Street . . . flaming'.[56] There was no night or day, only fire and 'a smoak so great, as darkened the Sun at noon-day'. From his garden, Pepys 'saw how horridly the sky looks, all on a fire . . . and, indeed, it was extremely dreadful, for it looks just as if it was at us; and the whole heaven on fire'.[57]

Almost the entire City of London had been transformed into a blazing inferno, spilling out towards the western and northern suburbs. In the east, it fought against the wind and finally ravaged Dunstan's in the east, sneaking precariously close to the Tower of London, whose White Tower contained vast gunpowder stores. On the west side of the city, it had a much easier passage and, with the wind behind it, became almost impossible to tackle. Pavements glowed red with the heat, and men, horses and carts were unable to get close enough to pull down houses.[58] Blackwell Hall, belonging to the Company of Clothiers and filled with linen, silks and other materials burnt to the ground; the losses for the cloth trade were huge. The iron chains lining the city streets melted, as did the hinges, bars, and gates of prisons.[59] As well as Bridewell Prison, Ludgate and Newgate were destroyed, but luckily their prisoners managed to escape.

Then, at 8 p.m., as the fire snarled down Watling Street, it started to scorch the wooden scaffolding coating St Paul's Cathedral, before encasing the historic stone structure in heat and flame. Even though it stood 'high above all things' in London, the fire initially took hold on the roof, but by 9 p.m., the entire cathedral had erupted into flames. The light from this was so bright, the schoolboy Taswell noted, that as he stood at the King's Bridge, he was able to read an entire edition of Terence that he had carried with him in his pocket.[60] In an echo of the fire two hundred years earlier, the great sheet of lead covering the roof melted in the intense heat and ran down the streets like, as Vincent wrote, 'snow before the sun'. Evelyn described how the stones of St Paul's 'flew like grenados'. The vaulted ceiling and beams fell onto the pavement and broke through into St Faith's with an enormous crash. Filled with books that had been packed away for safety, its contents added fresh fuel to the furnace.

Books weren't the only things stowed away from the fire. At some point before the building took alight, an elderly woman had found shelter on the east side of the cathedral, perhaps hoping that the stone walls of the godly building would protect her. Once the fire took hold, she sadly met her end; crackling under the fierce heat, her body transformed from flesh to fuel. The huge stones calcified under the pressure and the cathedral's many friezes, decorative columns, statues and ornaments crumbled, cracked and disintegrated.[61] On the west side, the affiliated school of St Paul's, which had stood for 160 years and provided the education of many of the country's leaders, was completely destroyed. The 153 pupils, including possibly a nine-year-old boy named Edmund Halley, were not present, but for the second time in less than two years, their formal education was interrupted.

It wasn't long before the Guildhall to the north-east of the cathedral was also taken. The outbuildings and roofing were quickly destroyed, yet the walls of the Guildhall itself stood firm, glowing white gold with the heat of the fire. These grand buildings have become symbols of the devastation the fire wrought on the city, but through London's network of landlords and tenants, the fire affected rich and poor, old and young. As it continued to push northward towards Holborn Bridge, the highest point of the Fleet River within the city walls, it took hold of an inn 'at the sign of the Rose'. It belonged to the Onslow family – who would later become one of the great slave-owning families of the eighteenth century – and was leased to an Edward and Dorothy Osborne. The premises were utterly destroyed, leaving both tenants and owners financially crippled.

By the end of Tuesday, despite his early concerns, Pepys's house was still standing. But the fire was stalking its way down Tower Street and close to All Hallows Church at the end of Seething Lane. Expecting the worst, but hoping for the best, he and his wife, Elizabeth, had remained at their home and that evening they dined on leftovers once again, this time a shoulder of mutton. With hardly anything left in his house, Pepys lay down to sleep on his assistant's quilt.

He was woken at 2 a.m. by his wife. She had heard that the fire had got to All Hallows Church. At once, Pepys gathered together the rest of his valuables, left his home with his wife, maid and assistant and chartered a boat to take them all to Woolwich. As they travelled along the Thames in the moonlight the group watched the whole city on fire behind them.

Dropping off his companions and his money and instructing them always to take care that at least one person remained with the valuable goods, Pepys returned to London. He couldn't bring himself to ask anyone on the way how things were in Seething Lane – he had convinced himself that his house would be destroyed. When he finally returned at 7 a.m., however, he found his house was in fact intact. What's more, heading towards the fire, he discovered that the use of gunpowder to create firebreaks near to All Hallows Church seemed to have halted the fire's progress.

He climbed the steeple of All Hallows Church, which had only been partially burnt, and 'there saw the saddest sight of desolation that I ever saw; everywhere great fires, oyle-cellars, and brimstone, and other things burning'. He walked into town, the ground like hot coals burning his feet, and found that Gracechurch Street, Fenchurch Street and Lombard Street had been turned to dust. He walked to Moorfields and bought some bread, before returning to the charred city and falling asleep. The fire had already done its worst, but continued in to Wednesday. To the west of the city, the Duke of York fought its progress that evening as it appeared to break out afresh near the Temple. His men blew up buildings and cut off the fire's path. Edmund Berry Godfrey, the Justice of the Peace for Westminster, behaved so bravely in fighting the fire there that, according to one report, 'the King would have knighted him, but he refused it', so instead Charles 'ordered a piece of plate of [worth] 50l' to be created for Godfrey, bearing his coat of arms.[62] An anonymous account explained that, 'by his [the Duke's] care, diligence, great labour, and seasonable commands' the fire was eventually and 'most happily . . . extinguished'.[63]

That same evening, the other side of the city, a hysteria had taken hold of the thousands of refugees stranded at Moorfields, Parliament Hill and other open spaces around Islington. A rumour had started that 50,000 Dutch and French immigrants were armed and about to march to Moorfields to cut throats, rape women and plunder. The mob armed themselves with whatever they could find and fell on any foreigners found in the crowds. With extraordinary care, members of the nobility and the trained guard quashed the violence and calmed the hostile masses. Moorfields was fast becoming a dystopian nightmare of a place. Evelyn described:

The poor inhabitants . . . some under tents, some under miserable huts and hovels, many without a rag, or any necessary utensils, bed or board, who from delicateness, riches, and easy accommodations in stately and well-furnished houses, were now reduced to extreme misery and poverty.[64]

When Monck finally arrived, on 7 September, the immediate horror was over. Some believed his presence might have altered the outcome of the fire – Sir Nathaniel Hobart commented that 'the Duke of Albemarle came this night to towne, happily if he had bin here before the Towne might have bin saved, but God was not pleased, & we must submit to his will'[65] – but there was also a sense that, as bad as it was, it could have been much worse. The protection of the suburbs surrounding the walls and the holding of the fire at the Tower of London, Cripplegate, the Temple and Leadenhall was directly linked to the efforts of the king, the duke and the nobility. Parliament would later praise 'the miraculous Blessing of God upon your Majesty's Endeavours for the Preservation of that Part of the City which is left',[66] and the contemporaneous ballad, *London's Lamentation*, set their actions to poetry:

> God gave a blessing to their hands,
> for by this means the flames grew lower,
> It did at once obey Commands,
> both at the Temple, and the Tower,
> At Pie-corner, and Aldersgate,
> The fire lost his Flaming state.

> At Holborn-bridge and Cripple-gate,
> and in the midst of Coleman-street,
> And Basing-hall it was laid flat,
> it did such opposition meet,
> Bishops-gate-street and Leaden-hall,
> To Cornhil-Standard are saved all.

The loss was tremendous. In four days, an estimated 70,000 people had been made homeless and 13,000 houses, 87 churches and 52 livery halls had been destroyed. The city gates of Ludgate, Newgate and Aldersgate were severely damaged. The Guildhall was a ruin, the Custom House was no more, St Paul's Cathedral was destroyed, Baynard's Castle was shattered, and the Royal Exchange had been burnt to the ground. The cost of the fire was estimated at £10 million. The Earl of Clarendon lamented that 'the most rich and wealthy parts of the city' had been turned to dust.[67] So total was the devastation that, as Sir Edward Atkyns described, 'you can hardly tell where such a Parish or Place was'.[68] Walking through the ruined city, he declared:

> there is nothing but stones and rubbish, and all exposed to the open air. So that you may see from one end of the Citty almost to ye other . . . and you can compare London (were it not for ye rubbish) to nothing more than an open field.'[69]

One Lady Elmes wrote that she was 'sure so sad a sight was never seen before as that city is now lying in ashes, besides the unimaginable loss the hole kingdom receives by it'.[70] Evelyn, 'with extraordinary difficulty' clambered 'over the heaps of . . . smoking rubbish'; frequently losing his bearings, the ground under his feet was so hot that 'it even burnt the soles of my shoes'. He saw the grandest of London's buildings reduced to dust, 'the fountains dried up and ruined, while the very waters remained boiling'. The burning continued deep inside the city's cellars and vaults with dark clouds billowing through the air.[71]

Those who had lost everything picked at the ruins of their homes and businesses 'like men in some dismal desert, or rather, in some great city laid waste by a cruel enemy', as Evelyn wrote. Walking through the city, one Giles Burke, found there to be 'nothing left but rubbish and ashes'.[72] Andrew Marvell captured the scene in his poem 'The Third Advice to a Painter':

> See how men all like ghosts, while London burns,
> Wander and each over his ashes mourns

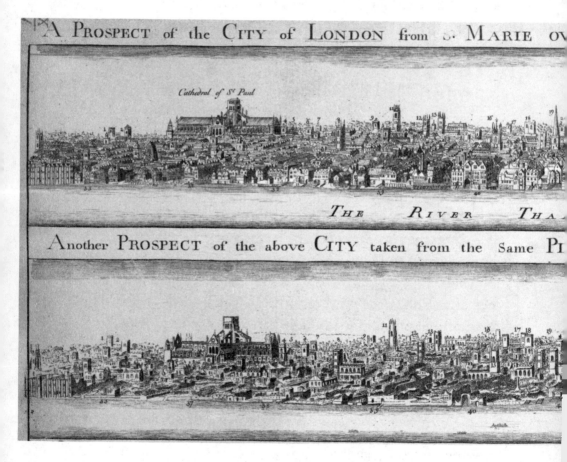

*A panoramic illustration of London before and after the Great Fire,
by Wenceslaus Hollar*

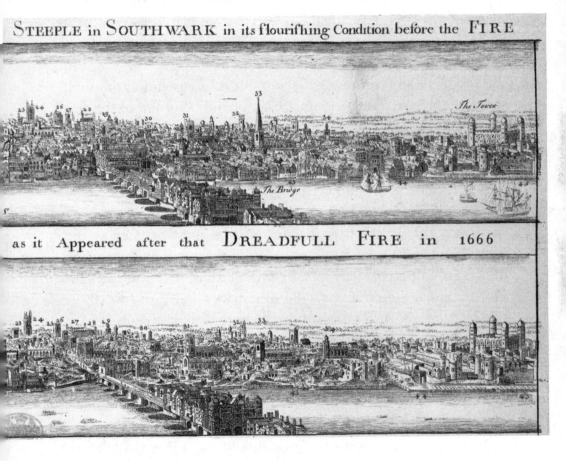

STEEPLE in SOUTHWARK in its flourishing Condition before the FIRE

The Tower

The Bridge

as it Appeared after that DREADFULL FIRE in 1666

Whether rich, poor, old or young, the damage was felt by all and, as Denis de Repas declared, 'Every one thinks his losse the greatest.'[73] Bulstrode Whitelocke, who was based in Chilton Foliat in Wiltshire, received word that his house in Fleet Street had been burnt to the ground; despite his son's and one Elizabeth Roberts's best efforts, he was told that 'only two loads of his goods [were] saved[,] the rest of them, & among them some of the best things, & books and writings were burnt'. His losses were worth an estimated £1,000, and included a house that he had leased out near to the Temple.[74] Richard Pierce, a cook and yeoman with a large and dependent family, claimed to have lost £4,000–£5,000 in the fire and had no means of recouping his trade unless the king granted him space at the Cooks' Company Halls (one of the few livery halls to survive). A widow named Ann Lloyd begged for a space at an almshouse near Bishopsgate Street after claiming to have lost 'all she had' to the fire,[75] while Mr and Mrs Dunston were too poor to rebuild their property in Thames Street.[76] The geographer and printer John Ogilby, who would go on to create the first detailed road maps in England, was almost ruined by the fire when much of his stock went up in flames, including issues of his new edition of *Aesop's Fables* with illustrations by Wenceslaus Hollar, and among one Dr Tillotson's losses was £100 worth of books.[77] Indeed, the book trade as a whole was hit especially hard by the fire, with estimated losses of £200,000.[77]

As soon as the immediate risk of fire was over, the king wrote to the Lord Mayor, instructing him to recall the aldermen and restore the governance of the city. They moved to Gresham College and set about re-establishing trade: markets were held at Bishopsgate Street, Tower Hill, Smithfield and Leadenhall Street, vendors were granted permission to set up temporary sheds at key locations, and 'honest and able persons' were appointed to ensure the fire did not restart in the various city wards. The first priority was to prevent the thousands of refugees starving. As such, neighbouring villages and towns were called upon to supply sustenance. Many constructed ramshackle shops on top of the ruins of their old ones. Michael and Betty Mitchell managed to find lodgings in Shadwell, and a month and a half after the fire Michael had completed his new shop 'in the room of his house that was burned'.[78] Appeals were made for people living in the suburbs to help with temporary shelter, and a general charitable collection from around the country was authorised, with many places donating generously.

The following day, orders were given for canvas that was origi-nally intended for the fleet to be sent to Moorfields and fashioned into tents for the thousands of stranded citizens, and rations of ship's biscuit were distributed. Despite these efforts, it seems that food was still in short supply, with 'bread, bear [sic], meat, all in scarcity & many want it', as Dr Denton wrote.[79] He also confessed to not daring to send any of his 'men out of doors for feare of being pressed to work at the fire'.[80] Fortunately the weather, which had conspired with the fire to wreak maximum damage on London, remained dry and warm. As Pepys wandered the city, his clothes 'all in dirt from top to bottom', he saw a singed cat appear from a pipe, hairless but very much alive; butts of sugar that lay exposed in the streets emptied by greedy hands and dropped into cups of beer; and women working hard to sweep water away from canals before becoming 'as drunk as devils'. That day he dined on a fried breast of mutton at his friend's house where there were 'a great many of us, but very merry, and indeed as good a meal, though as ugly a one, as ever I had in my life'.[81]

With the letter office shut down and the *London Gazette* para-lysed, the rest of England received only scraps of news relating to the fire. By Thursday, reports had reached as far as Berwick, with one Mr Scott writing to Joseph Williamson that local soldiers claimed to have seen 'the likeness of abundance of ships in the air'; Scott conceded that the vision was taken to be 'their strong imaginations'.[82] In Newcastle, while they knew a fire had taken place, an informer named Richard Forster complained that they had 'no perfect relation of how so famous a city should be consumed so suddenly', so were left to wonder whether 'the

Dutch, French, and fanatics had a hand in it' and entertained the rumour that many had been apprehended with 'balls of wild fire in their hands'.[83] At Eton, William Lord Maynard also wrote to Williamson and confessed that people 'grow depressed with stories of persons ruined'. Maynard revealed that there were fears that it might have been treachery, with tales of eight or nine men carrying gunpowder apprehended near Marylebone, of a papist nobleman setting a house on fire in Holborn, and of 'thousands of [other] such reports'.[84] In Swansea, John Mann wrote how they were in 'great fear of the consequences of a sad fire'.[85]

When news reached Norwich, the mayor of the city ordered bellmen to cry out around the city, innkeepers and inhabitants were instructed not to lodge strangers until they had been properly examined, and the local militia was made ready.[86] In Coventry, Ralph Hope wrote how it was 'impossible for pen to express the sad influence the calamitous & deplorable fall of poor London has generally had upon our sorrowfully sympathizing city', adding that many of Coventry's clothiers had been 'undone by it', because most 'had their whole estates lying there in cloth, and now all or the greatest part destroyed'.[87] Panic wasn't helped by those who liked to indulge in tall tales. On his way to Littlecote House to gather more information about the fire, Bulstrode Whitelocke bumped into one Sir Seymour Pyle who, he claimed, 'had too much wine'. Pyle revealed that there had been a great clash between 60,000 Presbyterians (supported by the French and Dutch) and the king's militia, which had resulted in the death and imprisonment of 30,000 of these rebels. Fortunately, as Whitelocke soon discovered, alcohol had gotten the better of Pyle's senses and he had been 'drunke & swearing & lying att almost every word'.[88]

It took well over a week for news of the fire to reach foreign shores. In Paris, as soon as reports arrived there was talk of little else with many of King Louis XIV's courtiers believing the loss to be considerable.[89] The enormity of the disaster was clear to all, with the Venetian ambassador in Paris writing that 'this accident . . . will be memorable through all the centuries'. Publicly, Louis XIV stated that he would not have 'any rejoicings about it, being such a deplorable accident involving injury to so many unhappy people', and offered his condolences to Charles and James's mother, his aunt, who was in France. He also offered to send aid in the shape of food provisions and anything else that might be required to relieve the suffering of those left destitute.[90] Privately, he was thrilled at the stroke of good fortune. The French king had made a mess of his summer campaign and his fleet was in no shape to fight. It was believed that England's magazine stores and navy supplies had been destroyed and that the English would be forced to retire. The Venetian ambassador believed that the incident would force England to abandon its 'high pretensions' and to beg for the French king's mercy and help.[91]

When news of the fire reached the Earl of Sandwich, who was still seconded to Spain as foreign ambassador, he played down the extent of the damage. He, truthfully, told his fellow diplomats that the fire had not affected the powder supplies, armouries or naval storehouses and that the gold, silver and jewels had been transported away before the fire hit the financial districts of London. Omitting the scale of the damage to London's livery companies and churches, he added that the loss had mainly affected buildings of minor importance and beauty.[92] Sandwich also revealed that Charles had ordered the city to be rebuilt in a 'more beautiful and stately form', which he reportedly hoped would change 'the compassion of their friends into admiration and [leave] their enemies confounded'.[93] The Duke of Savoy shared this hope and, writing to Charles to offer his condolences, expressed his belief that on the ruins of the old city 'another London city more beautiful' would be built that would carry Charles's name into posterity as the founder of the great new capital.[94]

There were attempts to comfort the citizens of London with similar assertions about the greatness of the future city, but many could think no further than the day in front of them; de Repas claimed that 'there is no certainty yet what they will doe'.[95] From the beginning, Thomas Vincent saw the fire as 'God's Terrible Voice' and mused:

The glory of London is now fled away like a Bird, the Trade of London is shattered and broken to pieces, her delights also are vanished, and pleasant things laid to waste; now no chaunting to the sound of the Viol, and dancing of the sweet Musick of other Instruments, now no drinking Wine in Bowls, and stretching upon beds of lust; now no excess of Wine and banquetings; no feasts in Halls and curious dishes; no amorous looks, and wanton dalliances; no ruffling silks, and costly dresses; these things in that place are at an end.[96]

8

A Phoenix in Her Ashes

So saying, her rash hand in evil hour
Forth reaching to the fruit, she plucked, she ate:
Earth felt the wound, and nature from her seat
Sighing through all her works, gave signs of woe,
That all was lost.

John Milton, Paradise Lost[1]

ENGLAND HAS MANY indigenous fruits, but the large sweet apple is not one of them. It originated in Central Asia, before Roman cultivation saw its distribution across southern and then northern Europe. By the seventeenth century, there were too many varieties of apple in England to list properly – from pomewaters, custards and blanderelles to bittersweets, queens and the pippin.[2] Whether grown to be cooked, turned into cider or simply eaten, apples were cultivated across the country, with orchards in the southern counties of Hertfordshire and Kent providing the stock that was sold in London. Of course, there were other fruits: at least 65 varieties of pear, 35 varieties of cherry, 61 varieties of plum and 6 varieties of apricot.[3] Strawberries blossomed in the south-west, berries and figs could be found across England, and oranges, which were difficult to grow in northern Europe, were imported from abroad. The humble apple, however, was by far the most abundant and versatile fruit in seventeenth-century England.

At a medium-sized farmstead in the hamlet of Woolsthorpe by Colsterworth in southern Lincolnshire, a small orchard of rare apple trees, known as the Flower of Kent, flourished in the gardens. During the spring these trees would be covered in flushed pink-white blossom and by late summer and early autumn their branches would be heavy with large sweet apples, used for cooking. The farmstead, known as Woolsthorpe Manor, was about a mile to the west of the Great North Road and located in an area of agricultural richness. Up until 1642, the limestone building and working fields had been owned by a prosperous yeoman farmer who had died just two months before the birth of his only child. This child was now a twenty-three-year-old man named Isaac Newton and, on a hazy autumn day in 1666, he sat beneath one of the apple trees in, as he later described, 'a contemplative mood'.

For all its rural beauty, Woolsthorpe was not where Newton wanted to be. He had in fact attempted to return to his university studies earlier that year, but the plague in Cambridge had proved to be far too virulent. Instead, he had new shelves constructed at his family home to accommodate the books he had brought back from Cambridge, and made frequent trips to the library at the nearby parsonage in Boothby Pagnell.[4] Newton might have been in exile, but he did not spent his time idly. Filling the pages of his notebooks with the results of experiments and observations, his time at Woolsthorpe resulted in some of the most significant scientific and mathematical discoveries of the entire century. As he later reflected, 'in those days I was in the prime of my age for invention'.[5]

Despite having no formal training in mathematics, Newton had created the first thorough work on calculus and geometry, by forming equations to measure integration (areas bound to curves) and differentiation (tangents to curves); a genre of mathematics that he referred to as 'the calculus of fluxions'. He had also experimented with optics, using a triangular glass prism to unravel 'the celebrated Phaenomena of colours'. Darkening his chamber except for a thin slice of light through his window, Newton placed the glass prism at the light's entrance so 'that it might be thereby refracted to the opposite wall'. In doing so, he discovered that white light consisted of integral composite colours, which revealed themselves when split. This discovery ran contrary to Robert Hooke's musings in his book *Micrographia*, which suggested that the colours were a result of, rather than revealed by, the prism. Individually, these were significant advances. Combined, they represented a remarkable achievement. Grouped with his final discovery of 1666, they marked Newton out as a scientific great.

Whatever he was contemplating as he sat under the apple tree on this autumnal day was brought to a sudden halt when, above him, a stem holding one of the plump apples strained and snapped. The speckled red fruit thumped to the ground and, in a flash, Newton had a groundbreaking epiphany. It became clear to him that the fruit had been drawn to the ground because gravitation worked to pull things together and hold everything onto the Earth, and that its gravitation must extend beyond the sky, into space, and to the moon itself. Following where Galileo and Kepler had led, and Einstein would later follow, in 1666, Newton had started:

> . . . to think of gravity extending to the orb of the Moon . . . and deduced that the forces which keep the Planets in their Orbs must be reciprocally as the squares of their distances from the centres about which they revolve . . .

At least, that is how the incident was told to, and recorded by, at least four different people during the course of Newton's long and illustrious life.[6] With its echoes of the tree of knowledge in the Garden of Eden, the strong image of a maverick genius unravelling the mysteries of the universe in isolation from wider society is difficult to shake. While there is no reason to doubt that Newton had something of an epiphany in his garden that year, his initial leap of understanding was followed by painstaking work to develop the mathematical equations and models that got to the crux of his understanding of gravitation. In fact, Newton's contribution was significant not for its eureka moment (others, including Robert Hooke, had made and would continue to make passing theories about the pull of objects and gravity), but for the fact that it moved away from, as the French scientist Alexis Clairaut wrote in 1727, 'a truth that is glimpsed' to 'a truth that is demonstrated'. Through the scrupulous use of calculus, Newton would demonstrate in his seminal text *Philosophiæ Naturalis Principia Mathematica* (1687) that gravitation and the movement of objects was demonstrable by mathematical connections.

While the Royal Society argued over the relative merits of Thomas Hobbes's latest work, privately Newton had proved himself as the leading mathematician of his age. For several years, however, his work would remain hidden and unpublished, with only its author aware of its significance. Newton's plague exile had worked to lay the groundwork for the subjects that would occupy his mind throughout the rest of his life, and ensure his place in history. His work on gravitation would be developed over the ensuing decades, but in 1666 he had already sowed the seeds of a vicious scientific battle between himself and Robert Hooke, who had developed his own theories about gravitation, that would begin in just over a decade's time, dragging the Royal Society into a fierce debate about plagiarism and academic ownership.

For now, 105 miles south of Newton's home in Lincolnshire, Hooke had a far more practical matter to deal with. Following the fire, his residence at Gresham College had become overrun by London's aldermen and financiers; so much so that several college occupants had been forced to vacate their offices and lodgings to make space for the city's powers of authority. The physician Dr Jonathan Goddard's offices were taken over by the City Chamberlain, and a Dr Horton's former lodgings, which were supposed to go to one Dr George Clifford, were found, as the records state, 'to be most commodious', and were comman-deered by the Deputy Town Clerk and the City Swordbearer. Space was also made for a Mr Godfrey, who had managed to preserve the records of the Company of Mercers. The Guildhall was too badly damaged to serve as a meeting place, so on the king's orders Gresham College had become the temporary centre of governance.

On 13 September 1666, 'a good, modest, and innocent look[ing]' woman, as Pepys once described her, enjoyed the pre-autumnal weather as she rode on horseback across the fields and gardens surrounding Whitehall. The twenty-seven-year old, who was dressed in a cavalier riding habit and a horseman's coat, with a hat and feather adorning her dark brown head of hair, had decided to leave the confines of the royal palace for some fresh air.[7] For this woman, the past year and a half had been defined by loss: her beloved mother had died thousands of miles away, her trusted (albeit flawed) confidant had been slaughtered during the ill-fated battle at Bergen, she had experienced the trauma of a miscarriage, and had watched her adopted capital city burn to the ground, all the while suffering the humiliation of her husband's extramarital relationships. The fresh rumours that his chief mistress, Lady Castlemaine, was pregnant again would prove to be false – in fact, his next child would be born to the actress Nell Gwynn three years later – but the gossip cannot have failed to pain a woman who, with every year and every miscarriage, moved further away from her prescribed role as a producer of royal heirs. However, Queen Catherine was no longer the innocent young woman who had arrived in England four years ago. Experience had matured her and, from now onwards, she would set about carving her own space within the capricious English court.

She had left her husband in the palace where he faced the unique task of deciding how best to rebuild a capital city. In truth, there were three pressing and interlinked issues he needed to address: first, to find a way to restore order, encourage trade and prevent rebellion; second, to devise a strategy for rebuilding London; and third, to manage the demands of an ongoing maritime war. On this day, it was the second of these three problems that the king was focused on. Instructions had already been given to the artist Wenceslaus Hollar to 'take an exact plan and survey of the city . . . after the calamity of the late fire',[8] and today the king and the Duke of York were joined by John Evelyn, who had created the second of three major proposals for a new London. The first, presented two days earlier by Christopher Wren, had been rooted in a baroque style with uniform streets and avenues, geometrically dependent on the western peak of a newly designed St Paul's Cathedral. The speed with which Wren had assembled his design engendered the disapproval of the Royal Society, whose members argued that he should have presented it to them first. The architect claimed, however, to have been 'so pressed to hasten it [his proposal], before other desseins [designs] came in that he could not possibly consult the society about it'.

He was right to be hasty. Seventeenth-century London had no shortage of polymathic thinkers with ideas on how to create a new city. Evelyn's design came from the same school of thought as Wren's. Based on his personal survey of the ruins, he proposed a new grid pattern, with widened streets and ordered gardens and piazzas, and noxious trades positioned outside the city walls to minimise the risk of fire. For over an hour, the king and the Duke of York pored over the particulars of the proposal. Charles, as the diarist recorded, seemed to be 'extremely pleased with what [Evelyn] had so early thought on'. The third major design, created by Robert Hooke, would be given the Royal Society's seal of approval when it was presented to members and the city aldermen and Lord Mayor at Gresham College over a week later. On seeing Hooke's plans, they were reported to be 'well pleased' with his design, and were urged by the Lord Mayor to present the plan to the king because it was 'far before that which was drawn up by the surveyor of the City [Peter Mills]'.

Over the ensuing weeks and months many unsolicited rebuilding plans would be put forward – from the design suggested by the cartographer Richard Newcourt, which consisted of grids and squares with a church in the centre of each, to the plan put forward by one Captain Valentine Knight, whose rather basic design had dozens of streets running east to west and included an idea to charge a canal toll to make extra revenue for the crown. Charles was reportedly angry with Knight's suggestion that the crown could make money out of London's misfortune, but what he thought of the rest of the designs is unclear. It is interesting, however, that on the very day he reviewed Evelyn's plans, a royal proclamation was drafted by the Lord Chancellor, declaring to the world that 'No man's loss in the late fire is comparable to his [the king's], but he hopes to live to see a much more beautiful city than that consumed'. It would be a city 'well provided against accidents by fire'. The construction of 'hasty and unskilful buildings' was forbidden, and the Lord Mayor was granted permission to pull down any premises erected that did not adhere to the regulations; those built in accordance with the guidelines, however, would be exempt from Hearth Tax for seven years.[9]

The need for action was imminent because London was fast becoming a dangerous place. The thick smoke that had clogged the air surrounding the city had, by now, mostly dissipated, but fires continued to burn in cellars and warehouses, fuelled by coal, oil and other combustible goods.[10] The temporary sheds and tents erected against the city walls for trade proved to be a poor substitute for real commerce. Many who journeyed through the city plundered the remains for treasure or mementos: Pepys took some glass from the Mercers's chapel whilst William Taswell took some metal from the remains of St Paul's Cathedral. Orders had been given for debris to be cleared away, but there was still much to do, and the ruined city became the dwelling place of unwholesome characters. Gangs started to operate within the ruins, pretending to offer wanderers a 'link' (a candlelit-escort) through the wrecked city, but it was claimed that 'when they catch a man single, [they] whip into a vault with him, knock him down, strip them from top to toe, blow out their links, and leave the persons for dead'. Writing to Lord Arlington's secretary, Joseph Williamson, the clerk at the General Letter Office, James Hickes, who had relocated to the north of the city, reported that 'there are many people found murdered and carried into the vaults amongst the ruins'. The murdered body of a woman was discovered after an apothecary's apprentice had been attacked and rammed into a vault containing her corpse. Without adequate watchmen, Hickes argued, 'no person dare, after the close of the evening, pass the streets amongst the ruins'.[11]

The human cost of the Great Fire of London is often thought to have been negligible. Indeed, in his vast work *The Present State of England*, Edward Chamberlayne reported that 'not above six or eight persons were burnt'.[12] There was undoubtedly enough warning for large swathes of London's population to vacate hazardous areas, and when news of the disaster reached the Essex vicar Ralph Josselin, he noted that 'few perished in the flames'.[13] But fire is a force that can take lives and destroy the evidence. During an earlier and much smaller fire near Tower Street in 1650, along with forty-three people known to have perished, commentators also reported finding 'parts of . . . bodies, and other bare bones, and other quite consumed' in the rubbish and debris 'so that no other account can be given of them'.[14] The Tower Street fire raged for just a couple of hours, but the Great Fire of London lasted four days, reaching temperatures of 1,700°C; any comparable evidence would have been largely destroyed. It would be reasonable to suppose that for every sick person who was helped out of their house, such as Edward Atkyns's sister, who 'being then very ill, all ye care was to remove her',[15] there were others with no one to aid them.

Even with London's depleted population following the plague, the number of recorded deaths in 1666 was still in the hundreds each week. Those with potentially life-threatening ailments such as consumption and dropsy would have been put at an even greater risk when transported without adequate care. Parish records for this time are incomplete, but there are hints that the death toll might have been far greater than previously supposed. At the parish of St Giles without Cripplegate, for example, the number of burials during the month of September went up by a third (presumably due to citizens from destroyed parishes using this surviving church), and there was a disproportionate rise (by two-thirds) in the number of deaths due to being 'aged', and an increase in deaths attributed to 'fright'.[16] Evelyn was convinced that many had died when he wrote about the foul smell in the air caused by 'some poor creatures' bodies, beds, and other combustible goods'. In his poem about the year 1666, John Dryden indicated the deaths of infants during the fire when he wrote: 'For helpless infants left amidst the fire'. It is also likely that in the presence of such a calamity, the importance of describing the sight of dead bodies became secondary to describing the sight of the destroyed city. Although the schoolboy William Taswell was taken aback by what he called a dead 'decrepid woman' near to the east walls of St Paul's Cathedral (vividly described as 'whole as to skin, meagre as to flesh, yellow as to colour'),[17] he confessed that it was something he had almost forgotten to include in his account of the fire. News of disasters is often exaggerated, but that does not mean there wasn't some truth in the reports that reached France of:

> . . . the terror and the death of those who were overwhelmed by the fall of roofs, by the ruin of the houses and by the press of those who were fleeing to save themselves and their goods is indescribable. The letters from London speak of the terrible sights of persons burned to death and calcined limbs, making it easy to believe the terror though it cannot be exactly described. The old, tender children and many sick and helpless persons were all burned in their beds and served as fuel for the flames.[18]

There were also deaths caused by exposure and poverty, including the seventy-year-old Jacobean dramatist James Shirley and his wife and one John Woodward, a butcher who was buried shortly after the fire outside the city walls.

One of the most curious deaths to occur in the aftermath of the disaster was that of the French watchmaker Robert Hubert. In an effort to allay public fears, a committee was put together towards the end of September to investigate the cause of the fire. Within days, Hubert came forward and confessed to orchestrating the catastrophe with the help of twenty-three accomplices. He certainly fitted the bill. Blame for the fire was levelled at a number of perpetrators – from the Dutch and Quakers, to dissatisfied merchants, God, and the dissolute court of Charles II – but in the immediate aftermath it was a French Catholic plot that was most feared. Thomas Vincent saw it that way, writing 'this doth smell of popish design, hatcht in the same place where the Gunpowder-plot was contrived, only that this was more successful'.[19] Many read more into old encounters than they might have ordinarily. One Mr Light recalled a 'zealous Papist' asking him in February 1665: 'You expect great things in '66, and think that Rome will be destroyed, but what if it be London?' Elizabeth Styles remembered a Frenchman telling her, five months before the fire, that at some point between June and October there would not be 'a house left between Temple Bar and London Bridge'.[20] There were also questions about the uncanny accuracy of the astronomer William Lilly's visual predictions in *Monarchy or No Monarchy*.

As a young Frenchman, Hubert was exactly the kind of perpetrator people wanted to fear, but there were two problems: firstly, his motive was questionable – he was a Protestant not a Catholic – and secondly he had a cast-iron alibi – he had been at sea when the fire broke out. Nevertheless, for some unknown reason the watchmaker gave a detailed account of his actions, explaining that he had thrown a fireball through the window of Farriner's bakery. To prove his guilt he led the committee to the exact site of the bakehouse in Pudding Lane. He was incarcerated and tried as a traitor. The jury – which included Thomas Farriner, who had managed to evade condemnation for his integral part in the outbreak of the fire – found him to be guilty. The Earl of Clarendon later confessed that 'Neither the judges, nor any present at the trial did believe him guilty; but that he was a poor distracted wretch, weary of his life, and chose to part with it.'[21] He was executed at Tyburn on 27 October 1666.

His execution did not stop the tightening of controls over Quakers and other religious dissidents. A Quaker in Windsor, for example, was apprehended after reportedly having a vision that 'they have had the pestilence and fire and other calamities, and yet are not amended, but a worse plague has yet to come on them and the nation'.[22] One Richard Leeming intercepted correspondence from a harness maker in London to a Quaker bearing the motto 'The man of sin shall fall and Christ shall reigne over all'.[23] Any texts deemed to be heretical or atheistic were suppressed, and a Commons committee was licensed to assess 'books as tend to atheism, blasphemy and profaneness' including (and in particular) Thomas Hobbes's *Leviathan*. In this climate of fear and accusation, Hobbes found the charge that he promoted atheism as 'the greatest defamation possible', but set about burning many of his papers and writing an appendix for the Dutch publication of *Leviathan* detailing why the work was not heretical, just to be safe.

Once the immediate fear of French and Dutch terror in the city had died down, it was widely accepted that the fire had been an act of God, not man – but this did not make the incident benign. The historian Edward Chamberlayne acknowledged that while many factors had contributed to the disaster – including, as he described, 'The Drunkenness or Supine negligence of the Baker, in whose House it began'[24] – to him it was 'Gods just anger, for the notorious impenitency of the Citizens, for their abetting and instigating the shedding of the precious innocent Blood' of Charles I.[25] The minister Edward Stillingfleet claimed that in order to make his displeasure known, 'God hath imployed a more furious element, which by its merciless and devouring flames might in a more lively manner represent unto us the kindling of his wrath.'[26] Even the committee tasked with investigating the fire eventually conceded that 'nothing hath yet been found to argue it to have been other than the hand of God upon us, a great wind, and the season so very dry'. The *London Gazette* told a similar story, deducing that:

> the whole was an unhappy chance, or to speak better the heavy hand of God upon us for our sins, shewing us the terrour of his Judgment in thus raising the fire, and immediately after his miraculous and never enough to be acknowledged Mercy in putting a stop to it when we were in the last despair, and that all attempts for the quenching it however industriously pursued, seemed insufficient.

Abroad, it wasn't the cause that concerned England's enemies, it was the effect. The Venetian ambassador in Paris thought that the fire would be 'worse than any defeat of her fleets, worse than the plague and than any other disaster, capable of making them change their government and principles',[27] reporting that 'cries are now heard on every hand, that since the House of Stuart came to the throne England has never enjoyed felicity but has suffered from incessant miseries'.[28] The *London Gazette* was quick to recognise the attempts of England's enemies 'to persuade the world abroad of great parties and disaffection at home against his majesties government'. However, it professed that the fire had actually engendered great affection for the king, even during a time when 'disorder might have been expected from losses, distraction, and almost desperation of some persons in their private fortunes, thousands of people not having had habitations to cover them'.[29] When news of the fire reached Antwerp, Aphra Behn wrote back to Whitehall that the Dutch had boasted that the English fleet was likely to retreat. Addressing the Commons shortly after the disaster, the king acknowledged that the Dutch and the French would delight in the news, and pushed for

Parliament to find adequate funds to continue the campaign, declaring that:

> if they were able this last Year to persuade this miserable People, whom they so mis-led, That the Contagion had so wasted the Nation, and impoverished us, that we could not be able to set out any Fleet, how will they be exalted with this last Impoverishment of this City, and contemn all reasonable Conditions of Peace?[30]

But there were no longer the funds to continue the war, and no reason to suppose an extended campaign would benefit the English. With gains and losses on both sides, terms would need to be agreed with all parties involved – namely, England, the Dutch Republic, France and Denmark. With the help of Swedish negotiators, who had advocated England's cause on the continent throughout the conflict, it looked as though the struggle would be resolved.

Meanwhile, in order to fulfil the king and Parliament's wish for a new city whose 'Beauty and Praise . . . shall fill the whole Earth', several obstacles needed to be overcome.[31] The first was to unravel the complex web of historic formal and informal agreements between tenants and landlords; Sir Nathaniel Hobart thought that the 'rebuilding of the Citty will not bee soe difficult as the satisfying all interests, there being many proprietors'.[32] For a long time, premises in London had not been clearly defined. Properties were joined together and intermixed, with parts sublet and other parts refashioned. The fire worked to amplify existing issues between tenants and landlords, with houses that remained intact placed at a premium. Writing to his wife in Essex, one Thomas Bromfield explained that 'Houses are ten times dearer than ever they were.'[33] Hobart himself feared that his landlord, who he described as being 'a person so odious that if his cause were just he would hardly find favour',[34] would end his tenancy. Likewise, many landlords suffered through the loss of revenue. Dr Denton's wife lost £86 per year in income and, as Denton wrote, after

Wenceslaus Hollar's Survey of the Great Fire of London, 1666

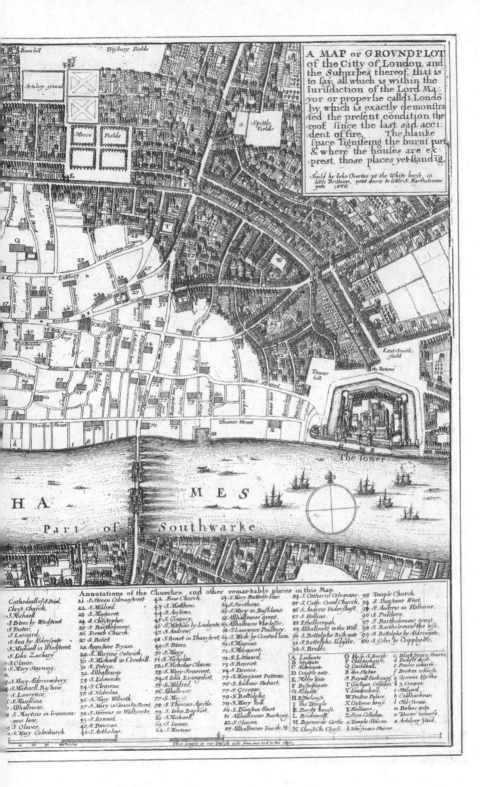

A MAP or GROVNDPLOT of the Citty of London and the Suburbes thereof, that is to say, all which is within the Iurisdiction of the Lord Mayor or properlie callct London, by which is exactly demonstrated the present condition thereof since the last sad accident of fire. The blanke space signifeing the burnt part & where the houses are exprest, those places yet standing.

Sould by Iohn Overton at the White horse, in little Brittaine, next doore to little S. Bartholomew gate. 1666.

The Tower

THA␣␣␣MES

Part of ␣␣␣ Southwarke

East Smithfield
Tower hill
the Posterne
Thames Street
Tower Street
Spittle Fields
Moore Fields
Artillery ground
Bunhill
Finsbury Fields

Annotations of the Churches, and other remarkable places in this Map.

Cathedrall of S. Paul,
Christ Church.
S. Michaell
S. Peters by Woodstreet
S. Foster,
S. Leonard,
S. Ann by Aldersgate
S. Michaell in Woodstreet
S. Iohn Zachary
S. Olaves,
S. Mary Stayning,

S. Mary Aldermanbery,
S. Michaell Bashaw,
S. Laurence,
S. Mawdlins,
Allhallowes,
S. Martins in Ironmongers lane,
S. Olaves,
S. Mary Colechurch.

21. S. Steven Colmanstreet
22. S. Mildred,
23. S. Margaret,
24. S. Christopher,
25. S. Bartholomew
26. French Church,
27. S. Benet,
28. Augustine Fryars,
29. S. Martins Outwich,
30. S. Michaell in Cornhill,
31. S. Peters,
32. Allhallowes,
33. S. Edmunds,
34. S. Clemens,
35. S. Nicholas,
36. S. Mary Wolnoth,
37. S. Mary in Gracestreet,
38. S. Stevens in Walbrooke,
39. S. Bennet,
40. S. Pancras,
41. S. Antholine.

42. Bow Church,
43. S. Matthew,
44. S. Austins,
45. S. Gregory,
46. S. Martins by Ludgate,
47. S. Andrew,
48. S. Benet in Thamstreet,
49. S. Peters
50. S. Mary,
51. S. Nicholas,
52. S. Nicholas Olaves,
53. S. Mary Somerset,
54. S. Iohn Evangelist,
55. S. Mildred,
56. Allhallowes,
57. S. Mary,
58. S. Thomas Apostls,
59. S. Iohn Baptist,
60. S. Michaell,
61. S. Iames,
62. S. Martins.

63. S. Mary Buttolfs lane,
64. S. Swithens,
65. S. Mary in Bushlane,
66. Allhallowes The lesser,
67. S. Laurence Poultney,
68. S. Mich: by Crooked lane,
69. S. Magnus,
70. S. Mary,
71. S. Margaret,
72. S. Leonard,
73. S. Bennet,
74. S. Dennis,
75. S. Margaret Pattens,
76. S. Andrew Hubart,
77. S. George,
78. S. Bottolphs,
79. S. Mary hill,
80. S. Dunstan East
81. Allhallowes Barking,
82. S. Olave,
83. Allhallowes Fanch: St.

84. S. Catharin Colemans,
85. S. Cath: Creed Church,
86. S. Andrew Vndershaft,
87. S. Hellins,
88. S. Ethelborough,
89. Allhallowes in the Wall,
90. S. Bottolphs Bishgate,
91. S. Bottolphs Algate,
92. S. Brides,

93. Temple Church,
94. S. Dunstans West
95. S. Andrew in Holborne,
96. S. Pulchers,
97. S. Bartholomew great,
98. S. Bartholomews the lesse,
99. S. Bottolph by Aldersgate,
100. S. Giles by Cripplegate.

A. Ludgate
B. Newgate
C. Aldersgate,
D. Cripple gate
E. Moore gate
F. Bushopsgate,
G. Aldgate,
H. E. posthouse,
I. the Temple
K. Dorset house,
L. Bridewell
M. Baynards Castle
N. ChrystCh: Cloyst:

O. Hosp: S. Barth:
P. Christopher,
Q. Guildhall,
R. the Stokes
S. Royall Exchange
T. Gresham Colledge,
V. Leadenhall,
W. Dukes Palace
X. Ossorne house
Y. Bedlame,
Z. Sion Colledge,
a. Temple Staires
b. Whitefriars Staires

c. Blackfryers Staires
d. Puddle docke.
e. Paules wharfe
f. Broken wharfe.
g. Queene Hythe
h. 3 Cranes
i. Stilard,
k. Coldharbour
l. Old Swan.
m. Belins gate
n. Tower wharfe
o. Artillery Yard.

This length at one English mile Answere one end to the other.

having 'a little time to recollect herself', would cry all day long.[35] In an effort to combat these tensions, several bills would be passed and a judiciary, known as the Fire Court, would be set up to sort out claims and counter-claims, and to assess where various properties had existed before the fire. Beginning in February 1667, with three magistrates working pro bono publico, the Fire Courts would later resolve hundreds and hundreds of cases and disputes, enabling the programme of rebuilding to begin as swiftly as possible.

Wren, Hooke and Evelyn were almost certainly versed in the utopian tracts of Thomas More and Francis Bacon. But while utopian cities might work on paper, it was clear that the reality of the situation in London left minimal room for change. Private ownership of the city's shops, houses and storehouses, as well as the livery halls under the jurisdiction of the powerful city guilds, meant that there was a vested interest in sustaining the status quo. The innovative rebuilding proposals were cast aside, and the first Rebuilding Act would be passed on 8 February 1667. While key changes were implemented – streets would be widened, a forty-foot gap would be made along the waterfront, the Fleet River would be canalised, the number of churches would be reduced, and trades that could result in fires were moved from high-risk areas – much of the street pattern remained the same. There was, however, one crucial difference: it was enshrined in law that new buildings had to be made of brick and stone. As such, the aesthetic of London would be changed for ever.

As the winter of 1666 arrived, despite Thomas Vincent's predictions, everyday life resumed. The theatres had reopened – although Thomas Killigrew complained that they were not as busy as they had once been. Over the course of the year, he had gone to considerable expense improving the performance space within his playhouse in Drury Lane: widening the stage and investing in new machinery. In December, Nell Gwynn trod the newly refurbished boards when she returned to the stage in James Howard's comedy *The English Monsieur*. Pepys went to see the play and wrote how he thought 'the women do very well; but, above all, little Nelly'. She was to dominate the theatre for the next couple of years. There was also an incident in November when Robert Smith, one of the leading actors of the Duke's Playhouse under William Davenant, got into a quarrel with, and then killed, another man over the contents of a play. Luckily for audience members who were saddened at the possible loss of one of their favourite actors, Smith was to return to the boards soon enough, specialising in villainous characters. Friction between playwrights, actors and patrons would continue, with actresses frequently pelted by rebuffed suitors, and rival playwrights, poets and patrons regularly conducting a war of words or satirising one another onstage: in 1679 the Earl of Rochester infamously orchestrated a beating of John Dryden.

A woman who within four years would be drawing in crowds to her debut play, *The Forc'd Marriage*, had written letters to Killigrew throughout the autumn but he paid them little attention. Aphra Behn's situation in Antwerp had shifted from fraught to desperate. Despite her months of service and success in reaching out to William Scot, she seems to have been all but stranded across the Channel, and had taken to addressing Killigrew and Lord Arlington directly to ask for money – even declaring to Arlington that her 'life or death [was] in his hands'. Not only was she in debt, but she had been forced to pawn her possessions, and feared that her money troubles might see her imprisoned.[36] The trust she had built with Scot was damaged by her inability to provide funds, and most of the information she had managed to send back to England could have just as easily been gleaned from Dutch newsbooks. She did, however, offer one piece of intelligence that would prove to be prescient. It was not the first time the rumour would be relayed back to Whitehall and it would not be the last, but within one of her many dispatches was intelligence from Scot that the Dutch had a secret plan to make a landed attack on England.[37]

On 15 November, streams of coaches headed to Whitehall Palace. A great ball was being held to celebrate the queen's twenty-eighth birthday. Although he wasn't a guest, from the loft of Whitehall Palace Pepys revelled in a resplendent candlelit view of diamonds, pearls, silks, gold and beauty. The king was dressed in a 'vest of some rich silke and silver trimming', and the Duke of York wore a cloth of silver. Also present were Prince Rupert, the Duke of Monmouth, the Duke of Buckingham, the Earl of Rochester, the Duchess of York, Lady Castlemaine, the queen's ladies-in-waiting – including Frances Stewart, who wore 'black and white lace' with her 'head and shoulders dressed with dyamonds' – and many more members of the nobility. The festivities went on until midnight and Pepys was convinced that he was 'never likely to see more gallantry while I live, if I should come twenty times'.

Yet behind the gilded veneer, a rot that would eat away at the Stuart dynasty had set in. The honeymoon period of Charles's kingship had come to an end, and Killigrew lamented how rather than rule as he should, the monarch 'now spends his time in imploying his lips and his prick about the Court, and hath no other imployment'. The ageing Earl of Clarendon was being usurped by the younger Lord Arlington, and would soon find himself blamed for the mismanagement of the Second Anglo-Dutch War and experience a dramatic fall from grace, that would force his exile. More seriously, a tension between the Duke of York and the king's illegitimate firstborn son, the Duke of Monmouth, had developed with whispers circulating that Monmouth – a man whom Pepys thought spent 'his time the most viciously and idly of any man' – had ambitions to be his father's heir.[38] Within two years, the Duke of York's interest in Catholicism would result in a secret conversion to the faith. In just under twenty years, Charles would be dead and James would order Monmouth's execution.

By February 1667, the war with the Dutch was believed to be as good as over. Orders were given to moor the largest of England's warships at Chatham in order to save money. They were to be protected by the fortified garrison at Sheerness as well as a huge metal chain-barrier. With peace negotiations underway, by May 1667 it seemed as though a deal would soon be made. There was just one problem – both England and the Dutch Republic harboured a secret. In England, Charles had privately agreed to support a French land attack on the Spanish Netherlands, in the hope that Gallic money could be used to fund the English fleet for another campaign against the Dutch. De Witt, however, was planning one last Dutch attack – a raid on English shores.

De Witt's audacious plan had been months in the making and his target would be the most prized dockyard of all, Chatham. Thought to be impenetrable, Chatham was accessed via the Medway River, which was full of shoals and twisty meanders. In June 1667, under de Ruyter's expert management, the Dutch fleet managed to steer along the Medway to orchestrate the raid. They captured the fort of Sheerness and the noise of the resultant battle was so loud that the guns could be heard as far away as Cambridge. Having recently returned to the university city, Isaac Newton heard the blasts and told his colleagues that the Dutch had beaten the English. When he was asked how he could be so certain, he explained that 'by carefully attending to the sound, he found it grew louder and louder, consequently came nearer; from whence he rightly infer'd that the Dutch were victors'.[39] He was, indeed, right.

The Dutch razed the dockyard to the ground: with trumpets blasting, drums beating and Dutch seamen cheering, fireships were sent to assault English warships at anchor. Gun batteries from the castle made little impact. The *Loyal London*, *Royal Oak* and *Royal James* were burnt, fifteen more warships were destroyed and, most crushing of all, the king's vessel, the *Royal Charles*, was towed away. It was, and still is, the most humiliating naval defeat in English history (not least because many of those on board the Dutch ships were actually English seamen), and a glorious triumph for the Dutch Republic. Until the raid on the

Medway, England could have made a case for being the victors of the war. Afterwards, England's position on the negotiating table was much less certain. There were profound psychological repercussions, and within a year a government inquiry would be launched into not only the Medway disaster but also the catastrophic decision to split the fleet ahead of the Four Days Fight. Within ten days of the raid, the peace treaty was completed and signed at Breda by all parties. The terms forced the English Navigation Acts to be restructured to favour the Dutch in their trade of goods from German principalities. Meanwhile, the Dutch retained Surinam and England kept the American out-post of New Netherland (which would later become New York and New Jersey).

When war with the Dutch broke out for the third time in 1672, many of the key players from the Second Anglo-Dutch War returned to the sea. The Earl of Sandwich was killed in action during the Battle of Solebay when his flagship the *Royal James* was attacked; when it washed up on the shore, his body was so charred that he was only recognised by his flag sash. He was given a state funeral for his services to England. Sir Edward Spragge never forgot the humiliation he suffered during the St James's Day Battle – while the rest of the English fleet had won a terrific victory, his rear-squadron had been battered by Admiral Tromp. During the Third Anglo-Dutch War he determined to kill him or die trying and achieved the latter, following a bloody duel. Sir Thomas Clifford, whose intelli-gence impressed during the Second Anglo-Dutch War, became one fifth of Charles II's infamous 'CABAL', a group of coun-sellors who were to become the king's chief advisers following the fall of the Lord Chancellor, the Earl of Clarendon. He resigned his post in the early 1670s, however, because of his Catholic faith. Suffering from melancholy, he committed suicide in 1673.

On the Dutch side, frictions between de Witt and supporters of the House of Orange escalated to such a degree that de Witt and his brother were lynched in 1672, an act that many suspected Tromp could have been behind. De Ruyter excelled once more during the Third Anglo-Dutch War, securing important victories against the English, but he died during a battle near Spain, following a leg injury. Tromp succeeded him as supreme commander of the Dutch navy in 1679. The young boy, William of Orange, grew into a man, became the Stadholder in 1672, married the Duke of York's daughter Mary and took the crown of England in 1688.

The most tangible legacy of 1665–6, however, is London itself. Immediately after the fire, there were whispers around court that the accident might actually be 'the greatest blessing that God ever conferred' upon Charles II for it had levelled the 'rebellious' city of London and forever opened its gates to royal power. It was political discourse that, according to Clarendon at least, displeased the king. The real legacy would be much more tangible.[40] It would take city surveyors Robert Hooke and Peter Mills nine weeks and over 1,200 feet of timber to stake out most of the streets and buildings that were ready for the rebuild. A tax on coal coming into London would be used to fund the construction of public buildings such as the Guildhall and parish churches. Some people did quite well out of the disaster: carpenters, masons and bricklayers were so busy with work that even the Treasury had difficulty procuring workmen. Conscious of the need to have a Custom House operational as soon as possible, 'for the publique trade of the citty and so consequently for the advantage of the whole body', authorisation was granted to press workmen. They would be paid their usual wage and released once the work was completed on a new Custom House in Mark Lane.[41] Daniel Defoe, who was only six years old at the time of the fire, recalled a period of great industry, declaring it to be 'incredible what a Trade this made all over the whole Kingdom, to make good the Want and to supply that Loss'.[42] By the end of 1667, 150 houses had been rebuilt, and by 1672, the majority of the new houses had been constructed and the livery companies were well on their way to completion. Writing in 1671, Chamberlayne declared:

> as if the late Fire had onely purged the City, the Buildings are become infinitely more beautiful, more commodious, and more solid (the three main vertues of all Edifices) then before; nay, as if the Citizens had not been any way impoverish'd, but rather inrich't by that huge Conflagration . . .[43]

It wasn't until 1669 that Christopher Wren was awarded the role of Master of Works, supported by Robert Hooke. In this capacity, he was responsible for the design of fifty churches across London. If a utopia wasn't possible, then Wren would make sure London was sprinkled with architectural genius, and it was in the detail that he really came alive. His churches embraced baroque style with clean lines, bold cupolas and white stone. His masterpiece was, of course, what Chamberlayne described as 'the Mother Church of the Mother City of this Kingdom':[44] St Paul's Cathedral. Work began on the cathedral in 1669 and it was declared officially complete on Christmas Day 1711. Its construction spanned the reigns of no fewer than five monarchs, and Wren, who was only two years younger than Charles II, managed to see its completion, before dying in 1723 aged ninety-one.

The emotional toll on the hundreds of thousands of people who experienced and survived the plague, war and fire is harder to quantify, but there are hints of its impact. Shortly after the Great Fire, a disturbing image of the printer Thomas Newcomb's behaviour emerges from the archives. Though he had managed to re-establish his printing business with commendable speed in the weeks and months following the fire, he was slow to pay the book-women who sold the *London Gazette* in the streets. One book-woman in particular, Mrs Andrews, complained that Newcomb was carrying 'himselfe more strangely' than ever before and that he was often either 'soo farr from these parts' or found near the 'Churchyard' (presumably the ruins of St Paul's

Churchyard) 'where the stench of earth is offensive & unwhole-some'.[45] Complaints were made against Sir William Batten, who was reported to be 'formerly a serious, honest man' who 'now rants and storms, calls their [seamen's] wives ill names'. For many months, Pepys suffered from nightmares that his house was ablaze. In March 1667, he was 'mightily troubled . . . with fears of fire, which', he confessed, 'I cannot get out of my head to this day since the last great fire'.[46] Despite his efforts to save Lime Street, John Vandermarsh would later have to contend with anti-Dutch xenophobia as he fought for the right to rebuild his lawfully leased property. Perhaps Sir Nathaniel Hobart best sums up the emotional effect of the fire: 'the image of this terrible judgment has made such an impression in the soules of every one of us, that it will not be effaced while we live'.[47]

In the immediate aftermath of the fire, Evelyn betrayed a senti-ment that appears to have been endemic in the unquestionably religious world of late-seventeenth-century England: that of guilt. It was widely accepted that the terrible fortune suffered by London, and England more generally, had been self-inflicted; just deserts for indulging in sin and committing acts of heresy or, as he wrote: 'the late dreadful conflagration, added to the plague and war, [were] the most dismal judgments that could be inflicted; but which indeed we highly deserved for our prodigious ingrati-tude, burning lusts, dissolute court, profane and abominable lives'.[48] Indeed, when Parliament met shortly after the fire, it was declared that it represented 'the Justice of God', and that those affected 'were not the greatest Sinners on whom the Tower of Siloam fell; and doubtless all our Sins did contribute to the filling up that Measure, which being full, drew down the Wrath of God upon that City'. Linking the conflagration to the plague, the anonymous author of a pamphlet entitled *Flagellum dei* further reflected that while the plague had predominantly ravaged the outer suburbs, the fire had been most active within the walls. It was, the author mused, 'As if it were design'd by Divine Providence, that each part should have its punishment, and none a double one'.[49] The author saw the fire as God's punishment for 'Rebellion, Pride, Whoring, Drunkenness, Gluttony, [and] Cheating'. Several months later, Evelyn once again wondered at the events of 1666: 'indeed it had been a year of prodigies in this nation, plague, war, fire . . .'.[50]

Yet amidst the tragedy and terror, there had also been great moments of triumph. John Dryden had spent the most part of 1665 and 1666 exiled from London at his family home in Charlton, Wiltshire, writing a series of essays called *Of Dramatick Poesie* and experiencing the joys of fatherhood after his wife had given birth to their first son, Charles. He had also penned a historical poem, 'For I have chosen the most heroic subject which any poet could desire', a work of 1,216 lines that followed the events of 1665–6 and would propel him to the position of Poet Laureate two years later. Published in 1667, it celebrated London's triumph over adversity and its survival against all odds. The poem was dedicated not to the king, a nobleman or wealthy patron, but to London itself, with Dryden noting that he was

> the first who ever presented a work of this nature to the Metropolis of any Nation, so is it likewise consonant to Justice, that he who was to give the first Example of such a Dedication should begin it with that City, which has set a pattern to all others of true Loyalty, invincible Courage, and unshaken Constancy.

It was a masterful work of persuasive propaganda, working to bind the people to their king. Beginning with the Battle of Lowestoft, it tracked the progress of the naval campaigns under the Duke of York, then the Earl of Sandwich, George Monck and Prince Rupert, alluding to the plague but focusing on maritime action. The poem's finale was a telling of the Great Fire of London. Royalist to the core but also sentimental, brave, and hopeful, Dryden named the poem *Annus Mirabilis: A Year of Wonders, 1666* and opined that the new London would 'stand a wonder to all Years and Ages . . . a *Phœnix* in her ashes'. He declared:

> Methinks already from this chemic flame,
> I see a city of more precious mould:
> Rich as the town which gives the Indies name,
> With silver paved, and all divine with gold.

Epilogue: After 1666

Charles II

CHARLES LIVED UNTIL 1685, becoming the longest reigning monarch of the seventeenth century. It was a period defined by national trauma, but also creative growth. Heavily criticised for his debauchery and licentiousness, where many monarchs might have failed Charles managed to hold his position and his country through the Great Plague, the Great Fire of London, two wars against the Dutch, an Exclusion Crisis, a Popish Plot, and pressure from his cousin and secret ally, Louis XIV, to convert openly to Catholicism. He left behind at least fourteen illegitimate children and a clutch of grieving mistresses. On his death at the age of fifty-five, one observer wrote:

> He is mightily lamented by every one, as well by his enemies as friends; and [I] heard a gentleman say that came from London, that the citty was in tears, and most of the towns through which he came. Yet perhaps it may be that they wept not so much for the love they bore him, as for fear that his brother who now reigns should be worse than he. Good God, prevent it![1]

James, Duke of York

James's wife, Anne, was to die of breast cancer in 1671, leaving James with three daughters and no male heir. With the introduction of the Test Act, which excluded Catholics from office, James II was forced to resign as Lord High Admiral of the navy. The king replaced the duke's position with a group of admiralty commissioners. He inherited the throne from his brother in 1685, but his reign was marked by its abrupt end three years later. Following the unexpected birth of a son in 1688 by his catholic second wife, Mary of Modena, fearful that James would try to force Catholicism on the country, a group of peers invited his daughter Mary and her husband William of Orange to take the English throne. James spent the rest of his life trying to win back his crown, before finally dying in 1701 of a brain haemorrhage. He was sixty-seven.

There was a moment in the eighteenth century when the Archbishop of Paris considered putting him forward to be canonised. The moment passed.

Margaret Cavendish

During her lifetime, Margaret Cavendish proved herself to be equal to her male contemporaries. She went on to write several important works of scientific theory, all published by Anne Maxwell. The works, however, were never critiqued by the Royal Society's official journal *Philosophical Transactions*, despite the journal reviewing a wide range of scientific tracts. In May 1667 she was invited to a Royal Society meeting where she witnessed some experiments and discussed science with the members, becoming the first woman to attend a meeting there. She was, unfortunately, never invited back and it would be two centuries before another woman would be allowed to attend a meeting. Excepting Queen Victoria, women were not permitted to become fellows of the Royal Society until 1945. She died at the age of fifty in 1673.

John Wilmot, 2nd Earl of Rochester

Immediately after 1666, the Earl of Rochester became the person he was probably always destined to be: a prolific poet, sometime playwright, libertine and rake. His lifestyle inspired the works of George Etherege, William Wycherley, Aphra Behn and John Dryden, though his activities also provoked censure. He left behind a body of work that has stood the test of time and a mythology that began to grow before his body was cold in the earth.

Elizabeth Malet clearly never left his mind, and on 29 January 1667 the pair eloped at a chapel in Knightsbridge, to the surprise of many. Of her feelings for Rochester, Elizabeth wrote:

> Though you still possess my heart,
> Scorn and rigor I must feign;
> There remains no other art
> Your love, fond fugitive, to gain.[2]

During the late 1660s and 1670s, Rochester befriended both Nell Gwynn and Aphra Behn. He died in 1680, aged thirty-three, from suspected syphilis and gonorrhoea. Following his death, Behn composed a poem in his honour, declaring:

> Mourn, mourn, ye Muses, all your loss deplore,
> The young, the noble Strephon is no more.
> Yes, yes, he fled quick as departing light,
> And ne'er shall rise from Death's eternal night,
> So rich a prize the Stygian gods ne'er bore,
> Such wit, such beauty, never graced their shore.

John Milton

John Milton's epic poem *Paradise Lost* was finally sold in 1667 to the bookseller Sam Symons,[3] after the Great Fire had brought another delay to its publication. Its author, on the suggestion of his friend Thomas Ellwood, had spent the majority of 1665 and 1666 writing a follow-up poem that would be called *Paradise Regained*; it would be published in 1671. Milton returned to London in 1667 and died in 1674, aged sixty-five. He was buried in the church of St Giles-without-Cripplegate, in Fore Street. His grave was disturbed towards the end of the eighteenth century by a group of drunken grave-robbers who pulled apart his skeleton.

George Monck

In his own lifetime, George Monck, the Duke of Albemarle, was a legendary figure whose support was crucial to Charles. When he died in 1670, aged sixty-one, he was given a full state funeral. Whether rightly or wrongly, his actions during the Second Anglo-Dutch War garnered much praise. In 1667, there were so many ballads printed about Monck that Pepys remarked: 'I observe that people have some great encouragement to make ballads of him of this kind. There are so many, that hereafter he will sound like Guy of Warwicke.'[4] A soldier at heart, the sea had never been his natural habitat which is perhaps evident in another extract from Pepys:

> It was pretty to hear the Duke of Albemarle himself to wish that they would come on our ground, meaning the French, for that he would pay them, so as to make them glad to go back to France again; which was like a general, but not like an admiral.[5]

Sir Christopher Wren and Robert Hooke

Together, Sir Christopher Wren and Robert Hooke designed the Royal Observatory at Greenwich, the new building for Bethlem Hospital, fifty churches across London and a monument to the Great Fire in the form of a magnificent column topped with a golden flame, which doubled as a scientific laboratory.

In the years to follow, Robert Hooke would reach out to a promising Cambridge scientist named Isaac Newton. He suggested that the scholar explore the idea of gravitation. Robert Hooke said of Wren, 'Since the time of Archimedes there scarce ever met in one man in so great perfection such a mechanical hand and so philosophical [a] mind.'[6]

Isaac Newton

Along with his later scientific achievements, most notably the publication of *Principia*, Isaac Newton also wrote extensively on the occult, religion and alchemy. He became President of the Royal Society and Master of the Royal Mint at the time the Bank of England was established, and in this latter capacity he reformed the English currency and clamped down on counterfeit coinage.

Newton's lasting legacy rests on his understanding of gravitation. In this, he was accused of plagiarism by Robert Hooke in 1687, who claimed that he had given Newton the notion of decreased gravitation and prompted the scientist's interest in the area. Newton died in 1727, aged eighty-four.

Aphra Behn

Aphra Behn sunk even lower before she made her ascent. She spent 1668 begging for help from the king to pay off debts of

£150, and was probably sent to a debtor's prison. Miraculously, the ineffective spy made a triumphant foray into playwriting, becoming one of the most prolific playwrights of her age. Her first work, *The Forc'd Marriage*, opened at the Duke of York's theatre in 1670 and was followed by dozens of other works of satire, most notably *The Rover*. She also wrote what is arguably one of the first novels in English, *Oroonoko*. Through her connection with Killigrew, she became acquainted with the Earl of Rochester, Nell Gwynn and the coterie of courts wits. She died in 1689, aged forty-eight.

At least nineteen of Aphra Behn's plays were staged in London and it is perhaps her preface to *Lucky Chance* that reveals the most about her character: 'I value Fame as much as if I had been born a Hero; and if you rob me of that, I can retire from the ungrateful World, and scorn its fickle Favours.'[7]

Michael and Betty Mitchell

Michael and Betty Mitchell moved into their home in Thames Street in early 1667. Betty gave birth to their daughter in May and Samuel Pepys's wife helped to deliver the baby, Elizabeth. The baby was to die soon after, but the couple would quickly have another, also named Elizabeth. Pepys and his wife attended the child's christening.

William Taswell

Early in 1667, William Taswell lost his beloved mother. She died at the age of forty-three giving birth to the young boy's sister, Maria. Taswell completed his studies at Westminster School and subsequently went to Oxford University. In 1673, his father remarried and reduced the allowance he offered his children so that he could live, as Taswell described, 'more luxuriously' with his new bride. Taswell fell into a depression, ashamed to reveal his poverty to his peers and, because he was thought a gentleman, unable to take work. At the time he was too young to take Holy Orders. He spent the rest of his life as a rector in Wood Norton, Norfolk.

Nell Gwynn

Nell lived a short life but, as mistress to Charles II, it was a full one. Throughout the late 1660s she dominated the London stage in comedic plays. Drawing on the precedent of Beatrice and Benedict in Shakespeare's *Much Ado About Nothing*, the sparring and quick-witted merry couple became a staple of Restoration theatre and Nell came to define the role of the witty female. Whether by accident or design, she become part of a ground-breaking band of women defying convention and exploiting new freedoms in the theatre.

As her relationship with the king became public knowledge, she drew in large crowds. In 1670, the former orange-seller bore the king a son whom she named Charles and who the king made the 1st Duke of St Albans. She died in 1687, aged thirty-seven.

Samuel Pepys

Fearful that he was losing his eyesight, Samuel Pepys stopped writing his diary on 31 May 1669. A couple of months later, Pepys and his wife travelled to Paris, armed with a letter from John Evelyn suggesting places to see and people to visit. Sadly, within days of their return to London Elizabeth became ill, dying on 10 November 1669. In 1673, his house in Seething Lane was destroyed by a fire that broke out at the Navy Board offices. It was not rebuilt. He was made Secretary of the Admiralty in 1674 and in 1683, as a result of his work on the Tangier Committee, he was sent to Tangier to help dismantle the colony. In 1686 he became President of the Royal Society, the year that Newton's *Principia* was published. He was also made Secretary to the Admiralty and MP for Harwich. In his fifties, during the reign of William and Mary, Pepys was accused of being a Jacobite. Although he never remarried, during the later 1670s he started a relationship with his housekeeper Mary Skinner, which would last until his death. He spent his final years in a house in Clapham and died in 1703, aged seventy. Almost thirty-four years after her death, Pepys was buried next to his wife at the church of St Olave Hart Street.

Acknowledgements

FIRST AND FOREMOST, I thank Sam Rideal for putting up with me this past year and a half. It is impossible to express how grateful I am for his patience, encouragement and support. Equally, Edie Rideal has provided endless encouragement, welcome distraction and constant joy. Writing a book is never a solitary endeavour and the highs and the lows we have shared together.

I would like to thank my agent Donald Winchester at Watson, Little who saw enough potential in half a dozen pages to take a chance on an unproven author. He has been a calm, reassuring and understanding presence throughout. I am also grateful to Mark Richards, my editor at John Murray, who immediately 'got' what I was trying to do with the book. Over the past year, his careful commentary and persistent belief both in me and the book have spurred me on and re-energised my interest in the book's protagonists. The team at John Murray are astonishingly good and have worked tirelessly behind the scenes, particularly Caroline Westmore, Martin Bryant, Candida Brazil, Juliet Brightmore and Ruby Mitchell. I am also grateful to editors and translators at Thomas Dunne Books and Unieboek.

Sarah Philpott, Dr Joanne Paul, Dr David Davies, Lara Thorpe and Ruth Wilson read the book in many states of completion. Their feedback, suggestions and conversation greatly enhanced the final work. I am particularly grateful to Lara Thorpe for sharing her unpublished research into the apothecary John Allin, and Sarah Philpott for her keen eye and endless patience. At UCL, I am grateful to Professor Eleanor Robson, Professor Michael Hebbert and most of all Professor Jason Peacey for not only sparking my interest in Stuart London, but for his kindness over the past few years, particularly in allowing me to take time away from my research to write a narrative history. Any mistakes are mine alone.

I must also mention Guy Walters, Dr Andrew Crome, Marit Leenstra from Crossrail, Steven Ellis from the *London* Wreck Project and Mark Dunkley from Historic England, who all kindly offered their ears and guidance at various points during my research. Anyone writing about the Great Plague and the Great Fire of London owes a debt of gratitude to the historians who have gone before, and I am no exception. George Walter Bell's meticulously researched books remain the benchmark by which all histories of the plague and fire are measured. I am also indebted to the recent works of Adrian Tinniswood, Neil Hanson, Stephen Porter and A. Lloyd and Dorothy C. Moote. Equally, J. D. Davies, J. R. Jones and Frank Fox have made invaluable contributions to our understanding of the Second Anglo-Dutch War and the late-seventeenth-century navy more generally. It is 2016, so gratitude is owed to the many marvellous men and women who have painstakingly assembled hundreds of thousands of state, parish and civic records online.

I am grateful to my closest friends Stephanie Blundell, Kimberley Gibbs, Jennie Kozlowski and Raseeta Williams for drawing me back into the present day and offering invaluable wine-fuelled distraction. Finally, I must acknowledge the huge debt I owe to my parents, David and Julie Ellis, my siblings, Simon, Christian, Hannah and Kathryn, and my grandparents, Harry and Heather Ellis and Maureen Davies. They have indulged my ego for (just over) three decades and their support and encouragement have never faltered.

Illustration Credits

© Alamy: 4 above right and 7 centre right/GL Archive, 5 above left/Ian G. Dagnall/National Portrait Gallery London, 7 above left/Heritage Image Partnership Ltd. © The British Library Board: 5 centre right/G.11599, 5 below left/598.e.1 frontispiece, 7 below/718.e.20.(9.). © Crossrail Ltd: 8 above right and centre left. Reproduced by kind permission of Steve Ellis of The *London* Shipwreck Trust: 8 below right. © National Maritime Museum, Greenwich, London: 1 below, 4 below, 6 below. © National Portrait Gallery, London: 3 above right. © National Portrait Gallery, London/Bridgeman Images: 1 above. © National Trust Photographic Library/Bridgeman Images: 3 above left and below. Warwick Castle, Warwickshire/Bridgeman Images: 4 above left. Wellcome Library: 2 above right and below. Yale Center for British Art, Bequest of Arthur D. Schlechter: 6 above.

Integrated maps: © The British Library Board: pp. 12–13/ Maps R.17.a.3, pp. 194–5/Maps K. Top.20.21, pp. 214–15/Maps Crace Port.2.54.

Notes

Prologue

1. For more about the origins of Punch see George Speaight, 'The Origin of Punch and Judy: A New Clue?', *Theatre Research International*, 20 (1995), pp. 200–6.

Chapter 1: The *London* Burns

1. Edward Chamberlayne, *The second part of the present state of England together with divers reflections upon the antient state thereof* (London, 1671), p.206.
2. John Milton, *Paradise Lost*, Book IX, lines 446.
3. Thomas Ellwood, *The history of the life of Thomas Ellwood: or an account of his birth, education, &c. with divers Observations on his Life and Manners when a Youth: and how he came to be convinced of the Truth; with his many Sufferings and Services for the same. – Also several other remarkable Passages and Occurrences. Written by his own hand. To which is added A supplement, by J. W.* (London, 1791), p.147.
4. John Gay, *Trivia* (London, 1716), p.13.
5. John Evelyn, *Fumifugium* (London, 1661), Preface.
6. Samuel Pepys, *The Diary of Samuel Pepys*, Vols 1–IX, ed. Robert Latham and William Matthews (HarperCollins, 1995), henceforth cited as Pepys's *Diary*, 1 February 1666.
7. John Graunt, *Natural and Political Observations Mentioned in a following Index, and made upon the Bills of Mortality* (London, 1676), p.55.
8. John Evelyn, *The Diary of John Evelyn*, Vol. II, ed. William Bray (M. Walter Dunne, 1901), henceforth cited as Evelyn's *Diary*, 9 February 1665; 1 July 1664.

9. Pepys's *Diary*, 20 February 1665.

10. Ibid., 11 August 1665.

11. 'Charles II – volume 114: March 1–15, 1665', in Mary Anne Everett Green (ed.), *Calendar of State Papers Domestic: Charles II, 1664–5* (London, 1864), p.244; Abbot Emerson Smith 'The Transportation of Convicts to the American Colonies in the Seventeenth Century', *American Historical Review*, 39.2 (1934): 232–49.

12. *Intelligencer Published for the Satisfaction and Information of the People* (London), Monday, 13 March 1665, Issue 20.

13. Ibid.

14. John Aubrey, *Letters Written by Several Eminent Persons in the Seventeenth and Eighteenth Centuries*, Vol. 2, Part 2 (1813), p.623.

15. Robert Hubert, *A catalogue of many natural rarities with great industry, cost, and thirty years travel in foraign countries / collected by Robert Hubert, alias Forges* (London, 1665); *Intelligencer*, Monday, 13 March 1665, Issue 20.

16. *Intelligencer*, Monday, 13 March 1665, Issue 20.

17. This figure is based on estimates by Restoration statistician John Graunt.

18. William Taswell, 'Autobiography and Anecdotes by William Taswell, D.D., sometime Rector of Newington, Surrey, Rector of Bermondsey and previously Student of Christ Church, Oxford. A.D. 1651–1682', *Camden Old Series*, 55 (1853), pp. 9–10.

19. Graunt, *Natural and Political Observations*, p.60.

20. Pepys's *Diary*, 13 May 1666.

21. In his diary entry dated 9 January 1664, Samuel Pepys writes how he was told by Elizabeth Howlett that 'Mrs Mitchell herself had a daughter before marriage, which is now near thirty years old, a thing I could not have believed.'

22. Kate Loveman, *Samuel Pepys and His Books: Reading, Newsgathering, and Sociability, 1660–1703* (Oxford University Press, 2015), p.170.

23. *Intelligencer*, Monday, 13 March 1665, Issue 20.

24. Ibid., Monday, 6 March 1665, Issue 19.

25. Anonymous, *The English and Dutch affairs Displayed to the Life both in matters of warr, state, and merchandize, how far the English engaged in their defence against the most potent monarchy of Spain, and how ill the Dutch have since requited the English for their extraordinary favours, not onely in the time of Queen Elizabeth their protector and defendress, but also in the time of King James, by their bloody massacree of them at Amboyna, their ingratitude to King Charles the First of glorious memory, and the true state of affairs as they now stand in the reign of our royal soveraign King Charles the Second / by a true*

lover and asserter of his countries honour (London: Printed by Thomas Mabb for Edward Thomas, 1664).

26. *Poor Robins character of a Dutch-man* (London, 1672), cited in Steve Pincus, 'From butterboxes to wooden shoes: the shift in English popular sentiment from anti-Dutch to anti-French in the 1670s', *Historical Journal*, 38 (1995), p.337.

27. Anonymous, *The Dutch Boare Dissected, or a Description of Hogg-Land. A Dutch man is a Lusty, Fat, two Legged Cheese-Worm: A Creature, that is so addicted to Eating Butter, Drinking fat Drink, and sliding, that all the World knows him for a slippery Fellow, an Hollander is not an High-lander, but a Low-lander; for he loves to be down in the dirt, and boar-like, to wallow therein* (London, 1665).

28. For more on this see Helmer J. Helmers, *The Royalist Republic*, (Cambridge University Press, 2015), p.203.

29. *Nederlandtsche nyp-tang* (1652), cited in ibid., p.204.

30. Steve Pincus, 'Popery, Trade and Universal Monarchy: The Ideological Context of the Outbreak of the Second Anglo-Dutch War', *English Historical Review*, Vol. 107, No. 422 (Oxford University Press, 1992), pp. 5–9.

31. For further details of Holmes's use of the spring-based pendulum watch see 5 March, *Philosophical Transactions*, 1665, Vol. 1, Nos 1–22, pp. 13–15. For quote about Holmes's personality see Pepys's *Diary*, 1 September 1661.

32. 6 March 1665, 'Venice: March 1665', in Allen B. Hinds (ed.), *Calendar of State Papers Relating to English Affairs in the Archives of Venice*, Vol. 34, 1664–1666 (London, 1933), pp. 81–93.

33. *Philosophical Transactions*, Vol. 1, pp. 190–1

34. 'Charles II – volume 113: February 19–28, 1665', in Everett Green (ed.), *Calendar of State Papers, 1664–5*, p.216.

35. The bill was printed by Richard Hodgkinson, living in Thames Street over against Baynard's Castle, 1664.

36. Charles Trollope has posed this theory based on archaeological evidence at the site. Of the five cannons retrieved from the sea, three were filled with cartridges; one was half-full and the other empty. He argues that it was when filling the fourth cannon that the explosion occurred. The wreck is split in two directly above the ship's hold, where the gunpowder was kept.

37. State Papers 29/114 f.147.

38. Pepys's *Diary*, 8 March 1665.

39. State Papers 29/114 f.132

40. State Papers 29/114 f.147

41. Pepys's *Diary*, 8 March 1665.
42. Ibid.
43. Evelyn's *Diary*, 9 March 1665.
44. State Papers 29/114 f.155
45. Pepys's *Diary*, 11 March 1665.
46. Evelyn's *Diary*, 16 May 1665.
47. Thomas Greene, *A Lamentation Taken up for London* (London, 1665), p.2.

Chapter 2: Outbreak

1. Roy Booth (ed.), *The Collected Poems of John Donne* (Wordsworth Poetry Library, 2002), p.27.
2. There is no unanimous consensus as to the biological nature of seventeenth-century plague. While DNA tests have revealed the presence of *Yersinia pestis* in skeletons from the period across Europe, it has been argued that the symptoms of seventeenth-century plague do not tally with modern bubonic plague. Alternative theories have ranged from it being Ebola (Susan Scott and Christopher Duncan, 2001), anthrax (Graham Twigg, 1984; John Findlay D. Shrewsbury, 1970), typhus or another unknown and extinct disease (Samuel K. Cohn, 2002).

    Research is ongoing, but this author takes the mainstream view that the Great Plague of 1665 was a virulent strain of bubonic plague with rat fleas as the primary vector. DNA evidence proves that *Yersinia pestis* was present during the period. The symptoms of modern bubonic plague do in fact tally with the symptoms of early modern bubonic plague. The way in which some cases of plague spread suggests a level of human to human transmission. Whether this was through pneumonic plague (evidence suggests that this was also present) or another vector is yet to be conclusively proven. Recent studies have demonstrated that human body lice can be efficient vectors of the disease and may have played a role, along with human fleas (*P. irritans*), in early modern epidemics.

    See S. Haensch, R. Bianucci, M. Signoli et al., 'Distinct Clones of *Yersinia pestis* Caused the Black Death', *PLOS Pathogens*, 7 October 2010; S. Ayyadurai, F. Sebbane, D. Raoult, M. Drancourt, 'Body Lice, *Yersinia pestis Orientalis*, and Black Death', *Emerging Infectious Diseases*, 2010;16 (5): 892–3; and Lars Walløe, 'Medieval and Modern Bubonic Plague: Some Clinical Continuities', *Medical History*, Supplement 27

(2008): 59–73. For a lively overview see John Kelly, *The Great Mortality: An Intimate History of the Black Death, the Most Devastating Plague of All Time* (HarperCollins, 2006).

3. For full details on the biology see B. Joseph Hinnebusch, Amy E. Rudolph, Peter Cherepanov et al., 'Role of Yersinia Murine Toxin in Survival of Yersinia Pestis in the Midgut of the Flea Vector', in *Science* (26 April 2002), Vol. 296, Issue 5568, pp. 733–5.

4. Nathaniel Hodges, *Loimologia or, an Historical Account of the Plague in London in 1665: With precautionary Directions against the like Contagion* (London, 1721), p.3.

5. See J. A. I. Champion (ed.), 'London's Dreaded Visitation: The Social Geography of the Great Plague in 1665', *Historical Geography Research Series* (1995).

6. Hodges, *Loimologia*, p.3.

7. In 1623, 897 houses were recorded in the area and by the end of the seventeenth century this had increased to 2,000.

8. Hodges, *Loimologia*, p.3.

9. Pepys's *Diary*, 8 May 1663.

10. George W. Stone, William Van Lennep, Emmett L. Avery, Arthur H. Scouten, Charles B. Hogan (eds), *The London Stage, Part I: 1660–1700* (Southern Illinois University Press, 1965), p.87.

11. 8 February 1667, 'Charles II – volume 191: February 6–14, 1667', in Mary Anne Everett Green (ed.), *Calendar of State Papers Domestic: Charles II, 1666–7* (London, 1864), p.502.

12. This victim was one 'Margarit Daughter of Dr. John Ponteus'; cited in A. Lloyd Moote and Dorothy C Moote, *The Great Plague: The Story of London's Most Deadly Year* (John Hopkins University Press, 2004), p.52.

13. *Intelligencer*, Monday, 17 April 1665, Issue 29.

14. Case discussed at court at Whitehall in the presence of Charles II, 28 April 1665, 1665 Jan. 2–1666 Apr. 27, Vol. 5, Privy Council Register 2/58.

15. Ibid.

16. Pepys's *Diary*, 28 April 1665.

17. Ibid., 30 April 1665.

18. 11 April 1665. 'Charles II – volume 117: April 1–11, 1665', in Everett Green (ed.), *Calendar of State Papers 1664–5*, pp. 102–3.

19. *Philosophical Transactions*, Vol. 1, p.94.

20. Robert Hooke, *Micrographia: or Some Physiological Descriptions of Minute Bodies Made by Magnifying Glasses with Observations and Inquiries Thereupon* (London, 1665), Schem. 34.

21. 'An Account of Micrographia, or the Philosophical Descriptions of Minute Bodies, Made by Magnifying Glasses', *Philosophical Transactions*, Vol. 1, pp. 27–32.

22. Pepys's *Diary*, 21 January 1665.

23. Graunt, *Natural and Political Observations*, Preface.

24. Pepys's *Diary*, 15 May 1665.

25. Ibid., 3 June 1665.

26. John Dryden, *An Essay of Dramatick Poesie* (London, 1668), p.1.

27. Evelyn's *Diary*, 3 June 1665.

28. George DeForest Lord (ed.), *Anthology of Poems of State Affairs: Augustan Satirical Verse 1660–1714* (Yale University Press, 1975), p.38.

29. Evelyn's *Diary*, 8 June 1665.

30. Pepys's *Diary*, 3 June 1665.

31. *Intelligencer*, Monday, 12 June 1665, Issue 45.

32. Taswell, 'Autobiography', pp. 9–10.

33. Pepys's *Diary*, 22 January 1666.

34. Thomas Vincent, *God's Terrible Voice in the City* (London, 1667), p.35.

35. J. R. Wardale, *Clare College Letters and Documents* (Macmillan and Bowes, 1903), p.51.

36. For description of New Churchyard see Vanessa Harding, 'Burial of the Plague Dead in Early Modern London', in J. A. I. Champion (ed.), *Epidemic Disease in London, Centre for Metropolitan History Working Papers Series*, No. 1, 1993, pp. 53–64. See Champion, 'London's Dreaded Visitation', pp. 56–7.

37. The Ramseys are an interesting family because it is traditionally thought that Mary was the first plague case in the area. Although her sister's cause of death is not observed in the records, it would be an odd coincidence if she had died of anything other than plague at this time.

38. London Metropolitan Archives, Bridewell Chapel, Bishops' transcripts of baptisms, marriages and burials, 1665–1666, DL/A/E/192/ MS10952A.

39. It is possible that Mary Godfrey's father was Thomas Godfrey who, according to Hearth Tax records, lived a stone's throw from the New Churchyard in 'Porters Alley'. St Giles without Cripplegate parish records list the burial of a 'Mary Godfrey' twice: the first on 31 August 1665 and the second on 2 September 1665. This could be a case of human error when recording deaths or a remarkable coincidence. Both entries have the father as listed as Thomas Godfrey, with the former citing him as a husbandman. Parish registers: London Metropolitan

Archives, St Giles Cripplegate, Composite register, 1663–1667, P69/ GIS/A/002/MS06419, Item 006 and Hearth Tax records: 'Hearth Tax: City of London 1666, St Giles (without) Cripplegate, Golding Lane West', in *London Hearth Tax: City of London and Middlesex, 1666* (Centre for Metropolitan History, 2011).

40. Burial register, see London Metropolitan Archives, St Olave Hart Street, Bishops' transcripts of baptisms, marriages and burials, 1665–1666, P69/OLA1/A/002/MS28869, p.30; Hearth Tax reference, see 'Hearth Tax: City of London 1666, St Olave Hart Street', in *London Hearth Tax*.

41. Cynthia Wall (ed.), *Daniel Defoe: A Journal of a Plague Year*, (Penguin, 2003), p.58.

42. Neil Cummins, Morgan Kelly and Cormac Ó Gráda, 'Living standards and plague in London, 1560–1665', *CAGE Online Working Paper Series* (Department of Economics, University of Warwick, 2013), pp. 9–10.

43. Graunt, *Natural and Political Observations*, p.13.

44. John Bell, *London's remembrancer, or, A true accompt of every particular weeks christnings and mortality in all the years of pestilence within the cognizance of the bills of mortality, being xviii years* (London, 1665), pp. 2–3.

45. 14 August 1665, 'Charles II – volume 129: August 11–22, 1665', in Everett Green (ed.), *Calendar of State Papers 1664–5*, pp. 516–17.

46. 'Venice: August 1665', in Hinds (ed.), *Calendar of State Papers . . . Venice*, pp. 172–86.

47. Pepys's *Diary*, 12 August 1665.

48. Joseph Frank Payne (ed.), *Loimographia an Account of the Great Plague of London in the Year 1665 by William Boghurst an Apothecary* (London, 1894), p.29.

49. Frances Parthenope Verney and Margaret M. Verney (eds), *Memoirs of the Verney Family from the Restoration to the Revolution 1660 to 1696: Compiled from the Letters and Illustrated by the Portraits at Claydon House*, Vol. IV, (London, 1899), p.118.

50. Hodges, *Loimologia*, p.22.

51. John Bell, *London's remembrancer*, p.17.

52. Hodges, *Loimologia*, pp. 8–9.

53. Anonymous, *Famous and effectual medicine to cure the plague* (London, 1670).

54. Hodges, *Loimologia*, p.48.

55. Ibid., p.128.

56. Ibid., p.13.

57. Ibid., p.181.

58. Vincent, *God's Terrible Voice*, p.38.

59. William Munk, *The Roll of the Royal College of Physicians in London*, Vol. 1, 1518–1700 (London, 1878), p.334.
60. Hodges, *Loimologia*, p.15.
61. Pepys's *Diary*, 12 February 1666.
62. Ibid., 16 February 1666.
63. Ibid., 3 September 1666.
64. Taswell, 'Autobiography', pp. 9–10.
65. Thomas Clarke, *Meditations in my confinement, when my house was visited with the sickness in April, May and June, 1666, in which time I buried two children, and had three more of my family sick* (London, 1666), p.9.
66. Ibid., p.10.
67. Payne (ed.), *Loimographia*, p.57.
68. Hodges, *Loimologia*, p.11.
69. Vincent, *God's Terrible Voice*, pp. 44–8.
70. Pepys's *Diary*, 14 September 1665.

Chapter 3: The Turning Tide

1. Lord (ed.), *Anthology of Poems of State Affairs*, p.41.
2. The practice of giving naval opportunity to well-bred young men developed significantly during the Dutch Wars. See J. D. Davies, *Gentlemen and Tarpaulins: The Officers and Men of the Restoration Navy* (Clarendon Press, 1991).
3. Pepys's *Diary*, 18 September 1665.
4. J. R. Jones, *The Anglo-Dutch Wars of the Seventeenth Century* (Longman, 1996), p.23.
5. Ibid., p.161.
6. R. C. Anderson, (ed.), *The Journals of Sir Thomas Allin, 1660–1678*, Vol. 1 (Navy Records Society, 1929), p.240.
7. R. C. Anderson (ed.), *The Journal of Edward Montagu, First Earl of Sandwich, Admiral and General at Sea, 1659–1665* (Navy Records Society, 1929), p.243.
8. Ibid., p.244.
9. Ibid., p.247.
10. Jones, *The Anglo-Dutch Wars*, p.17.
11. Dagomar Degroot, '"Never such weather known in these seas": Climatic Fluctuations and the Anglo-Dutch Wars of the Seventeenth Century, 1652–1674', *Environment and History*, Vol. 20, No. 2, May 2014, pp. 239–73.

12. Pepys's *Diary*, 20 May 1664.

13. J. D. Davies, *Pepys's Navy: Ship, Men and Warfare, 1649–1689* (Seaforth Publishing, 2008), p.35.

14. Treglown (ed.), *The Letters of John Wilmot*, pp. 46–9.

15. Ibid., p.43.

16. Anderson (ed.), *Journal of Edward Montagu*, p.252.

17. Treglown (ed.), *The Letters of John Wilmot*, p.43.

18. This is just one example of many observations recorded by Isaac Newton in his notebook while studying for his BA at Cambridge from 1661 to 1665. It is found within the Portsmouth Collection at Cambridge University Library, *Certain Philosophical Questions*, MS Add.3996, folio 109r.

19. *Certain Philosophical Questions*, MS Add.3996, folio 3r.

20. Payne (ed.), *Loimographia*, p.54.

21. Walter George Bell, *The Great Plague in London* (Folio Society, 2001), p.86.

22. Ibid.

23. Clarke, *Meditations*, p.6.

24. 4 August 1665, 'Charles II – volume 129: August 11–22, 1665', in Everett Green (ed.), *Calendar of State Papers 1664–5*, p.502.

25. 7 August 1665, ibid., p.506.

26. 15 August 1665, ibid., pp. 517–19.

27. Walter George Bell, *The Great Plague*, p.86.

28. Ibid., pp. 87–8.

29. Ibid., p.88.

30. M. Bell, '"Her usual practices": The later career of Elizabeth Calvert, 1664–75', *Publishing History* (1994), 35, 5.

31. Margaret Cavendish, *Philosophical Letters: or, Modest Reflections Upon Some Opinions in Natural Philosophy Maintained by Several Famous and Learned Authors of this Age, Expressed by Noble Letters* (London, 1664).

32. Evelyn's *Diary*, 30 May 1667.

33. Harleian MS 6828, fols. 510–23, British Library.

34. Evelyn's *Diary*, 27 April 1667.

35. Ibid., 18 April 1667.

36. Pepys's *Diary*, 11 April 1667 (NB: this could also be the 'Queen of Sweden', in either case, the meaning is retained).

37. State Papers 29/132 f.97

38. Ellwood, *The history of the life of Thomas Ellwood*, p.143.

39. Ibid., p.146.

40. John Milton, *The readie and easie vvay to establish a free commonwealth and*

the excellence therof compar'd with the inconveniences and dangers of readmitting kingship in this nation (London, 1660), p.23.

41. Ellwood, *The history of the life of Thomas Ellwood*, pp. 143–8.
42. Treglown (ed.), *The Letters of John Wilmot*, pp. 46–9; Anderson (ed.), *Journal of Edward Montagu*, p.262.
43. Anderson (ed.), *Journal of Edward Montagu*, p.262.
44. T. H. Lister, *Life and administration of Edward first Earl of Clarendon; with Original Correspondence and Authentic Papers Never Before Published*, Vol. III (London, 1837), pp. 393–5.
45. Treglown (ed.), *The Letters of John Wilmot*, pp. 43–5.
46. Lister, *Life and administration*, pp. 394–5.
47. Ibid.
48. State Papers 29/129 f.58
49. 25 August 1665, Everett Green (ed.), *Calendar of State Papers 1664–5*, p.532.
50. State Papers 29/132 f.127
51. 12 August 1665, Everett Green (ed.), *Calendar of State Papers 1664–5*, pp. 514–15.
52. 10 September 1665, Ibid., pp. 557–8.
53. Pepys's *Diary*, 9 September 1665.
54. 17 August 1665, Everett Green (ed.), *Calendar of State Papers 1664–5*, pp. 520–2.
55. Jones, *The Anglo-Dutch Wars*, p.57.
56. Ibid., p.23.
57. Evelyn's *Diary*, 25 September 1665.
58. Pepys's *Diary*, 22 November 1665.
59. J. J. Cartwright (ed.), *Memoirs and Travels of Sir John Reresby* (London, 1904) p.145.
60. Pepys *Diary*, 13 July 1663.
61. Antonia Fraser, *Charles II* (Weidenfeld & Nicolson, 1979), p.311.
62. Pepys's *Diary*, 17 November 1665.
63. 'The second parliament of Charles II: Sixth session (Oxford) – begins 9/10/1665', in *The History and Proceedings of the House of Commons*, Vol. I, 1660–1680 (London, 1742), pp. 85–92.
64. Ibid.
65. *Newes Published for Satisfaction and Information of the People* (London, England), Thursday, 24 August 1665, Issue 65.
66. State Papers 29/129 f.81.
67. Richard Ward (ed.), *The Manuscripts of his Grace the Duke of Portland preserved at Welbeck Abbey*, Vol. III (London, 1894), p.293.

68. Andrew Clark (ed.), *The Life and Times of Anthony Wood, antiquary, of Oxford, 1632–1695, described by Himself* (Oxford, 1891), p.68.
69. Ibid.
70. Ward (ed.), *The Manuscripts of his Grace the Duke of Portland*, p.296. Prostitutes were often subjected to the 'ducking stool' a device in which a victim would seat, strapped in by an iron bar, and then be 'ducked' or submerged in a pool of water. It was designed to humiliate the victim.
71. For description of Ralph Montagu see State Papers 29/131 f.73. For remarks about the Duchess of York and Henry Sidney see Pepys's *Diary*, 9 January 1666.
72. Pepys's *Diary*, 22 November 1665.
73. Benedict de Spinoza (trans. R. H. M. Elwes), *On the Improvement of the Understanding / The Ethics / Correspondence* (Dover Publications, 1955), p.294.

Chapter 4: The Fateful Year

1. Vincent, *God's Terrible Voice*, p.153.
2. London, England, Baptisms, Marriages and Burials, 1538–1812, City of London, St Botolph's Church, Aldgate, 1653–1675, f.85. www.ancestry.com
3. Ibid., p.81.
4. Pepys's *Diary*, 5 January 1666.
5. *Oxford Gazette*, Issue 16, 8 January 1666.
6. Pepys's *Diary*, 30 January 1666.
7. Ruth Norrington (ed.), *My Dearest Minette: The Letters Between Charles II and His Sister Henrietta, Duchesse D'Orléans* (Peter Owen, 1996), p.130.
8. Vincent, *God's Terrible Voice*, p.54.
9. John Bell, *London's remembrancer*, p.15.
10. Ibid., p.16.
11. E. Cotes, *London's dreadful visitation, or, A collection of all the bills of mortality for this present year* (London, 1665), p.2.
12. Ibid., p.3.
13. Ellwood, *The history of the life of Thomas Ellwood*, pp. 148–9.
14. Vincent, *God's Terrible Voice*, p.53.
15. Pepys's *Diary*, 23 March 1666.
16. The marriage took place on 28 February 1666. See Sir George John Armytage, *Allegations for marriage licences: issued by the Vicar-General of the Archbishop of Canterbury, 1660 to 1668* (London, 1892), pp. 165–6.

17. According to the 1662 Hearth Tax records where her husband David Maxwell is listed as being the owner of the property.

18. Margaret Cavendish, *The description of a new world, called the blazing world* (London, 1666), To the Reader, p.4.

19. 'Hearth Tax: City of London 1666, St Margaret New Fish Street' in *London Hearth Tax*.

20. They were wed on 9 July 1637 at the parish church of St Helen Bishopsgate. London Metropolitan Archives, St Helen Bishopgate, Composite register: baptisms 1598–1654, marriages 1606–1653, burials 1598–1630, P69/HEL/A/002/MS06831, Item 001.

21. London Metropolitan Archives, St Mary, Whitechapel, Register of burials, June 1658–September 1670, P93/MRY1/059.

22. Pepys's *Diary*, 5 January 1666.

23. Ibid., 28 January 1666.

24. Evelyn's *Diary*, 29 January 1666.

25. Pepys's *Diary*, 29 January 1666.

26. Evelyn's *Diary*, 26 May 1703.

27. Pepys's *Diary*, 29 January 1666.

28. Letter dated 22 February 1666 and written by William Coventry on behalf of James, Duke of York in J. R. Powell and E. K. Timings (eds), *The Rupert and Monck Letter Book 1666: Together with Supporting Documents* (Navy Records Society, 1969), p.15.

29. State Papers 29/148 f.51

30. Philip E. Jones (ed.), *The Fire Court: Calendar to the Judgments and Decrees*, Vol. II (William Clowes & Sons, 1966), p.255.

31. John Childs, 'The Sales of Government Gazettes during the Exclusion Crisis, 1678–81', *English Historical Review*, Vol. 102, No. 402 (January 1987), p.104.

32. 'Charles II – volume 165: July 27–31, 1666', in Mary Anne Everett Green (ed.), *Calendar of State Papers Domestic: Charles II, 1665–6* (London, 1864), pp. 584–8.

33. State Papers 29/147 f.19

34. *London Gazette*, 1 February 1666–5 February 1666, Issue 24.

35. Pepys's *Diary*, 31 January 1666.

36. State Papers 29/147 f.42.

37. Pepys's *Diary*, 19 February 1666.

38. Ibid.

39. Henry Oldenburg (ed. and trans. A. Rupert Hall and Marie Boas Hall), *The Correspondence of Henry Oldenburg*, Vol. III, 1666–1667 (University of Wisconsin Press, 1966), pp. 57–60.

40. Pepys's *Diary*, 19 February 1666.

41. State Papers 29/151 f.44. News letter, written by Henry Muddiman.

42. Michael McKeon, 'Sabbatai Sevi in England', *AJS Review*, Vol. 2 (April 1977), pp. 131–69.

43. Pepys's *Diary*, 28 February 1666.

44. Anonymous, 'A New Letter Concerning the Jewes' [written by Serrarius], (London, 1666), pp. 1–5.

45. Evelyn's *Diary*, 18 October 1666.

46. John Sheffield, *The Works of John Sheffield, Earl of Mulgrave and the Duke of Buckingham*, Vol. II (London, 1723), p.54.

47. George Etherege, *Man of Mode* (London, 1676), p.87.

48. David M. Vieth (ed.), *The Complete Poems of John Wilmot Earl of Rochester* (Yale University Press, 2002), p.60.

49. Pepys's *Diary*, 25 February 1666.

50. Treglown (ed.), *The Letters of John Wilmot*, p.198.

51. Pepys's *Diary*, 23 February 1668.

52. Treglown (ed.), *The Letters of John Wilmot*, p.198.

53. Pepys's *Diary*, 21 April 1666.

54. Ibid., 18 April 1666.

55. 'Volume 71: November 8–December 31, 1700', in Joseph Redington (ed.), *Calendar of Treasury Papers, Vol. 2, 1697–1702* (London, 1871), pp. 437–8.

56. Pepys's *Diary*, 26 March 1666.

57. Ibid., 25 February 1667.

58. Alan MacFarlane (ed.), *The Diary of Ralph Josselin, 1616–1683* (Oxford University Press, 1991), 5 April 1666. The fast day is noted also by Pepys and Evelyn.

59. Evelyn's *Diary*, 5 April 1666.

60. Pepys's *Diary*, 8 April 1666.

61. Ibid., 22 April 1666.

62. Powell and Timings (eds), *The Rupert and Monck Letter Book*, p.31.

63. Ibid., p.13.

64. Ibid., p.37.

65. *London Gazette*, 5 April 1666–9 April 1666, Issue 42.

66. Nathaniel Hodges's letter dated 8 May 1666 is included within *An account of the first rise, progress, symptoms and cure of the plague: being the substance of a letter from Dr Hodges to a person of quality* (London, 1721), p.35

67. Nathaniel Hodges, *Vindiciae medicinae et medicorum: an Apology for the Profession and Professors of Physic* (London, 1666), p.5

68. Powell and Timings (eds), *The Rupert and Monck Letter Book*, pp. 4–5.

69. Ibid., p.13.
70. Evelyn's *Diary*, 8 May 1666.

Chapter 5: The Red Sea

1. John Dryden, *Annus Mirabilis: The Year of Wonders, 1666* (London, 1667).
2. Anderson (ed.), *Journals of Sir Thomas Allin*, p.269.
3. 'Miscarriages of the War'. 'House of Commons Journal, Volume 9: 31 October 1667', in *Journal of the House of Commons, Volume 9, 1667–1687* (London, 1802), pp. 10–14.
4. 'A true narrative of the engagement between His Majesty's fleet and that of Holland, begun June 1st, 1666, at 2 o'clock afternoon, and continuing till the 6th, at 10 o'clock at night', State Papers 29/158 f.3.
5. 'Miscarriages of the War' in *Journal of the House of Commons*, pp. 10–14.
6. 'Venice: June 1666, 16–30', in Hinds (ed.), *Calendar of State Papers . . . Venice*, p.6.
7. Ibid., p.16.
8. Letter from William Clarke to Joseph Williamson, State Papers SP 29/157 f.79.
9. 'Miscarriages of the War' in *Journal of the House of Commons*, pp. 10–14.
10. Samuel Pepys quoting reports given to William Penn after the event, Pepys's *Diary*, 4 July 1666.
11. Ibid., 11 June 1666.
12. From a conversation Pepys had with Halsall after the battle. Pepys's *Diary*, 24 June 1666.
13. Letter from William Clarke to Joseph Williamson, State Papers 29/157 f.79.
14. 'A true narrative of the engagement between His Majesty's fleet and that of Holland . . .', State Papers 29/158 f.3
15. Monck led with the Red Squadron from the *Royal Charles*, supported by Vice Admiral Joseph Jordan on the *Royal Oak* and newly promoted Rear Admiral Robert Holmes on the *Defiance*; followed by the White Squadron, led by Admiral George Ayscue on the *Prince*, Vice Admiral Sir William Berkeley on the *Swiftsure* and Rear Admiral Captain John Harman on the *Henry*; the Blue Squadron took the rear, led by Admiral Jeremiah Smith, Vice Admiral Thomas Teddeman and newly promoted Rear Admiral Captain Richard Utber on the *Rupert*. See

letter from William Clarke to Joseph Williamson, State Papers 29/157 f.79.

16. The Dutch artist Willem van de Velde was on one of the Dutch ships during the battle and sketched what he saw, turning his sketches into paintings on his return. From these paintings we get a sense of the scenes as the fleets engaged.

17. 'A true narrative of the engagement between His Majesty's fleet and that of Holland . . .', State Papers 29/158 f.3.

18. 'Venice: June 1666, 16–30', in Hinds (ed.), *Calendar of State Papers . . . Venice*, p.15.

19. Davies, *Pepys's Navy*, pp. 39–40.

20. 'A true narrative of the engagement between His Majesty's fleet and that of Holland . . .', State Papers 29/158 f.3

21. Anonymous pamphlet translated from Dutch, 'A Relation of the Passages in the Battel at Sea, Between the Fleet of England and the United Neitherlands: Collected according to the charge & order of the Lords States General' (24/14 June, 1666), p.5.

22. Anderson (ed.), *Journals of Sir Thomas Allin*, p.269.

23. Pepys's *Diary*, 24 June 1666. Reiterated in 'Miscarriages of the War' in *Journal of the House of Commons*, pp. 10–14.

24. Pepys's *Diary*, 3 June 1666.

25. Anderson (ed.), *Journals of Sir Thomas Allin*, p.269.

26. State Papers 29/158 f.56.

27. 4 June 1666. "Charles II – volume 158: June 1–14, 1666', in Everett Green (ed.), *Calendar of State Papers 1665–6*, pp. 428–9.

28. Ibid.

29. State Papers 29/158 f.88

30. Ibid.

31. 'Venice: June 1666, 16–30', in Hinds (ed.), *Calendar of State Papers . . . Venice*, p.15.

32. State Papers 29/158 f.54

33. Evelyn's *Diary*, 24 March 1672.

34. Pepys's *Diary*, 4 June 1666.

35. Ibid., 3 June 1666.

36. Ibid.; State Papers, 3 June, William Coventry to Lord Arlington.

37. Evelyn's *Diary*, 9 February 1665.

38. Vieth (ed.), *The Complete Poems of John Wilmot*, p.40.

39. Evelyn's *Diary*, 1 June 1666.

40. Pepys's *Diary*, 2 June 1666.

41. Though usually a Guinea ship, the *Great Gift*, or the *Gift*, was in the

vicinity during this time, recorded as being fitted at Sheerness on 18 June, ready to rejoin the fleet.

42. State Papers 29/158 f.56.
43. Ibid.
44. *London Gazette*, 4 June 1666–7 June 1666, Issue 59.
45. State Papers 29/158 f.54.
46. Narrative of the engagement between the English and Dutch fleets. Sent from the *Royal Charles*, 8 June 1666, State Papers 29/158 f.118
47. Powell and Timings (eds), *The Rupert and Monck Letter Book*, p.63.
48. *London Gazette*, 4 June 1666–7 June 1666, Issue 59.
49. 'Venice: June 1666, 16–30', in Hinds (ed.), *Calendar of State Papers . . . Venice*, p.15.
50. Thomas Clifford to Lord Arlington, 5 June 1666, State Papers 29/158 f.88.
51. 4 June 1666, State Papers 29/158 f.54
52. A true narrative of the engagement between His Majesty's fleet and that of Holland . . .', State Papers 29/158 f.56.
53. Ibid.
54. Ibid.
55. Pepys's *Diary*, 3 June 1666.
56. Ibid.
57. Narrative of the engagement between the English and Dutch fleets, State Papers 29/158 f.118.
58. Thomas Clifford to Lord Arlington, 5 June 1666, State Papers 29/158 f.88.
59. Narrative of the engagement between the English and Dutch fleets. State Papers 29/158 f.118.
60. Dryden, *Annus Mirabilis*, lines 417–21.
61. 'Miscarriages of the War' in *Journal of the House of Commons*, pp. 10–14.
62. Thomas Clifford to Lord Arlington, 5 June 1666, State Papers 29/158 f.88.
63. Ibid.
64. Ibid.
65. 'A Relation of the Passages in the Battel at Sea . . .', p.12.
66. 'A true narrative of the engagement between His Majesty's fleet and that of Holland . . .', State Papers 29/158 f.56.
67. Pepys's *Diary*, 4 June 1666.
68. Ibid.
69. 'A true narrative of the engagement between His Majesty's fleet and that of Holland . . .', State Papers 29/158 f.56.

70. Thomas Clifford to Lord Arlington, 5 June 1666, State Papers 29/158 f.88.

71. Narrative of the engagement between the English and Dutch fleets, State Papers 29/158 f.118.

72. 'Venice: June 1666, 16–30', in Hinds (ed.), *Calendar of State Papers . . . Venice*, p.1.

73. Narrative of the engagement between the English and Dutch fleets, State Papers 29/158 f.118.

74. 'Venice: June 1666, 16–30', in Hinds (ed.), *Calendar of State Papers . . . Venice*, p.15.

75. Thomas Clifford to Lord Arlington, 5 June 1666, State Papers 29/158 f.88.

Chapter 6: Fantastic Fortune

1. Aphra Behn, *The Rover, or, The Banish't Cavaliers* (London, 1677), p.49.

2. June 6 1666, 'Charles II – volume 158: June 1–14, 1666', in Everett Green (ed.), *Calendar of State Papers 1665–6*, p.430.

3. Pepys's *Diary*, 6 June 1666.

4. Evelyn's *Diary*, 6 June 1666.

5. Pepys's *Diary*, 7 June 1666.

6. Ibid., 24 June 1666.

7. Ibid., 8 June 1666.

8. *London Gazette*, 11 June 1666–14 June 1666, Issue 61.

9. 'Venice: June 1666, 16–30', in Hinds (ed.), *Calendar of State Papers . . . Venice*, p.15.

10. Ibid.

11. Ibid.

12. *London Gazette*, 7 June 1666–11 June 1666, Issue 60.

13. 'Venice: June 1666, 16–30', in Hinds (ed.), *Calendar of State Papers . . . Venice*, p.20.

14. 'A Relation of the Passages in the Battel at Sea . . .', p.16.

15. Pepys's *Diary*, 10 July 1666.

16. Evelyn's *Diary*, 18 June 1666.

17. 17 July 1666, 'Charles II – volume 163: July 15–20, 1666', in Everett Green (ed.), *Calendar of State Papers 1665–6*, p.547.

18. Powell and Timings (eds), *The Rupert and Monck Letter Book*, p.62.

19. 'Miscarriages of the War in *Journal of the House of Commons*, pp. 10–14;

letter from Monck and Rupert to Lord Arlington, dated June 24 1666, 23 June 1666. 'Charles II – volume 159: June 15–25, 1666', in Everett Green (ed.), *Calendar of State Papers 1665–6*, p.455.

20. 23 June 1666, 'Charles II – volume 159: June 15–25, 1666', in Everett Green (ed.), *Calendar of State Papers 1665–6*, pp. 453–4.

21. Ibid.

22. Pepys's *Diary*, 2 July 1666.

23. Ward (ed.), *The Manuscripts of his Grace the Duke of Portland*, p.297.

24. 9 July 1666, 'Charles II – volume 162: July 8–14, 1666' in Everett Green (ed.), *Calendar of State Papers 1665–6*, p.512.

25. 23 June 1666. 'Charles II – volume 159: June 15–25, 1666', in Everett Green (ed.), *Calendar of State Papers 1665–6*, p.449.

26. 1 July 1666. 'Charles II – volume 161: July 1–7, 1666', in Everett Green (ed.), *Calendar of State Papers 1665–6*, pp. 485–6.

27. 30 June 1666. 'Charles II – volume 160: June 26–30, 1666', in Everett Green (ed.), *Calendar of State Papers 1665–6*, p.477.

28. 9 July 1666. 'Charles II – volume 162: July 8–14, 1666' in Everett Green (ed.), *Calendar of State Papers 1665–6*, pp. 512–16.

29. State Papers 29/162 f.23.

30. Pepys's *Diary*, 22 July; and the *London Gazette* confirms as much.

31. Gilbert Burnet, *Some Passages of the Life and Death of the Right Honourable John, Earl of Rochester: Who Died the 26th of July 1680: Written by His Own Direction on His Death-Bed* (London, 1875), p.10.

32. Ibid., p.4.

33. 3 July 1666, 'Charles II – volume 161: July 1-7, 1666', in Everett Green (ed.), *Calendar of State Papers 1665–6*, pp. 493–7.

34. State Papers 29/163 f.174.

35. Ibid.

36. Pepys's *Diary*, 27 July 1666.

37. Burnet, *Life and Death of . . . John, Earl of Rochester*, p.6.

38. 27 July 1666, Sir Thomas Allin to Williamson; 27 July, Sir Thomas Clifford to Lord Arlington. 'Charles II – volume 165: July 27–31, 1666', in Everett Green (ed.), *Calendar of State Papers 1665–6*, pp. 579–80.

39. 27 July 1666, Sir Thomas Clifford to Lord Arlington. 'Charles II – volume 165: July 27–31, 1666', in Everett Green (ed.), *Calendar of State Papers 1665–6*, p.580.

40. *Intelligencer*, Monday, 13 March 1665, Issue 20.

41. 11 July 1666, Wednesday noon, *Royal Charles*, Sir Thomas Clifford to Lord Arlington; 'Charles II – volume 162: July 8–14, 1666', in Everett Green (ed.), *Calendar of State Papers 1665–6*, pp. 523–4.

42. Ibid.

43. For Vandermarsh see State Papers 29/163 f.26; for Mrs D'Ecluse and Jacomyna see 17 July 1666 (Mrs D'Ecluse made a request to travel to Dort just before the prisoner ship left England), 'Charles II – volume 163: July 15–20, 1666', in Everett Green (ed.), *Calendar of State Papers 1665–6*, p.544.

44. Behn's most recent biographer, Janet Todd, has commendably attempted to trace the young Aphra, making a convincing case for her to have been one 'Eaffrey Johnson' who was born in December 1640 to Bartholomew and Elizabeth Johnson: see Janet Todd, *The Secret Life of Aphra Behn* (Rutgers University Press, 1996), p.14.

45. Alan Marshall, '"Memorialls for Mrs Affora": Aphra Behn and the Restoration Intelligence World', *Women's Writing*, Vol. 22, No. 1, February 2015, pp. 13–33.

46. See the opening of Behn's letter to Killigrew, 31 August 1666, State Papers 29/169 f.157.

47. Apra Behn's Letter 16 August 1666, State Papers 29/167 f.209.

48. Ibid.

49. Marshall, '"Memorialls for Mrs Affora" . . .', *Women's Writing*, pp. 13–33.

50. Ibid.

51. For further examples see Marshall, '"Memorialls for Mrs Affora" . . .', *Women's Writing*, pp. 13–33.

52. Exact date unknown, February 1665. 'Charles II – volume 113: February 19–28, 1665', in Everett Green (ed.), *Calendar of State Papers 1664–5*, p.218.

53. 'A true and perfect narrative of the great and signal success of a part of His Majesty's fleet under his Highness Prince Rupert and his Grace the Duke of Albemarle, burning 160 Dutch ships within the Vlie', p.3; also found in State Papers 29/167 f.1.

54. 11 August 1666, *Royal James*, Letter from Prince Rupert and the Duke of Albemarle to the king. 'Charles II – volume 167: August 9–16, 1666', in Everett Green (ed.), *Calendar of State Papers 1666–7*, p.32.

55. 'A true and perfect narrative of the great and signal success of a part of His Majesty's fleet . . .', p.6; also found in State Papers 29/167 f.1.

56. Ibid., p.5; also found in State Papers 29/167 f.1.

57. 'Venice: August 1666', in Hinds (ed.), *Calendar of State Papers . . . Venice*, p.62.

58. 'A true and perfect narrative of the great and signal success of a part of His Majesty's fleet . . .', p.6; also found in State Papers 29/167 f.1

59. 'Venice: August 1666', in Hinds (ed.), *Calendar of State Papers . . . Venice*, p.62.
60. 'A true and perfect narrative of the great and signal success of a part of His Majesty's fleet . . .', pp. 6–7; also found in State Papers 29/167 f.1.
61. Ibid.
62. Anderson. (ed.), *Journals of Sir Thomas Allin*, p.283.
63. Aphra Behn to Jas Halsall, 27 August, State Papers 29/169 f.47.
64. 'Venice: August 1666', in Hinds (ed.), *Calendar of State Papers . . . Venice*, p.62.
65. Pepys's *Diary*, 15 August 1666.
66. Anonymous, *Sir Robert Holmes his bonefire: or, The Dutch doomsday* (1666).
67. Evelyn's *Diary*, 25 August 1666.
68. Adrian Tinniswood, *His Invention so Fertile: A Life of Christopher Wren* (Pimlico, 2002), pp. 126–30.
69. *Philosophical Transactions*, Vol. 1, pp. 248–54.
70. Ibid., p.289.
71. 'Charles II – volume 170: September 1–8, 1666', in Everett Green (ed), *Calendar of State Papers 1666–7*, p.99.

Chapter 7: Fire! Fire! Fire!

1. Lord (ed.), *Anthology of Poems of State Affairs*, pp. 45–59.
2. Ward (ed.), *The Manuscripts of his Grace the Duke of Portland*, pp. 301–2.
3. Edward Atkyns, 'XV. Copy of a Letter to Sir Robert Atkyns, Knight of the Bath, Lord Chief Baron of the Exchequer, and Speaker of the House of Lords, in the Reign of King William, from his brother Sir Edward Atkyns, who was also Lord Chief Baron of the Exchequer', *Archaeologia: or Miscellaneous tracts relating to antiquity, 1770–1992* (1821), p.105.
4. Evelyn's *Diary*, 5 September 1666.
5. Edward Hyde, *Continuation of the Life of Edward Earl of Clarendon, Lord High Chancellor of England, and Chancellor of the University of Oxford. Being a Continuation of His History of the Grand Rebellion, from the Restoration to his Banishment in 1667. Written by Himself* (London, 1759), p.764.
6. *London Gazette*, 3 September 1666–10 September 1666, Issue 85.
7. Vincent, *God's Terrible Voice*, p.50.
8. Ibid., p.55.

9. Jones (ed.), *The Fire Court*, pp. 190–1.
10. Ibid., pp. 90–1.
11. Ibid., p.243.
12. Ibid., p.196.
13. Pepys's *Diary*, 2 September 1666.
14. Ibid.
15. Taswell, 'Autobiography', pp. 10–11.
16. Ibid., p.12.
17. Evelyn's *Diary*, 3 September 1666.
18. Ibid.
19. Hyde, *Continuation of the Life of Edward Earl of Clarendon*, p.611.
20. Evelyn's *Diary*, 5 September 1666.
21. Vincent, *God's Terrible Voice*, p.54.
22. Ibid., p.53.
23. *London Gazette*, 3 September 1666–10 September 1666, Issue 85.
24. List of five post stations appointed during the fire of London, written by Lord Arlington, State Papers 29/170 f.140.
25. 'Charles II – volume 170: September 1–8, 1666', in Everett Green (ed.), *Calendar of State Papers 1666–7*, pp. 95–6.
26. Evelyn's *Diary*, 3 September 1666.
27. Atkyns, 'XV. Copy of a Letter to Sir Robert Atkyns . . .', *Archaeologia*, p.106.
28. Windham Sandys to Viscount Scudamore; quoted in Adrian Tinniswood, *By Permission of Heaven: The Great Fire of London* (Pimlico, 2004), p.64; and Walter George Bell, *The Great Fire of London*, p.316.
29. T. B Howell Esq., William Cobbett and David Jardine (eds.), *A Complete Collection of State Trials and Proceedings for High Treason and other Crimes and Misdemeanors from the Earliest Period to the Year 1783, With Notes and other Illustrations*, Vol. VI (London, 1816), p.849.
30. Taswell, 'Autobiography', pp. 13–14.
31. Vincent, *God's Terrible Voice*, pp. 54–5.
32. Evelyn's *Diary*, 5 September 1666.
33. Taswell, 'Autobiography', p.12.
34. Jones (ed.), *The Fire Court*, p.255.
35. Pepys's *Diary*, 2 September 1666.
36. Taswell, 'Autobiography', p.11.
37. Vincent, *God's Terrible Voice*, p.57.
38. Hyde, *Continuation of the Life of Edward Earl of Clarendon*, p.661.
39. Taswell, 'Autobiography', p.11.
40. Howell, *A Complete Collection of State Trials and Proceedings*, p.848.

41. Atkyns, 'XV. Copy of a Letter to Sir Robert Atkyns . . .' *Archaeologia*, p.105.

42. Ward, (ed.), *The Manuscripts of his Grace the Duke of Portland*, p.298.

43. Taswell, 'Autobiography', p.11.

44. *Kuttze jedoch warhafftiger Relation von dem erschrechkichen Feuer-Brunst welcher den, 12,13,14,15,16 Septembris die Stadt London getroffen*, quoted in translation by Walter George Bell, *The Great Fire of London in 1666*, p.331.

45. Hyde, *Continuation of the Life of Edward Earl of Clarendon*, p.664.

46. Ibid.

47. Verney and Verney (eds), *Memoirs of the Verney Family*, p.255.

48. Pepys's *Diary*, 4 September 1666.

49. Evelyn's *Diary*, 7 September 1666.

50. Vincent, *God's Terrible Voice*, p.54.

51. Hyde, *Continuation of the Life of Edward Earl of Clarendon*, p.674.

52. Ellwood, *The history of the life of Thomas Ellwood*, p.153. Farriner's time at Bridewell: London, Bethlem Hospital patient admission registers and casebooks 1683–1932, Bridewell and Bethlem Minutes of the Governors 1627–1643, BCB–07, pp. 46, 64.

53. Atkyns, 'XV. Copy of a Letter to Sir Robert Atkyns . . .', *Archaeologia*, p.107

54. *London Gazette*, 3 September 1666–10 September 1666, Issue 85.

55. Hyde, *Continuation of the Life of Edward Earl of Clarendon*, p.665.

56. Evelyn's *Diary*, 4 September 1666.

57. Pepys's *Diary*, 4 September 1666.

58. Evelyn's *Diary*, 6 September 1666.

59. Ibid., 7 September 1666.

60. Taswell, 'Autobiography', p.12.

61. Evelyn's *Diary*, 7 September 1666.

62. Verney and Verney (eds), *Memoirs of the Verney Family*, p.140.

63. Anonymous, *A True and Exact RELATION OF THE Most Dreadful and Remarkable Fires, [. . .] happened since the Reign of King WILLIAM the Conqueror, to this present Year 1666. In the Cities of London and Westminster and other Parts of ENGLAND* (1666).

64. Evelyn's *Diary*, 5 September 1666.

65. Verney and Verney (eds), *Memoirs of the Verney Family*, p.142.

66. 'The second parliament of Charles II: Seventh session – begins 18/9/1666', in *The History and Proceedings of the House of Commons*, pp. 92–100.

67. Hyde, *Continuation of the Life of Edward Earl of Clarendon*, p.671.

68. Atkyns, 'XV. Copy of a Letter to Sir Robert Atkyns . . .', *Archaeologia*, p.106.

69. Ibid.

70. Quoted in Verney and Verney (eds), *Memoirs of the Verney Family*, p.142.

71. Evelyn's *Diary*, 7 September 1666.

72. Ward (ed.), *The Manuscripts of his Grace the Duke of Portland*, p.298.

73. Ibid., p.299.

74. Ruth Spalding (ed.), *The Diary of Bulstrode Whitelocke, 1605–1675* (Oxford University Press, 1991), p.710.

75. 'Charles II – volume 171: September 9–16, 1666', in Everett Green (ed.), *Calendar of State Papers 1666–7*, p.121.

76. Jones (ed.), *The Fire Court*, pp. 90–1.

77. Atkyns, 'XV. Copy of a Letter to Sir Robert Atkyns . . .', *Archaeologia*, p.107.

78. Pepys's *Diary*, 24 October 1666.

79. Verney and Verney (eds), *Memoirs of the Verney Family*, p.141.

80. Ibid.

81. Pepys's *Diary*, 6 September 1666.

82. 9 September 1666, 'Charles II – volume 171: September 9–16, 1666', in Everett Green (ed.), *Calendar of State Papers Domestic 1666–7*, p.108.

83. 11 September 1666, Newcastle, Richard Forster to Williamson, 'Charles II – volume 171: September 9–16, 1666', in Everett Green (ed.), *Calendar of State Papers 1666–7*, p.116.

84. 9 September 1666, Eton, W. Lord Maynard to Williamson. "Charles II – volume 171: September 9–16, 1666', in Everett Green (ed.), *Calendar of State Papers 1666–7*, pp. 109–10.

85. 10 September 1666, 'Charles II – volume 171: September 9–16, 1666', in Everett Green (ed.), *Calendar of State Papers 1666–7*, pp. 111–14.

86. Ibid.

87. 9 September, Coventry. Ralph Hope to Williamson. State Papers 29/171 f.13.

88. Spalding (ed.), *The Diary of Bulstrode Whitelocke*, pp. 709–10.

89. 'Venice: September 1666', in Hinds (ed.), *Calendar of State Papers . . . Venice*, p.84.

90. Ibid., p.82.

91. Ibid., p.77.

92. Ibid., p.94.

93. Ibid.

94. Translated from the French. State Papers 92, *Secretaries of State: State*

Papers Foreign, Savoy and Sardinia, 1579–1780, Vol. 24 (1651–1670), f. 119.

95. Ward (ed.), *The Manuscripts of his Grace the Duke of Portland,* p.299.
96. Vincent, *God's Terrible Voice,* p.61.

Chapter 8: A Phoenix in Her Ashes

1. John Milton, *Paradise Lost,* Book IX, lines 780–4.
2. C. Anne Wilson, *Food and Drink in Britain: From the Stone Age to the 19th Century* (Academy Chicago, 1991), pp. 330–1.
3. H. P. R. Finberg and Joan Thirsk, *The Agrarian History of England and Wales: 1500–1640* (Cambridge University Press, 1967), p.196.
4. Ackroyd, Peter, *Newton* (Nan A. Talese, 2008), p.26.
5. Ibid., p.25.
6. Ackroyd, *Newton,* p.27.
7. Description of Queen Catherine comes from John Evelyn's *Diary,* 13 September 1666.
8. 10 September 1666, 'Charles II – volume 171: September 9–16, 1666', in Everett Green (ed.), *Calendar of State Papers 1666–7,* pp. 111–14.
9. 13 September 1666. 10 September 1666, 'Charles II – volume 171: September 9–16, 1666', in Everett Green (ed.), *Calendar of State Papers 1666–7,* pp. 120–3.
10. Atkyns, 'XV. Copy of a Letter to Sir Robert Atkyns . . .', *Archaeologia,* p.108.
11. 12 September 1666, 'Charles II – volume 181: December 8–15, 1666', in Everett Green (ed.), *Calendar of State Papers 1666–7,* p.340.
12. Chamberlayne, *The . . . present state of England* (London, 1671), p.110.
13. MacFarlane (ed.), *Diary of Ralph Josselin,* 9 September 1666.
14. Anonymous, *Death's Master-Peece or A true relation of that great and sudden fire in Tower-street, London, &c.* (London, 1650).
15. Atkyns, 'XV. Copy of a Letter to Sir Robert Atkyns . . .', *Archaeologia,* p.107.
16. Church of England Parish Registers, 1538–1812, City of London, St Giles, Cripplegate, 1663–1667, f.181–2. www.ancestry.com.
17. Taswell, 'Autobiography', p.13.
18. 'Venice: September 1666', in Hinds (ed.), *Calendar of State Papers . . . Venice,* p.77.
19. Vincent, *God's Terrible Voice,* p.10.
20. *A true and faithful account of the several informations exhibited to the hounourable*

committee appointed by the Parliament to inquire into the late dreadful burning of the city of London together with other informations touching the insolency of popish priests and Jesuites . . . England and Wales. Parliament. House of Commons. Committee to Enquire into the Burning of London (London, 1667).

21. Hyde, *Continuation of the Life of Edward Earl of Clarendon*, p.671

22. 'Preface', in Everett Green (ed.), *Calendar of State Papers 1666–7*, pp. vii–xxxii.

23. 10 September 1666, State Papers 29/171 f.26.

24. Chamberlayne, *The . . . present state of England*, p.110.

25. Ibid., p.112.

26. Edward Stillingfleet, *A Sermon Preached before the Honourable House of Commons 10/10/1666* (London, 1666), p.14.

27. 'Venice: September 1666', in Hinds (ed.), *Calendar of State Papers . . . Venice*, p.77.

28. Ibid.

29. *London Gazette*, 3 September 1666–10 September 1666, Issue 85.

30. 'The second parliament of Charles II: Seventh session – begins 18/9/1666', in *The History and Proceedings of the House of Commons*, pp. 92–100.

31. Ibid.

32. Verney and Verney (eds), *Memoirs of the Verney Family*, p.143.

33. Ward (ed.), *The Manuscripts of his Grace the Duke of Portland*, pp. 299–301.

34. Verney and Verney (eds), *Memoirs of the Verney Family*, p.143.

35. Ibid.

36. 3 November 1666, Antwerp, 'Charles II – volume 177: November 1–11, 1666', in Everett Green (ed.), *Calendar of State Papers 1666–7*, p.236.

37. 21 September 1666, 'Charles II – volume 172: September 17–24, 1666', in Everett Green (ed.), *Calendar of State Papers 1666–7*, p.145.

38. Pepys's *Diary*, 16 December 1666.

39. Westfall, *Never at Rest: A Biography of Isaac Newton* (Cambridge University Press, 1983), p.194.

40. Hyde, *Continuation of the Life of Edward Earl of Clarendon*, p.674.

41. 'Entry Book: September 1666', in William A. Shaw (ed.), *Calendar of Treasury Books, Volume. 1, 1660–1667* (London, 1904), p.728.

42. Wall (ed.), *Daniel Defoe: A Journal*, p.214.

43. Chamberlayne, *The . . . present state of England*, p.112.

44. Ibid., p.198.

45. 12 November 1666, 'Charles II – volume 178: November 12–21, 1666', in Everett Green (ed.), *Calendar of State Papers 1666–7*, pp. 254–7.

46. Pepys's *Diary*, 24 March 1666.
47. Verney and Verney (eds), *Memoirs of the Verney Family*, p.142.
48. Evelyn's *Diary*, 10 October 1666.
49. Anonymous, *Flagellum dei, or, A collection of the several fires, plagues, and pestilential diseases that have hapned in London especially, and other parts of this nation from the Norman Conquest to this present* (London, 1668).
50. Evelyn's *Diary*, 6 March 1667.

Epilogue: After 1666

1. Abraham De la Pryme, *The Diary of Abraham De la Pryme, the Yorkshire antiquary* (Durham, Surtees Society, 1870), p.7.
2. Vieth (ed.), *The Complete Poems of John Wilmot*, p.10.
3. 'A transcript of the registers of the Worshipful Company of Stationers, from 1640–1708, A.D.', ed. G. E. Briscoe Eyre (London, 1913), Vol. 2, p.374.
4. Pepys's *Diary*, 6 March 1667.
5. Ibid., 4 April 1667.
6. J. A. Bennet., *The Mathematical Science of Christopher Wren* (Cambridge University Press, 2002), p.43.
7. Aphra Behn, *The Luckey Chance, or, An Alderman's Bargain a Comedy as is Acted by their Majesty's Servants* (London, 1687), Preface.

Bibliography

Primary Sources

An account of the first rise, progress, symptoms and cure of the plague: being the substance of a letter from Dr Hodges to a person of quality (London, 1721)

Anderson, R. C. (ed.), *The Journal of Edward Montagu, First Earl of Sandwich, Admiral and General at Sea, 1659–1665* (Navy Records Society, 1929)

——, *The Journals of Sir Thomas Allin, 1660–1678*, Vol. 1 (Navy Records Society, 1929)

Armytage, Sir George John (ed.), *Allegations for marriage licences: issued by the Vicar-General of the Archbishop of Canterbury, 1660 to 1668* (London, 1892)

Atkyns, Edward, 'XV. Copy of a Letter to Sir Robert Atkyns, Knight of the Bath, Lord Chief Baron of the Exchequer, and Speaker of the House of Lords, in the Reign of King William, from his brother Sir Edward Atkyns, who was also Lord Chief Baron of the Exchequer', *Archaeologia: or Miscellaneous tracts relating to antiquity, 1770–1992* (1821)

'A transcript of the registers of the Worshipful Company of Stationers, from 1640–1708, A.D.', ed. G. E. Briscoe Eyre (London, 1913), Vol. 2

Behn, Aphra, *The Rover, or, The Banish't Cavaliers* (London, 1667)

——, *The Luckey Chance, or, An Alderman's Bargain a Comedy as is Acted by their Majesty's Servants* (London, 1687)

Bell, John, *London's remembrancer, or, A true accompt of every particular weeks christnings and mortality in all the years of pestilence within the cognizance of the bills of mortality, being xviii years* (London, 1665)

Bunyan, John, *Grace Abounding to The Chief of Sinners,* (London, 1666)

Burnet, Gilbert, *Some Passages of the Life and Death of the Right Honourable John Earl of Rochester: Who Died the 26th of July 1680: Written by His Own Direction on His Death-Bed* (London, 1875)

Cartwright, J. J. (ed.), *Memoirs and Travels of Sir John Reresby* (London, 1904)

Calendar of State Papers Domestic: Charles II, 1665–6, ed. Mary Anne Everett Green (London, 1864)

Calendar of State Papers Domestic: Charles II, 1666–7, ed. Mary Anne Everett Green (London, 1864)

Calendar of State Papers Relating to English Affairs in the Archives of Venice, Vol. 34, 1664–1666, ed. Allen B. Hinds (London, 1933)

Calendar of State Papers Relating to English Affairs in the Archives of Venice, Vol. 35, 1666–1668, ed. Allen B. Hinds (London, 1935)

Cavendish, Margaret, *Philosophical Letters: or, Modest Reflections Upon Some Opinions in Natural Philosophy Maintained by Several Famous and Learned Authors of this Age, Expressed by Noble Letters,* (London, 1664)

——, *The description of a new world, called the blazing world* (London, 1666)

Chamberlayne, Edward, *The second part of the present state of England together with divers reflections upon the antient state thereof* (London, 1671)

Church of England Parish Registers, 1538–1812 (London: London Metropolitan Archives)

Clark, Andrew (ed.), *The Life and Times of Anthony Wood, antiquary, of Oxford, 1632–1695, described by Himself* (Oxford, 1891)

Clarke, Thomas, *Meditations in my confinement, when my house was visited with the sickness in April, May and June, 1666, in which time I buried two children, and had three more of my family sick* (London, 1666)

Cotes, E., *London's dreadful visitation, or, A collection of all the bills of mortality for this present year* (London, 1665)

Death's Master-Peece or A true relation of that great and sudden fire in Tower-street, London, &c. (London, 1650)

Defoe, Daniel, *A Journal of the Plague Year* (1722, ed. C. Wall, 2003)

De la Pryme, Abraham, *The Diary of Abraham De la Pryme, the Yorkshire antiquary* (Durham: Surtees Society, 1870)

Dryden, John, *Annus Mirabilis: The Year of Wonders, 1666* (London, 1667)

——, *An Essay of Dramatick Poesie* (London, 1668)

The Dutch Boare Dissected, or a Description of Hogg-Land. A Dutch man is a Lusty, Fat, two Legged Cheese-Worm: A Creature, that is so addicted to Eating Butter, Drinking Fat Drink, and sliding, that all the vvorld knows him for a slippery Fellow, an Hollander is not an High-lander, but a Low-lander; for he loves to be down in the dirt, and boar-like, to wallow therein (London, 1665)

Ellwood, Thomas, *The history of the life of Thomas Ellwood: or an account of his birth, education, &c. with divers Observations on his Life and Manners when a Youth: and how he came to be convinced of the Truth; with his many Sufferings and Services for the same. – Also several other remarkable Passages and Occurrences. Written by his own hand. To which is added A supplement, by J. W.* (London, 1791)

The English and Dutch affairs Displayed to the Life both in matters of warr, state, and merchandize, how far the English engaged in their defence against the most potent monarchy of Spain, and how ill the Dutch have since requited the English for their extraordinary favours, not onely in the time of Queen Elizabeth their protector and defendress, but also in the time of King James, by their bloody massacree of them at Amboyna, their ingratitude to King Charles the First of glorious memory, and the true state of affairs as they now stand in the reign of our royal soveraign King Charles the Second / by a true lover and asserter of his countries honour (London, 1664)

Etherege, George, *The Man of Mode* (London, 1676)

Evelyn, John, *Fumifugium* (London, 1661)

——, *The Diary of John Evelyn, Vol. II*, ed. William Bray (M. Walter Dunne, 1901)

Famous and effectual medicine to cure the plague (London, 1670)

Flagellum dei, or, A collection of the several fires, plagues, and pestilential diseases that have hapned in London especially, and other parts of this nation from the Norman Conquest to this present (London, 1668)

Gay, John, *Trivia* (London, 1716)

Graunt, John, *Natural and Political Observations Mentioned in a following Index, and made upon the Bills of Mortality* (London, 1676)

Greene, Thomas, *A Lamentation Taken up for London* (London, 1665)

The History and Proceedings of the House of Commons, Vol. 1, 1660–1680 (London, 1742)

Hodges, Nathaniel, *Vindiciae medicinae et medicorum: an Apology for the Profession and Professors of Physic* (London, 1666)

——, *Loimologia or, an Historical Account of the Plague in London in 1665: With precautionary Directions against the like Contagion* (London, 1721)

Hooke, Robert, *Micrographia: or Some Physiological Descriptions of Minute Bodies Made by Magnifying Glasses with Observations and Inquiries Thereupon* (London, 1665)

Howell, T. B Howell Esq., *A Complete Collection of State Trials and Proceedings for High Treason and other Crimes and Misdemeanors from the Earliest Period to the Year 1783, With Notes and other Illustrations*, ed. William Cobbett and David Jardine, Vol. VI (London, 1816)

Hubert, Robert, *A catalogue of many natural rarities with great industry, cost, and thirty years travel in foraign countries / collected by Robert Hubert, alias Forges* (London, 1665)

Hyde, Edward, *Continuation of the Life of Edward Earl of Clarendon, Lord High Chancellor of England, and Chancellor of the University of Oxford. Being a Continuation of His History of the Grand Rebellion, from the Restoration to his Banishment in 1667. Written by Himself* (London, 1759)

Intelligencer Published for the Satisfaction and Information of the People (London, 1665), issues 1–94

Jones, Philip, E. (ed.), *The Fire Court: Calendar to the Judgments and Decrees*, Vols I and II (William, Clowes & Sons, 1966)

Josselin, Ralph, *The Diary of Ralph Josselin, 1616–1683*, ed. Alan MacFarlane (Oxford University Press, 1991)

Lilly, William, *Monarchy or no monarchy in England. Grebner his prophecy concerning Charles, son of Charles, his greatnesse, victories, conquests. The Northern Lyon, or Lyon of the North, and chicken of the eagle discovered who they are, of what nation. English, Latin, Saxon, Scotish and Welch prophecies concerning England in particular, and all Evrope in generall. Passages upon the life and death of the late King Charles. AEnigmaticall types of the future state and condition of England for many years to come* (London, 1651)

London Gazette, 4 June 1666–7 June 1666

London Hearth Tax: City of London and Middlesex, 1666 (Centre for Metropolitan History, 2011)

MacFarlane, Alan (ed.), *The Diary of Ralph Josselin, 1616–1683* (Oxford University Press, 1991)

Milton, John, *The readie and easie way to establish a free commonwealth and the excellence therof compar'd with the inconveniences and dangers of readmitting kingship in this nation* (London, 1660)

——, *Paradise Lost* (London, 1667)

'Miscarriages of the War'. 'House of Commons Journal Volume 9: 31 October 1667', in *Journal of the House of Commons, Volume 9, 1667–1687* (London, 1802)

Munk, William, *The Roll of the Royal College of Physicians in London*, Vol. 1, 1518–1700 (London, 1878)

Newes Published for Satisfaction and Information of the People, Sep. 03, 1663–Dec. 28, 1665 (London)

Newton, Isaac, *Quaestiones quaedem Philosophicae (Certain Philosophical Questions), Trinity College Notebook (1661–1665)*, MS ADD.3996, Cambridge University Library

Norrington, Ruth (ed.), *My Dearest Minette: The Letters Between Charles II and His Sister Henrietta, Duchesse D'Orléans* (Peter Owen, 1996)

Oldenburg, Henry (ed. and trans. A. Rupert Hall and Marie Boas Hall), *The Correspondence of Henry Oldenburg*, Vol. III, 1666–1667 (University of Wisconsin Press, 1966)

Payne, Joseph Frank (ed.), *Loimographia an Account of the Great Plague of London in the Year 1665 by William Boghurst an Apothecary* (London, 1894)

Pepys, Samuel, *The Diary of Samuel Pepys*, ed. Robert Latham and William Matthews, Vols I–IX (HarperCollins, 1995)

Philosophical Transactions, Vol. I (1665–6) and Vol. II (1666–7), (Royal Society of London, 1963)

Powell, J. R., and E. K. Timings (eds), *The Rupert and Monck Letter Book 1666: Together with Supporting Documents* (Navy Records Society, 1969)

A Relation of the Passages in the Battel at Sea, Between the Fleet of England and the United Neitherlands: Collected according to the charge & order of the Lords States General (24/14 June 1666)

'The second parliament of Charles II: Seventh session – begins 18/9/1666', in *The History and Proceedings of the House of Commons*, Vol. I, 1660–1680 (London, 1742)

Sheffield, John, *The Works of John Sheffield, Earl of Mulgrave and the Duke of Buckingham, Vol. II* (London, 1723)

Sir Robert Holmes his bonefire: or, The Dutch doomsday (London, 1666)

State Papers 29, *Secretaries of State: State Papers Domestic, Charles II, 1664–1667*, Vols 195–213 (National Archives)

State Papers 92, *Secretaries of State: State Papers Foreign, Savoy and Sardinia, 1579–1780*, Vol. 24 (1651–1670) (National Archives)

Spalding, Ruth (ed.), *The Diary of Bulstrode Whitelocke 1605–1675* (Oxford University Press, 1991)

Spinoza, Benedict de (trans. R. H. M. Elwes), *On the Improvement of the Understanding / The Ethics / Correspondence* (Dover Publications, 1955)

Stillingfleet, Edward, *A Sermon Preached before the Honourable House of Commons 10/10/1666* (London, 1666)

Taswell, William, 'Autobiography and Anecdotes by William Taswell, D.D., sometime Rector of Newington, Surrey, Rector of Bermondsey and previously Student of Christ Church, Oxford. A.D. 1651–1682', *Camden Old Series*, 55 (1853)

Treglown, Jeremy (ed.), *The Letters of John Wilmot, Earl of Rochester* (Oxford: Blackwell, 1980)

A True and Exact RELATION OF THE Most Dreadful and Remarkable Fires, [. . .] happened since the Reign of King WILLIAM the Conqueror, to this present Year 1666. In the Cities of London and Westminster and other Parts of ENGLAND (London, 1666)

A true and faithful account of the several informations exhibited to the hounourable committee appointed by the Parliament to inquire into the late dreadful burning of the city of London together with other informations touching the insolency of popish priests and Jesuites . . . England and Wales. Parliament. House of Commons. Committee to Enquire into the Burning of London (London, 1667)

A True and perfect narrative of the great and signal success of a part of His Majesties fleet under His Highness Prince Rupert, and His Grace the Duke of Albemarle: burning one hundred and sixty Dutch ships within the Ulie, as also the town of Brandaris upon the island of Schelling, by some commanded men under the conduct of Sir Robert Holmes, the eighth and ninth of this instant August: published by especial command (London, 1666)

Verney, Frances Parthenope and Verney, Margaret M. (eds), *Memoirs of the Verney Family During the Seventeenth Century II* (Longmans, Green and Co., 1907)

Vieth, David, M. (ed.), *The Complete Poems of John Wilmot Earl of Rochester* (Yale University Press, 2002)

Vincent, Thomas, *God's Terrible Voice in the City*, (London, 1667)

Ward, Richard (ed.), *The Manuscripts of his Grace the Duke of Portland preserved at Welbeck Abbey*, Vol. III (London, 1894)

Selected Secondary Sources

Ackroyd, Peter, *Newton* (Nan A. Talese, 2008)

Ayyadurai, S., Sebbane, F., Raoult, D., Drancourt, M., 'Body Lice, *Yersinia pestis* Orientalis, and Black Death', *Emerging Infectious Diseases*, 2010; 16 (5), 892–3

Beattie, J. M., *Policing and Punishment in London 1660–1750: Urban Crime and Limits of Terror* (Oxford University Press, 2004)

Bell, M., '"Her usual practices": The later career of Elizabeth Calvert, 1664–75', *Publishing History* (1994), 35, 5

Bell, Walter George, *The Great Fire of London* (John Lane, 1923)

——, *The Great Plague in London* (Folio Society, 2001)

Bennett, J. A., *The Mathematical Science of Christopher Wren* (Cambridge University Press, 2002)

Champion, J. A. I. (ed.), *Epidemic Disease in London* (London, Centre for Metropolitan History, 1993)

——, 'London's Dreaded Visitation: The Social Geography of the Great Plague in 1665', *Historical Geography Research Series* (1995)

Childs, John, 'The Sales of Government Gazettes during the Exclusion Crisis, 1678–81', *English Historical Review*, Vol. 102, No. 402 (January 1987), pp. 103–6

Cooper, Michael, *'A More Beautiful City': Robert Hooke and the Rebuilding of London after the Great Fire* (Sutton Publishing, 2003)

Cummins, Neil, Morgan Kelly and Cormac Ó Gráda, 'Living standards and plague in London, 1560–1665', *CAGE Online Working Paper Series* (Department of Economics, University of Warwick, 2013)

Davies, J. D., *Gentlemen and Tarpaulins: The Officers and Men of the Restoration Navy* (Clarendon Press, 1991)

——, *Pepys's Navy: Ship, Men and Warfare, 1649–1689* (Seaforth Publishing, 2008)

Degroot, Dagomar, '"Never such weather known in these seas": Climatic Fluctuations and the Anglo-Dutch Wars of the Seventeenth Century, 1652–1674', *Environment and History*, Vol. 20, No. 2, May 2014, pp. 239–73 (35)

Falkus, Christopher, *The Life and Times of Charles II* (Weidenfeld and Nicolson, 1992)

Finberg, H. P. R. and Joan Thirsk, *The Agrarian History of England and Wales: 1500–1640* (Cambridge University Press, 1967)

Fox, Frank, L. *The Four Day's Battle of 1666* (Seaworth Publishing, 2009)

Fraser, Antonia, *Charles II* (Weidenfeld & Nicolson, 1979)

Gaskill, Malcolm, *Crime and Mentalities in Early Modern England* (Cambridge University Press, 2000)

Hall, Marie Boas, *Henry Oldenburg: Shaping the Royal Society* (Oxford University Press, 2002)

Haensch, S., R. Bianucci, M. Signoli et al., 'Distinct Clones of *Yersinia pestis* Caused the Black Death', *PLOS Pathogens*, 7 October 2010

Helmers, Helmer J., *The Royalist Republic* (Cambridge University Press, 2015)

Hinnebusch, B. Joseph, Amy E. Rudolph, Peter Cherepanov et al., 'Role of Yersinia Murine Toxin in Survival of Yersinia Pestis in the Midgut of the Flea Vector', in *Science* (26 April 2002), Vol. 296, Issue 5568, pp. 733–5.

Holland, Bart K., 'Treatments for Plague: Reports from Seventeenth Century Epidemics', *Journal of the Royal Society of Medicine* (June 2000), Vol. 93, pp. 332–4.

Hollis, Leo, *The Phoenix: The Men Who Made London* (Weidenfeld & Nicolson, 2009)

Jardine, Lisa, *On a Grander Scale: The Outstanding Career of Sir Christopher Wren* (HarperCollins, 2002)

Jones, J. R., *The Anglo-Dutch Wars of the Seventeenth Century* (Longman, 1996)

Kelly, John, *The Great Mortality: An Intimate History of the Black Death, the Most Devastating Plague of All Time* (HarperCollins, 2006)

Lord, George DeForest (ed.), *Anthology of Poems of State Affairs: Augustan Satirical Verse 1660–1714*, (Yale University Press, 1975)

Loveman, Kate, *Samuel Pepys and His Books: Reading, Newsgathering, and Sociability, 1660–1703* (Oxford University Press, 2015)

McDonnell, Sir Michael KBE, *The Annals of St Paul's School* (Cambridge University Press, 1959)

McGuire, J. E., and Martin Tammy (eds), *Certain Philosophical Questions: Newton's Trinity Notebook* (Cambridge University Press, 2002)

McKeon, Michael, 'Sabbatai Sevi in England', *AJS Review*, Vol. 2 (April 1977), pp. 131–69

Marshall, Alan, '"Memorialls for Mrs Affora": Aphra Behn and the Restoration Intelligence World', *Women's Writing*, Vol. 22, No. 1 (February 2015), pp. 13–33

Moote, A. Lloyd and Dorothy C. Moote, *The Great Plague: The Story of London's Most Deadly Year* (John Hopkins University Press, 2004)

Myers, Robyn (ed.), *The London Book Trade: Topographies of Print in the Metropolis from the Sixteenth Century* (Oak Knoll Press, 2003)

Pincus, Steve, 'Popery, Trade and Universal Monarchy: The Ideological Context of the Outbreak of the Second Anglo-Dutch War', *English Historical Review*, Vol. 107, No. 422, pp. 5–9

——, 'From butterboxes to wooden shoes: the shift in English popular sentiment from anti-Dutch to anti-French in the 1670s', *Historical Journal*, 38 (1995), pp. 333–61

Smith, Abbot Emerson, 'The Transportation of Convicts to the American Colonies in the Seventeenth Century', *American Historical Review*, 39.2 (1934): 232–49

Speaight, George, 'The Origin of Punch and Judy: A New Clue?', *Theatre Research International*, 20 (1995), pp. 200–6

Stevenson, Christine, *The City and the King: Architecture and Politics in Restoration London* (Yale University Press, 2013)

Stone, George W., William Van Lennep, Emmett L. Avery, Arthur H. Scouten, Charles B. Hogan (eds), *The London Stage, Part 1: 1660–1700* (Southern Illinois University Press, 1965)

Adrian Tinniswood, *His Invention so Fertile: A Life of Christopher Wren* (Pimlico, 2002)

——, *By Permission of Heaven: The Great Fire of London* (Pimlico, 2004)

Todd, Janet, *The Secret Life of Aphra Behn* (Rutgers University Press, 1996)

Tomalin, Claire, *Samuel Pepys: The Unequalled Self* (Penguin, 2003)

Wall, Cynthia (ed.), *Daniel Defoe: A Journal of a Plague Year* (Penguin, 2003)

Walløe, Lars, 'Medieval and Modern Bubonic Plague: Some Clinical Continuities', *Medical History, Supplement 27* (2008), 59–73

Wardale, J. R., *Clare College Letters and Documents* (Macmillan and Bowes, 1903)

Westfall, Richard S., *Never at Rest: A Biography of Isaac Newton* (Cambridge University Press, 1983)

Wilson, C. Anne, *Food and Drink in Britain: From the Stone Age to the 19th Century* (Academy Chicago, 1991)

Index

References to images are in *italics*; references to notes are indicated by n.